Locke on Knowledge, Politics and Religion

Also available from Bloomsbury

Chinese and Indian Ways of Thinking in Early Modern European Philosophy, by Selusi Ambrogio
Faith and Reason in Continental and Japanese Philosophy, by Takeshi Morisato
Finding Locke's God, by Nathan Guy
Johann Bernhard Basedow and the Transformation of Modern Education, by Robert B. Louden
The Philosophy of Anne Conway, by Jonathan Head

Locke on Knowledge, Politics and Religion

New Interpretations from Japan

Edited by Kiyoshi Shimokawa and Peter R. Anstey

BLOOMSBURY ACADEMIC
LONDON • NEW YORK • OXFORD • NEW DELHI • SYDNEY

BLOOMSBURY ACADEMIC
Bloomsbury Publishing Plc
50 Bedford Square, London, WC1B 3DP, UK
1385 Broadway, New York, NY 10018, USA
29 Earlsfort Terrace, Dublin 2, Ireland

BLOOMSBURY, BLOOMSBURY ACADEMIC and the Diana logo are trademarks of
Bloomsbury Publishing Plc

First published in Great Britain 2021
This paperback edition published 2023

Copyright © Kiyoshi Shimokawa, Peter R. Anstey and Contributors, 2021

Kiyoshi Shimokawa and Peter R. Anstey have asserted their right under the Copyright, Designs and Patents Act, 1988, to be identified as Editors of this work.

For legal purposes the Acknowledgements on p. viii constitute an extension of this copyright page.

Cover design by Charlotte Daniels
Cover image: John Locke (1632–1704), portrait by Michael Dahl, oil on canvas, c.1696.
© IanDagnall Computing / Alamy Stock Photo.

All rights reserved. No part of this publication may be reproduced or transmitted in any form or by any means, electronic or mechanical, including photocopying, recording, or any information storage or retrieval system, without prior permission in writing from the publishers.

Bloomsbury Publishing Plc does not have any control over, or responsibility for, any third-party websites referred to or in this book. All internet addresses given in this book were correct at the time of going to press. The author and publisher regret any inconvenience caused if addresses have changed or sites have ceased to exist, but can accept no responsibility for any such changes.

A catalogue record for this book is available from the British Library.

Library of Congress Cataloging-in-Publication Data

Names: Shimokawa, Kiyoshi, editor. | Anstey, Peter R., 1962-editor.
Title: Locke on knowledge, politics and religion: new interpretations from Japan / edited by Kiyoshi Shimokawa and Peter R. Anstey.
Description: London; New York: Bloomsbury Academic, 2021. | Includes bibliographical references and index. |
Identifiers: LCCN 2021007652 (print) | LCCN 2021007653 (ebook) | ISBN 9781350189188 (hb) | ISBN 9781350189195 (epdf) | ISBN 9781350189201 (ebook)
Subjects: LCSH: Locke, John, 1632-1704. | Philosophy, Japanese–21st century.
Classification: LCC B1297.L625 2021 (print) | LCC B1297 (ebook) | DDC 192–dc23
LC record available at https://lccn.loc.gov/2021007652
LC ebook record available at https://lccn.loc.gov/2021007653

ISBN: HB: 978-1-3501-8918-8
PB: 978-1-3501-8922-5
ePDF: 978-1-3501-8919-5
eBook: 978-1-3501-8920-1

Typeset by Deanta Global Publishing Services, Chennai, India

To find out more about our authors and books visit
www.bloomsbury.com and sign up for our newsletters.

Contents

List of Illustrations	vi
Contributors	vii
Acknowledgements	viii
Abbreviations	ix

Introduction: Locke and Japan *Kiyoshi Shimokawa*	1

Part I Knowledge and experimental method

1	Locke and non-propositional knowledge *Peter R. Anstey*	29
2	Boyle and Locke on primary and secondary qualities: A reappraisal *Shigeyuki Aoki*	52
3	Berkeley's experimental method in *An Essay Towards a New Theory of Vision* *Yasuaki Nakano*	74

Part II Law and politics

4	A defence of Locke's consent theory against Hume's critique *Takumichi Kojo*	101
5	Locke's political constitutionalism: A re-examination of his idea of the prerogative *Ryuichi Yamaoka*	119
6	The death penalty and a Lockean impossibilism *Masaki Ichinose*	145

Part III Religion and toleration

7	Locke's harm argument and the largeness of toleration *Kiyoshi Shimokawa*	169
8	Salvation and reasonableness in Locke's *Reasonableness of Christianity* *Keisuke Takei*	189
9	Locke on sex, marriage and the state *J. K. Numao*	214

Index	241

Illustrations

Figure

1.1	Two circles and an equilateral triangle	34

Tables

2.1	Boyle's Primary Affections and Secondary Qualities	58
2.2	The Primary and Secondary Quality Distinction in the First and Fourth Editions of the *Essay* and Wynne's *Abridgement* (1700)	64
2.3	*Essay* II. iv and viii Compared	66
9.1	Locke's Responses to Adultery, Fornication and Polygamy	228

Contributors

Peter R. Anstey, professor of Philosophy, Department of Philosophy, University of Sydney, Australia.

Shigeyuki Aoki, professor of Philosophy, Department of Philosophy, Chuo University, Japan.

Masaki Ichinose, professor of Philosophy, Department of Human Sciences, Musashino University, Japan.

Takumichi Kojo, associate professor of Philosophy, Department of Policy Studies, Aichi Gakuin University, Japan.

Yasuaki Nakano, lecturer in Philosophy, Gakushuin University and Keio University, Japan.

J. K. Numao, associate professor of Foreign Languages and Liberal Arts, Faculty of Science and Technology, Keio University, Japan.

Kiyoshi Shimokawa, professor of Philosophy, Department of Philosophy, Gakushuin University, Japan.

Keisuke Takei, associate professor of the History of Social Thought, Department of Economics, Fukuoka University, Japan.

Ryuichi Yamaoka, professor of Political Science, Open University of Japan, Japan.

Acknowledgements

Eight of the nine chapters that comprise this volume were initially presented at the John Locke Conference held in Tokyo at Gakushuin University in December 2016. I would like to extend my gratitude to the colleagues and students in the Department of Philosophy and the Faculty of Letters, who offered encouragement and helped organize the conference. I would also like to thank Gakushuin University for sponsoring Professor Peter Anstey as a visiting research fellow and allowing him to participate in the conference. As co-editor of this volume, Anstey has offered invaluable help, and I am truly grateful for his editorial skills and judicious decisions. Without his assistance, I could not have produced this volume in the present form.

I would like to thank Iwanami Shoten for permission to reprint Ryuichi Yamaoka, 'Rikkenshugi to seijiteki rializumu: Jon Rokku kokuotaikenron no kento', *Shiso*, no. 1144 (2019): 5–31; and Koyo Shobo for permission to reprint material from Takumichi Kojo, *Rokku Rinrigaku no Saisei* (Kyoto: Koyo Shobo, 2017), ch. 2: 32–46, and ch. 7: 122–35.

Kiyoshi Shimokawa
Gakushuin University, Tokyo

Abbreviations

Berkeley All citations of lifetime publications are from *The Works of George Berkeley, Bishop of Cloyne*, 9 vols, eds A. A. Luce and T. E. Jessop, London: Thomas Nelson and Sons, 1948–1957.

NTV *An Essay Towards a New Theory of Vision, Works of George Berkeley*, vol. 1.

PC *Philosophical Commentaries: Transcribed from the Manuscript and Edited with an Introduction and Index by George H. Thomas; Explanatory Notes by A. A. Luce*, eds A. A. Luce and G. H. Thomas, New York: Garland Publishing, 1989. First published in 1976.

PHK *A Treatise Concerning the Principles of Human Knowledge, Works of George Berkeley*, vol. 2.

TVV *The Theory of Vision or Visual Language Vindicated and Explained, Works of George Berkeley*, vol. 1.

Boyle

Forms and Qualities *The Origin of Forms and Qualities*, in *The Works of Robert Boyle*, 14 vols, eds M. Hunter and E. B. Davis, London: Pickering and Chatto, 1999–2000, vol. 5: 281–491. 1st edn 1666.

Filmer

Patriarcha *Patriarcha and Other Writings*, ed. J. P. Sommerville, Cambridge: Cambridge University Press, 1991.

Hume

Treatise *A Treatise of Human Nature*, vol. 1, eds D. F. Norton and M. J. Norton, Oxford: Clarendon Press, 2007, 1st edn, 1739–40. Cited by book, part, section and paragraph number, e.g. *Treatise* 3.2.2.14.

Locke

EPIS   *Epistola de Tolerantia, A Letter on Toleration*, ed. R. Klibansky, trans. J. W. Gough, Oxford: Clarendon Press, 1968, 1st edn, 1689.

Essay   *An Essay concerning Human Understanding*, ed. P. H. Nidditch, Oxford: Clarendon Press, 1975, 4th edn, 1700. Cited by book, chapter and paragraph number, e.g. *Essay* IV. iii. 6.

Letter   *A Letter Concerning Toleration and Other Writings*, ed. M. Goldie, Indianapolis: Liberty Fund, 2010.

Reasonableness   *The Reasonableness of Christianity*, ed. J. C. Higgins-Biddle, Oxford: Clarendon Press, 1999, 1st edn, 1695.

Second Letter   *A Second Letter Concerning Toleration*, in *The Works of John Locke*, 10 vols, London: T. Tegg, 1823, vol. 6: 61–137.

Third Letter   *A Third Letter for Toleration*, in *The Works of John Locke*, 10 vols, London: T. Tegg, 1823, vol. 6: 141–546.

TT   *Two Treatises of Government*, ed. P. Laslett, Cambridge: Cambridge University Press, 1988, 3rd printing 1698. Cited by treatise and section number, e.g. TT II. 28.

Newton

Principia   *The Principia: Mathematical Principles of Natural Philosophy*, trans. I. B. Cohen and A. Whitman, Berkeley: University of California Press, 1999, 3rd edn, 1726.

Introduction: Locke and Japan

Kiyoshi Shimokawa

It may be surprising to many readers that Locke scholarship has been flourishing in Japan for several decades. But what is even more surprising is that recent years have seen a remarkable increase in the number of scholarly and critical treatments of various aspects of Locke's philosophical thought in Japan. This is a new phenomenon, which has been evident since the 1990s. Unfortunately, however, present-day Japanese Locke scholarship is virtually unknown to those who live outside of Japan. The reason is simple. There is one major obstacle: many scholars and philosophers continue to write only in Japanese, and their works remain inaccessible to readers who do not understand the language. Japanese scholarship remains largely monolingual, particularly in the fields of philosophy and intellectual history. This is unfortunate because recent Japanese scholarship on Locke has much to offer, and its fruits should be widely shared by scholars and students the world over.

 The present collection of chapters is a first step towards remedying this situation. It is meant to bring recent work by eight Japanese scholars to the attention of Anglophone readers, and thereby to stimulate further research and scholarly debate. This is the first collection in English on Locke, written largely by Japanese scholars. Here I say 'largely', not 'solely', for there is one significant exception.[1] One of the contributors to this volume is Peter Anstey, who is Australian. The collection is actually a product of the Locke conference held at Gakushuin University, Tokyo, in December 2016. The conference was held on the occasion of Professor Anstey's visit to the university as a research fellow. The chapters contained in this volume, with the exception of that by Takumichi Kojo (Chapter 4), were originally presented at the conference, where Anstey provided incisive comments on each paper and played a vital role in stimulating the discussions. All of them were revised and updated later for publication, again with the assistance of Anstey. Thus, the present collection should be seen as arising from the international collaboration between him and the Japanese contributors.

This collection covers three areas of Locke's philosophical thought. The areas are broadly indicated by the title of the volume, but a more exact demarcation of the areas is found in the heading of each of the three parts of the book: knowledge and experimental method (Part I), law and politics (Part II), and religion and toleration (Part III). The nine chapters discuss not only specific key aspects of Locke's thought, but its wider intellectual milieu (e.g. Boyle and Berkeley). They seek to challenge and criticize established interpretations, and replace them with novel alternatives. The book also contains several chapters which provide insights into some of the significant practical issues facing us today, including constitutionalism, capital punishment, toleration, sex and marriage. The fresh insights, as well as the criticisms and alternatives it offers, are intended to advance Locke scholarship further and facilitate international collaboration.

1 Locke and Japan: First encounters

In order to help the reader to locate themes in the present volume in their broader historical context, I shall offer here an account of the development of Japanese Locke scholarship. I begin with its pre-history, that is, the two isolated moments when Locke and Japan first encountered each other. Locke read about Japan in the 1660s, and a Japanese scholar encountered Locke in the 1830s. A glimpse at those moments of engagement helps us to understand our place in history.

Locke's encounter with Japan took place sometime in the 1660s. He learned about the Japanese persecution of *Kirishitan* (i.e. Christians). The word, as used in Japanese history, refers to Catholics in the sixteenth and seventeenth centuries. Locke probably read an English translation of the Dutch book[2] which contained a description of the persecution that began in Japan in 1614. It was written by a Dutchman named François Caron, who had lived in Japan between 1619 and 1641, and his account was subsequently included in a number of English books. Locke also read an account of the persecution written by John Humphrey in his anonymous *A Proposition for the Safety and Happiness of the King and Kingdom* of 1667.[3] On the basis of his reading, Locke wrote a striking passage[4] about the severity of the Japanese persecution of Catholics in *An Essay Concerning Toleration* (1667). In this work he also touched on the cause of the persecution. Locke stated that it had nothing to do with any attempt to establish the uniformity of religion within the nation. Rather, it had to do with the fact that 'the doctrine of popish priests, gave them [sc. the Japanese government] that religion was but their pretense' while 'empire [was] theire designe', so that it 'made them fear the subversion of their state'.⁵

Locke has a point here, which may need further explanation. Catholic missionary activities in Japan began in the middle of the sixteenth century. The Jesuits sponsored by Portugal, and the Dominicans and Franciscans supported by Spain, were very successful in making a large number of converts, among whom were some *daimyo*, or powerful feudal lords of Japan. It is only natural that the subsequent rulers who wanted to unify Japan feared that the missionaries were a threat to national unity, which might lead ultimately to military conquest. Christianity was also perceived as fuelling a rebellion of the people.⁶ Thus in 1587, Toyotomi Hideyoshi promulgated the Purge Directive Order to the Jesuits, and in 1612 and 1613 Tokugawa Ieyasu banned Christianity and expelled all Christian missionaries from the country, laying the foundation for the isolationist foreign policy known as *sakoku* (literally, 'closed country'), which for more than two centuries strictly limited Japan's transactions with the West to its trade with the Dutch.

Let us now turn to the 1830s when the name 'Locke' first appeared in Japanese literature. It was the time when the Tokugawa government's long-standing isolationist foreign policy was just beginning to be questioned by its critics. Takano Choei⁷ (1804–1850) was one such critic. He was a prominent scholar trained in *Rangaku* (Dutch studies). Like Locke, he studied medicine. He wrote medical books and translated Dutch books. By using the knowledge he acquired from Dutch sources, he tried to promote the study of Western sciences in Tokugawa Japan.

Takano wrote a short history of Western philosophy, the first of its kind in Japan, in his 1835 notebook entitled 'Bunken Manroku' (A Set of Miscellaneous Observations). This short history originally had no title, but it has come to be called 'Seiyo Gakushi no Setsu' (Doctrines of Western Philosophers).⁸ Takano started his narrative with Thales, Pythagoras, Socrates, Plato and Aristotle. When he moved on to the modern era, he briefly mentioned Copernicus, Galileo and Descartes, and stressed that Newton, Leibniz and Locke were the three truly great modern philosophers. Takano transliterated Locke's name as 'Lok-ke', just as he struggled with the pronunciation of the two other names. He stated that 'Lok-ke, in particular, investigated the matter relating to the human mind and, on the basis of reason and experience, he determined the limits of human understanding' (Takano 1978b: 196, my translation). This is the first statement about Locke ever to appear in Japanese literature.

Takano's encounter with Locke was made possible through Dutch connections, and it is plausible that his fairly accurate description of Locke was based on one of the Dutch books he acquired. The Tokugawa government had completely prohibited Christianity in the early seventeenth century, and banned almost all transactions between Japanese and Western people. But it allowed an exception for trade. The Dutch were permitted to trade and have a diplomatic relationship with Japan under strict conditions through Dejima, a small fan-shaped island constructed in the bay of Nagasaki. It served as a Dutch trading post from 1641 to 1854, and for many years the island remained the only window through which knowledge about Western sciences and philosophy could be learned. This explains why Takano was a scholar in Dutch studies.

Takano, however, was critical of the government's isolationist policy, which involved the expulsion of foreign ships – Russian, British and American ships in particular. They had frequently approached Japan for various purposes, such as catching whales, demanding a supply or trade, bringing back Japanese castaways and making an expedition, and this caused a serious concern about the defence of Japanese coasts. In 1838 Takano anonymously published a book entitled *Bojutsu Yumemonogatari* (The 1838 Tale of a Dream), where he criticized the Tokugawa shogunate's handling of an incident in 1837 involving the American ship *Morrison*.[9] The government became furious, seeing it as a serious threat to the supremacy it had sustained over the rest of the nation, as well as to the consistent application of the expulsion policy. They arrested and imprisoned Takano, together with Watanabe Kazan and other progressive scholars who were dedicated to Dutch studies. This crackdown took place in 1839, and it is known as *Bansha no Goku* (imprisonment of the barbaric society of scholars).[10] Takano, being treated as having a commoner's status, received a heavy sentence of life imprisonment. Though he later managed to escape from prison, he had to go underground and live a fugitive's life under a pseudonym until he was re-arrested and died a tragic death.

As we can see from this narrative, the study of Western knowledge was a risky business in those days. There may not have been a direct causal link between Takano's encounter with Locke and his imprisonment or his tragic death. But I do want to highlight the fact that Takano, like later generations of Japanese scholars who studied Locke's philosophy and politics, sought to defend freedom, or freedom from the oppressive measures the government imposed on its people.

2 The first stage: Introducing Locke's ideas (1868–1945)

Japan abandoned its isolationist policy and opened its doors to Western, imperialist powers, with the coming of the mighty Black Ships in 1853 which were led by the American Commodore Matthew Perry. Being faced with their guns and acts of intimidation, the Tokugawa government had no choice but to sign an unequal treaty with the United States and open its ports. They also had to sign similar treaties with Russia, Britain, France and the Netherlands. Then in 1868, there occurred a restoration of monarchy, which marked the end of the Tokugawa government and signified a return to the emperor's rule. A new era of Meiji (literally, 'enlightened reign') started in 1868. From this point onwards, Japan underwent profound changes, transforming itself from an isolated feudal society to a modern, industrialized nation. In this process of modernization, Japan selected and adopted a number of Western scientific, technological, political, legal and philosophical ideas. It is in this context of modernization that we can properly understand the rise of the Japanese study of any Western thought, including Locke's. (The reader should note that in transliterating the Japanese language herein, I follow the standard rule of Romanization adopted in Japan, which is based on the Hepburn system. This rule requires us to use the letter 'r', without permitting the use of 'l'. If we follow it, the name 'John Locke' is bound to appear as 'Jon Rokku'.[11])

We may treat the period of 1868–1945 as the first stage which prepared the way for the rise of Locke scholarship in Japan. This is the period during which Locke's views on education, knowledge, ethics, politics and economics began to be discussed and disseminated through books and papers. There are at least four salient features of the literature of this period.[12]

First, Locke's views on education attracted the special attention of educators during the Meiji era (1868–1912) because they provided clues as to when to teach reading or how to deal with corporal punishment, and because there was an expectation that one could learn from it something about how to turn children into the leaders of a modern nation. Locke's *Some Thoughts Concerning Education* was translated into Japanese in 1893 and 1894. Second, Locke's empiricist epistemology attracted the attention of Nishi Amane, the author of *Hyakugaku Renkan* (Encyclopaedia, 1870) and other philosophical works on human nature. Nishi stressed that in Locke's view, experience, or sensation in particular, is the source of ideas, that is, those items which come to be written on the 'white paper' of the mind. He also touched on Locke's association of ideas.

Nishi was an influential thinker who created a large portion of modern Japanese philosophical vocabulary. A number of authors in the late nineteenth and early twentieth centuries commented on Locke's epistemological and ethical views in their books on the history of philosophy or of Western ethics. At least two books discussed Locke's empiricism: Kobayashi Sumie and Nishitani Kendo's *Rokku no Tetsugaku to Kyōiku Shichō* (Locke's Philosophy and His Thought on Education, 1929) and Oshima Masanori's *Rokku* (Locke, 1938). From 1916 to 1941 Oshima lectured on British and American philosophy at Tokyo Imperial University, but this was the exception. He was the first and only professor to lecture on that subject there or in any other imperial university. A partial translation of *An Essay concerning Human Understanding* by Hatta Shuzo appeared in 1930.[13] Another expanded translation by Kato Uichiro, which still omitted seven chapters of the *Essay*, was published in two volumes in 1940.[14] It should be added that Kato was one of Oshima's students.

Third, certain portions of Locke's political philosophy attracted the attention of scholars in the 1920s, which corresponded to the period of Taishō democracy. It was the time of a strong democratic movement for wider representation in politics, which resulted in universal male suffrage in 1925. Scholars debated questions about the right of resistance found in Locke. Some questioned how Locke could ever justify monarchy if he were really committed to democratic principles, and they seized upon the notion of 'moderation' to characterize Locke's political thought. Fourth, Locke's ideas on economics, labour and property rights were taken up in articles by a few distinguished scholars on economic thought in the 1910s.[15]

It should be noted, however, that the literature of this period often discussed Locke in rough comparison with other thinkers (e.g. Hobbes or Adam Smith), or in the broader context of the history of Western philosophy and ethics. Unlike the literature of the post-1945 period, it seldom concentrated on Locke, nor did it seem to delve into a deep analysis of the relevant issues, though there were a few significant exceptions.

3 The second stage: The progress of Locke scholarship (1946–89)

I have referred earlier to the process of modernization. Yet Japan emerged not only as an industrialized nation but also as an imperialist power which invaded and colonized other Asian countries. This imperialist power was finally defeated by the Allied Forces in 1945. Japan's surrender liberated Japanese scholars from the old imperialist ideology that had portrayed the nation as unique and superior under the emperor system. At the same time, they began to make strenuous efforts to study modern Western thought in an attempt to understand what modernity was really like, or to explore the ways in which such democratic values as liberty and equality could really be embodied in their own society.

I cannot trace in any detail the development of Locke scholarship from 1946 to 1989. Nor can I offer an account which does justice to the works produced during this long period.[16] Here I can only indicate some general tendencies and salient features of the literature on Locke from the period, mentioning only a few exemplary works.

The Locke scholarship of the period exhibits one remarkable tendency: the primary focus definitely shifted from education and general philosophy (as was the case with the pre-1945 literature) to *political* philosophy. Sonoko Yamada conducted a survey of the Japanese literature on Locke for the period of 1946–69, and showed that there had been a sharp increase in the number of books and articles published on politics, in comparison with other subjects.[17] What is more important, this primary focus on political philosophy, or, to be more exact, social and political philosophy, has continued to be the primary feature of Japanese Locke scholarship even to this day.

The shift to politics occurred partly because in 1946 Japan adopted a new Constitution, which had been originally drafted by the GHQ (General Headquarters) under the leadership of General Douglas MacArthur, and reviewed and revised by the Japanese government. Among other things, it incorporated the principle of popular sovereignty and that of trust. The former principle was used to change what had previously been the emperor's supreme, sacred status into something that is merely dependent on the will of the people.[18] Since both principles are found in Locke's 'Second Treatise', there is good reason for enquiring into the text. In fact, in 1948 Shiro Kiyomiya published an article entitled 'Nihonkoku Kenpō to Rokku no Seijishisō' (The Constitution of Japan and Locke's Political Thought), comparing the Constitution with Locke's political principles.[19]

But the adoption of the Constitution is only one of the reasons why scholars turned to Locke's political ideas. There is another, more fundamental, reason. Many scholars in the early years of the post-war period were groping for modern principles of political society, be they liberal, democratic or socialist, which would seem to them to help rebuild their own political society after the devastation of the war. So some scholars began to work on Locke, in the hope that they might find in his works some attractive principles, or at least their root ideas. Keiichi Matsushita's book *Shimin Seijiriron no Keisei* (The Making of the Political Theory of Citizens, 1959) is one of the earliest works on Locke which sought to find modern individualistic principles, together with a new bottom-up theory of government which incorporated the English principle of trust and the right to a revolution. Shoji Tanaka was a leading Locke scholar from the late 1960s onwards, who published a comprehensive work discussing natural law, property and politics. In the Preface he looked back and wrote: 'Locke scholarship [in Japan] began to make real progress only after the war', because scholars really wanted to 'go back to the roots of the idea of Western democracy' and 'see what they are' (Tanaka 1968: i). The search for some modern principles of political society has remained one of the most important motivations for many Japanese scholars. It should be added that since Locke's principles are broad enough to encompass the principles of natural law, rights, property and family, as well as those of political power as such, Locke's text came to attract a wide range of scholars, those working in philosophy, politics, law and the history of social and economic thought. The first complete Japanese translation of the *Two Treatises* by Kaichi Matsuura appeared in 1948.[20] Three translations of the 'Second Treatise' were published from the mid-1950s to the late 1960s.[21]

The second, prominent feature of the Japanese Locke scholarship of this period is that scholars tended to work on narrowly defined areas of thought (e.g. epistemology, medicine, natural law, property, toleration). Of those areas, two deserve special notice: epistemology and toleration.

First, epistemology. In the pre-war Japanese academic world, 'Western philosophy' was almost synonymous with 'German philosophy' since it was the philosophy mainly taught and studied in the imperial universities and old-style, elite high schools.[22] But after 1945, British and American philosophy came to prominence. They came to be treated with respect, and the study of Locke's epistemology and British empiricism became a legitimate subject to be studied. Quite a few articles were written on Locke's epistemology, though there appeared very few book-length treatments of the *Essay* during the period from 1945 to 1989.[23] The first complete translation, by Haruhiko Otsuki, of *An Essay concerning Human Understanding* did not appear until 1977.[24] Locke's Latin essays on the law of nature, which contained his early epistemology, were translated in 1962.[25]

Second, Locke's theory of toleration began to emerge as a new subject of research. This is in sharp contrast with the pre-war situation where only a few articles briefly touched on it. Locke sought to separate the care of souls from the power of the magistrate, and defended the separation of church and state, as part of his argument for the state's duty of toleration. But neither the separation nor the state's duty could have become a voice of the people or a subject of serious study in pre-war Japan. In 1868, the Meiji government started to elevate Shintō to the status of a national religion while destroying Buddhist temples and abolishing their previous privileges. Though the government appeared to change the policy of directly controlling religions (as it would manifestly infringe religious liberty), it adopted a new way of controlling school education by the Imperial Rescript on Education (1890). Then it finally came to strengthen and establish, from the 1930s to the end of the Pacific War, the system of *Kokka Shintō* (State Shintō) as an ideological machine to induce and compel its people to worship the emperor and mobilize them for the war. Shintō was now treated as the overarching Japanese tradition linked by its rituals to the emperor, who derived his legitimacy through his ancestors from the Sun Goddess Amaterasu.[26] This was claimed by the government to be the 'non-religious' tradition to which all religions, including Buddhism and Christianity, were to be subordinated.[27] It is in this manner that State Shintō came to suppress religious liberty in pre-war Japan.[28]

The Shintō Directive (1945), issued to the government by Occupation authorities, abolished State Shintō. The Directive's aim was 'to separate religion from the state, to prevent the misuse of religion for political ends, and to put all religions, faiths and creeds upon exactly the same basis' (Hardacre 1989: 169).[29] It banned 'all propagation and dissemination of militaristic or ultranationalistic ideology' in anything connected with Shintō (Hardacre 1989: 136). Subsequently, Article 20 of the new Constitution clearly stipulated the principle of the separation of church and state, and guaranteed individual religious liberty. It is only after this that Japanese scholars began a serious study of Locke's theory of toleration, with awareness of its relevance to the constitutional separation of church and state. Some essays on Locke and toleration began to appear in journals. In 1962, Masao Hamabayashi produced the first Japanese translation of *A Letter Concerning Toleration*, praising it as having enormous significance for religious liberty while also being surprised at the fact that this work had never been translated. It was followed by another translation.[30] Then in 1970, Akira Hirano published a Latin/Japanese facing-page translation of *Epistola de Tolerantia*.[31] In 1978, Kimimasa Inoue published a book on Locke's theory of toleration, taking into account his predecessors' arguments as well as his own.[32] Inoue also published an English edition of *An Essay Concerning Toleration* together with a piece entitled 'Toleratio'.[33]

The third, salient feature of the Locke scholarship of this period is that Japanese scholars learned a great deal from the growing output of English-speaking Locke scholars from the 1960s onwards, and often commented on their works in their own publications. For many Japanese scholars, it was an intellectually thrilling experience to read new editions of Locke's works (e.g. Nidditch's *Essay*, Laslett's *Two Treatises*, von Leyden's *Essays on the Law of Nature*, Abrams's *Two Tracts on Government*). On the other hand, they also found it exciting to learn from the new interpretations which were offered by Locke scholars in Britain and North America (e.g. C. B. Macpherson and James Tully on property, John Dunn on God, Richard Ashcraft on radicalism).

As Locke scholarship in the West became increasingly diversified with respect to its subject matter, its Japanese counterparts followed a similar pattern. In 1980, thirteen Japanese scholars were able to get together and publish a collection of essays on Locke, which covered most of the major areas of his thought, ranging from epistemology, natural philosophy and philosophy of language to natural law, property, political power and economics, and from toleration and religion to education.[34] In 1970, Tomofumi Hattori published the first Japanese translation of *The Reasonableness of Christianity* together with *A Discourse of Miracles* (Locke 1970b). In the late 1980s, Takashi Kato in his *Jon Rokku no Shisō Sekai* (The World of John Locke's Thought, 1987) sought to focus on the significance of Christianity for Locke's thought, and clarified the connections between *The Reasonableness of Christianity* and Locke's comments on demonstrable morality and revelation in the *Essay*.

4 The third stage: In search of more critical and scholarly treatments (1990–2020)

Let us now move on to the Locke scholarship of the most recent period. Since this concerns present-day scholarship, I should be careful and avoid being partial. For lack of space, however, I will have to be selective once again. It is fair to say that the prominent feature of the third stage is that scholars have aspired to take more critical approaches to, or give more scholarly treatments of, Locke's works than the previous generations did. Their critical stance may be seen, at least in part, as a consequence of the infiltration into Japan of the method of analytic philosophy practised in Britain and the United States. But it may also be seen as a result of each individual scholar's firm commitment to clarity. Their aspiration to high standards of scholarship may be explicable largely as a result of each new generation's endeavour to go beyond previous scholarly achievements. Besides, Japanese scholars now have more opportunities to do research abroad and visit the Bodleian Library to check Locke's manuscripts with their own eyes, than did previous generations. Moreover, they are also better informed of the general state of Locke scholarship.

The 1990s and 2000s saw the publication of two books on Locke's epistemology written by Yasuhiko Tomida: *Rokku Tetsugaku no Kakusareta Ronri* (A Hidden Logic of Locke's Philosophy, 1991) and *Kannensetsu no Nazotoki* (Solving the Puzzle of the Theory of Ideas, 2006). Tomida criticized the 'imagist' interpretation of Locke's theory of ideas, laying bare Berkeley's and his followers' misreading of Locke. What he offered instead is a complex naturalistic interpretation: Locke developed a scientific version of the representative theory of perception by accepting the corpuscular hypothesis, and then positing the 'things themselves', though he also retained the ordinary vocabulary of direct realism. Masaki Ichinose, one of the contributors to this volume, provided a novel interpretation that Locke's philosophy (which includes, in his view, not only his theory of knowledge but political theory) rests on the particular concept of a person he developed in his account of personal identity.[35]

In the field of natural rights, property and politics, there appeared five important books on Locke from the late 1990s to the late 2000s. In 1997 Nagamitsu Miura published *Jon Rokku no Shiminteki Sekai* (The Civil World of John Locke), where he presented his critical appraisal of Locke. While Miura criticized Locke's theory of toleration for excluding Catholics and for failing to dismantle the Church of England, he also argued that his theory of property acquisition, with his theory of just war, served to destroy the lives of native Americans. In the same year, the libertarian legal philosopher Susumu Morimura, in his *Rokku Shoyūron no Saisei* (The Rebirth of a Lockean Theory of Property, 1997), provided a reconstructive, libertarian defence of Locke's justificatory arguments for property acquisition, while he also critically examined the recent Locke literature on property (by Stephen Buckle, Barbara Arneil, A. John Simmons and others) and rejected alternative compact theories of property like Hume's. By contrast, my own *Jon Rokku no Jiyūshugi Seijitetsugaku* (The Liberal Political Philosophy of John Locke, 2000)[36] presented Locke as a classical liberal who stands in need of revision. It offered a close analysis of Locke's concept of property, taking into account the views of Grotius, Pufendorf and other natural lawyers. It then undertook to clarify, criticize and revise Locke's arguments for toleration, property acquisition, political obligation, justice and the public good, with a view to creating a more egalitarian theory of rights and politics. Three years later, Locke's constitutionalism received the special attention of the constitutional scholar Koji Aikyo, who examined its historical as well as its theoretical context in his *Kindai Rikkenshugi Shisō no Genzō* (The Original Image of Modern Constitutionalist Thought, 2003). Finally, Nagamitsu Miura developed his earlier view and published a very powerful critique of Locke's defence of colonialism and the dispossession of native Americans, in the book entitled *Jon Rokku to Amerika Senjūmin (John Locke and the Native Americans*, 2009).[37] It should be added that Hiroyuki Ito's unabridged translation of the *Two Treatises of Government* appeared in this period.[38]

In the area of religion and toleration, Goko Seno published *Rokku Shūkyōshisō no Tenkai* (The Development of Locke's Religious Thought, 2005). In this 716-page book, Seno considers the religious views of Locke's contemporaries, especially those who participated in the Trinitarian Controversy; then he goes on to explain Locke's own views; and finally, he reviews his controversies with Proast, Edwards and Stillingfleet. The following year, Sonoko Yamada published *Jon Rokku Kan'yōron no Kenkyū* (A Study of John Locke's *Essay Concerning Toleration*, 2006) which aimed at clarifying Locke's view of toleration, church and the Church of England. This book contains a Japanese translation of *An Essay Concerning Toleration*, based on her examination of Locke's four manuscripts.

Thus, we see Locke scholarship really flourished in Japan up until the late 2000s. This trend continued into the 2010s. Yamada published a sequel volume in 2013, *Jon Rokku no Kyōkairon* (John Locke's Theory of Church), which included a welcome translation of the whole of Locke's critical notes on Stillingfleet in Bodleian Library MS Locke c. 34. Then younger scholars, some of whom were supervised by the previous generation of Locke scholars, completed their PhDs and started publishing books. Kenichiro Imamura's *Rōdō to Shoyū no Tetsugaku* (A Philosophy of Labour and Property, 2011) re-examined Locke's labour theory of property, taking into account previous interpretations and criticisms. Keisuke Takei examined Locke's critique of Bagshaw, Samuel Parker and Stillingfleet to clarify his own view of church and the state in his *Kokka, Kyōkai, Kojin* (The State, Church and Individuals, 2016). And Takumichi Kojo reinterpreted Locke's consent theory and defended it as a viable theory of political obligation in *Rokku Rinrigaku no Saisei* (Resurrecting Locke's Ethics, 2017).

Other young scholars have followed suit. Taku Sasaki has discussed Locke's account of free will, determinism and responsibility in *Jon Rokku no Dōtoku Tetsugaku* (John Locke's Moral Philosophy, 2017). Takuya Furuta has reconsidered Filmer's political thought, and related it to Japanese intellectual contexts in *Robāto Firumā no Seijishisō* (The Political Thought of Robert Filmer, 2018). And Yuichi Watanabe has treated the right of subsistence as fundamental to Locke's theory of rights, and critically examined his account of the right of the needy and the rights of children as well as his labour theory of property in *Jon Rokku no Kenriron: Seizonken to sono Shatei* (John Locke's Theory of Rights: The Right of Subsistence and its Scope, 2020). On the other hand, some of the senior or retired professors have spent their time and energy producing new translations (in paperback) of *The Two Treatises of Government*, *Of the Conduct of the Understanding*, *A Letter Concerning Toleration* and *The Reasonableness of Christianity*.[39] There is also a translation of Filmer's works.[40] Thus, there is now a plethora of new books on Locke, with new translations available to general readers and students.

In giving this account of the development of Locke scholarship, I have not touched on the question of what sorts of disagreements and debates have existed among Japanese scholars about the interpretation or evaluation of Locke's philosophical thought. I should briefly comment on this issue because some readers may want to know something about the clash of opinions among Japanese scholars.

It is worth pointing out, however, that instead of engaging in debates among themselves, most Japanese scholars have sought to understand and evaluate Locke's own views by carefully reading his writings on the one hand, and by critically examining the output of Anglophone scholars on the other. If we look for debates going on in the work of Japanese scholars, we are likely to find that they tend not to be with their Japanese colleagues, but with some important historical figures or some recent Anglophone scholars who have provided new or influential interpretations. This is especially true of the works which appeared in the first two periods of Locke scholarship discussed earlier. After all, there was only a limited number of Japanese Locke scholars in those days, and they were not equally interested in pursuing the same set of problems. This made it difficult for polemical exchanges to take place. Nevertheless, there were occasional disagreements on specific issues. For instance, quite a few scholars in the second period searched for modern principles of politics in Locke, but they were also puzzled by the fact that conclusions of Locke's political philosophy seemed moderate despite its radical premises. So they often characterized his political philosophy as moderate, compromising or Janus-faced.[41] But some scholars, Keiichi Matsushita for instance, dissented from this characterization, and persisted in seeing great liberating potential in Locke's individualistic principles. There were also disagreements about the nature and status of the right of resistance,[42] and about whether Locke's labour theory of appropriation is truly liberating and gives benefit to everyone, or it instead ends up justifying the exploitation of labour-power through wage contracts.[43] It must be conceded, though, that those disagreements did not amount to a sustained debate among scholars.

However, a change does seem to be taking place in the most recent period of Locke scholarship (1990s to the present day). With the increase of Locke specialists, scholars now have more opportunities to refer to each other's work and engage in debates. While there seems to be no recent debate in the area of epistemology or toleration, there are a few debates and disagreements in the area of social and political philosophy. Two disputes in which I myself have been involved may well be relevant to the concerns of the broader community of Locke scholars. First, there is a debate on how we should understand the concept of a person which Locke used in the *Two Treatises*, and how it is connected with the concept of a person he developed in the *Essay*. As I said earlier, in 1997 Ichinose provided the interpretation that Locke used in his political theory the concept of a person which he developed in his account of personal identity (added to the second edition of the *Essay*). Locke stated that the term 'person' stands for 'a thinking intelligent Being, that has reason and reflection, and can consider it self as it self, the same thinking thing in different times and places' (*Essay* II. xxvii. 9). Ichinose interprets this concept of a person as a forensic concept, one which is required by a court of justice for ascribing responsibility and giving reward or punishment. One feature of this concept, according to Ichinose, is that 'it clearly incorporates a body' (Ichinose 1997: 92–3). He stresses that the concept of a person used in moral contexts is a bodily existence (Ichinose 1997: 93–4), and claims that Locke used one and the same concept of a person both in his account of personal identity and in his account of property, especially in putting forward the proposition that 'every Man has a *Property* in his own *Person*' (TT II. 27; Ichinose 1998: 70–3). I have offered a critical response to this interpretation, arguing that 'person' in the *Essay* refers to a mental entity (constituted by the same consciousness) which can be separated from a particular body, whereas 'person' in the *Two Treatises* is not a mental entity but an object of one's property (i.e. exclusive right of disposal).[44] 'Person' in the latter sense refers to an individual human being with particular attributes and powers, as distinguished from a thing or a lower animal. On my own account, this usage of the term is derived from Roman law and modern natural jurisprudence, and has nothing to do with the theological concerns which underpin Locke's account of personal identity. I also point out that though the concept of a person used in the *Two Treatises* is not inherently committed to the dualistic mind/body metaphysics, we often reduce it to a human body for practical purposes or to keep conceptual coherence intact.⁴⁵ This debate on Locke's concept of a person raises questions about Locke's actual use of the term 'person', and about the coherence of the concept of having a property in one's own person, that is, of 'self-ownership'. It has, in consequence, influenced Imamura's later discussion of Locke's theory of property acquisition.⁴⁶

Another debate concerns how Locke's labour theory of appropriation can function, in the colonial context, as a theory which dispossesses native Americans of their lands. In Miura 2009, Miura detects in Locke's theory more than one argument for dispossession. Like Tully, however, he treats Locke as endorsing the 'vacancy' argument (which Tully calls the agricultural argument). This argument proceeds from the premise that the lands which native Americans have traditionally used for hunting and other purposes can be regarded as vacant and common because their use is not legitimate (i.e. they have not engaged in sedentary agriculture), to the conclusion that it is legitimate for the settlers to appropriate those vacant lands by their own labour.⁴⁷ I myself have criticized this attribution of the vacancy argument to Locke for lacking textual support. I have argued, instead, that Locke's unilateralism makes possible an arbitrary judgement of settlers regarding what is vacant, or what constitutes injury to native Americans, and that this, rather than the vacancy or agricultural argument, is what really explains how Locke's theory can turn into a theory of dispossession.⁴⁸ This debate raises questions about what counts as vacancy and how injury is to be judged, as well as how Locke's theory of appropriation can really serve to justify the dispossession of native Americans.

5 The present collection (2021)

We now come to the present collection. It contains eight chapters by Japanese scholars, which I believe represent the scholarly and critical treatments characteristic of contemporary Japanese scholarship on Locke. They also exhibit, to some extent, the post-war tendency to focus on social and political issues. As I said at the beginning of this Introduction, this collection is intended to challenge and criticize established interpretations of Locke, and replace them with new alternatives. I would like to indicate what sorts of established interpretations are criticized, and what alternatives are proposed. I merely provide a 'screenshot' of the points of interest of each chapter, without going into details.

Part I discusses the nature of knowledge and takes up two kinds of experimental method. In Chapter 1, Peter Anstey rejects the widespread view that all knowledge for Locke is propositional. He argues, instead, that Locke accepts a form of non-propositional knowledge. The perception of the agreement and disagreement of ideas, according to Anstey, is akin to what Bertrand Russell called knowledge by acquaintance. He presents a careful, four-step analysis of Locke's view of the acquisition of knowledge, in order to show how the mind proceeds from perceiving to affirming, then to assenting and finally to verbalizing propositions.

In Chapter 2, Shigeyuki Aoki discusses the significance of Locke's experimental method for understanding Boyle's and Locke's views on the distinction between primary and secondary qualities. He claims that Boyle's influence on Locke's treatment of the PQ/SQ distinction was actually stronger than has been supposed in the recent secondary literature. In drawing the PQ/SQ distinction, according to Aoki, Locke relied heavily on the natural philosophy of his day, Boyle's corpuscularianism in particular. At the same time, he claims that Locke removed the scholastic jargon inherent in Boyle, and rejected his *a priori* treatment of the PQ/SQ distinction.

In Chapter 3, Yasuaki Nakano challenges Stephen Gaukroger's view, widely shared by others, that Berkeley is no more than an arch-metaphysician. Nakano claims, instead, that Berkeley is an experimental philosopher, and that he is not opposed to the autonomy of phenomenal explanation. He argues that in *An Essay Towards a New Theory of Vision*, Berkeley explains visual perception by phenomenal causes without recourse to metaphysical causes. He also shows that his explanatory procedure is in line with Newton's method of analysis. Thus, Nakano concludes that there is a continuous line of experimental philosophy running from Locke via Berkeley to Hume.

Part II discusses three different doctrines found in Locke's theory of law and politics. In Chapter 4, Takumichi Kojo challenges the received view that Hume's critique effectively demolished Locke's consent theory. Kojo rejects the descriptive component of Hume's critique as irrelevant to Locke. Neither the state of nature nor the original contract serves as a historical device for Locke; rather, they perform normative functions. Kojo also criticizes Hume's normative claim that a tacit consent is not freely given. To defend Locke's view, he argues that in order for a tacit consent to be valid, it must first conform to the law of nature, which prohibits any forced consent. Second, it must also be preceded by the establishment of a democratically elected legislature. Kojo concludes that Locke's consent theory can successfully justify the obligation to obey a particular government, while Hume ends up justifying any de facto government.

In Chapter 5, Ryuichi Yamaoka clarifies the nature and status of Locke's constitutionalism by re-examining his idea of royal prerogative. Yamaoka rejects the common supposition that in order to defend constitutionalism, one has to be a legal theorist who recommends the inflexible government of laws. Instead, he portrays Locke as a political theorist who incorporated a realistic sense of politics to cope with emergencies. In fact, Locke affirmed royal prerogative and allowed for a wide range of king's discretion. Yamaoka addresses the question how Locke was able to reconcile constitutionalism with discretionary power. He offers an analysis of seventeenth-century controversies, and shows that Locke learned a great deal from Filmer and other opponents and put their royalist arguments to a contrary use. Yamaoka claims that the concept of trust plays a crucial role in legitimizing royal prerogative, and suggests that modern liberals can learn from Locke's ideological struggle.

In Chapter 6, Masaki Ichinose addresses the issue of punishment with a particular focus on the death penalty. In spite of Locke's remark in section 3 of the 'Second Treatise' which indicates his approval of the death penalty, Ichinose claims to show that Locke's theory of rights logically implies that the death penalty is impossible. This view is what Ichinose calls an 'impossibilist view of the death penalty', or impossibilism for short. It is an equivalent of the view that the death penalty is conceptually incoherent, just as 'a round square' is. The impossibilist view is a logical consequence of Locke's theory of rights because Locke claims that nobody can forfeit his or her own life as a whole, while he also holds that punishment is explicable in terms of one's forfeiture of a right. Ichinose spells out its implications and suggests that it might shed light on people's ambivalence towards the death penalty.

Part III discusses issues relating to religion and toleration. My own chapter, Chapter 7, challenges the influential view, held by John Dunn and others, that Locke extended toleration only to Christians, or to Protestants in particular. It claims, instead, that Locke's theory is much more inclusive, embracing non-Christians like Jews, Muslims and native Americans, as well as all Christians. To show this, I focus on Locke's 'harm argument', which says that nobody ought to be punished by the magistrate unless he or she harms others. The chapter explains how Locke deployed it to expand the scope of toleration which would have remained much narrower if Locke had relied solely on the other arguments available to him. It also criticizes the received view that Locke excluded Catholics. I argue that Locke opposed the exclusion of any group of people on religious grounds, and point out that when Locke did defend exclusion (as in the case of atheists), he adopted the non-religious criterion of harming others.

In Chapter 8, Keisuke Takei takes up the doctrine of salvation presented in Locke's *Reasonableness of Christianity*, and considers its components to clarify his understanding of the nature of Christianity. Takei pays close attention to two of the main components of the doctrine of salvation: the unity of inner belief with outward behaviour, and the way Jesus carries out his mission. Takei leaves aside the method, commonly taken by other scholars, of locating the *Reasonableness* in a particular theological controversy. Instead, he focuses on the idea of Christ as an exemplar who achieves the unity of his inner belief and his outward behaviour. On Takei's account, Christians who seek salvation have to believe that Jesus is the Messiah, and they come to believe it by observing his miracles and good works. To be saved, however, they also have to repent their sins and obey Jesus's commands. The doctrine of salvation, understood in this way, is perfectly consistent with Locke's view that ordinary people, as reasonable creatures, can understand Christianity by reading the Bible. The Bible presents the example of Jesus, which clearly shows what true Christianity is.

In Chapter 9, J. K. Numao ventures into largely unexplored territory, and seeks to present a coherent picture of Locke's view of the state's relationship to sex and marriage. In the first part of the chapter, Numao examines Locke's views of what were generally thought to be sexual immoralities in the seventeenth century, such as adultery, fornication, incest, polygamy and sodomy. He considers whether or not Locke believed that those sexual practices and relationships ought to be tolerated by the state, and shows that he decided on the matter on the basis of natural law rather than on Christian scriptural teachings. In the second part, Numao considers whether a Lockean theory of sex and marriage might be able to vie with contemporary accounts which often go beyond marriage. Numao argues that while Locke's vision puts an emphasis on procreation and the preservation of the human species, allowing the state to protect and privilege marriages, it nevertheless has the openness, flexibility and thus robustness to compete with contemporary liberal and libertarian accounts of sex and marriage.

I have provided a preview of each chapter, but readers of this volume will discover more arguments and criticisms than I have indicated. Locke's philosophical thought deserves careful scrutiny not only because it is of historical interest, but also because it still remains important and influential in shaping the actual world we live in today. The following pages will also set new agenda for further research and scholarly debate. As Peter Anstey pointed out more than a decade ago, one of the unfortunate features of Locke scholarship as it developed in the recent past was 'a lack of cross-fertilisation' of ideas, found among the scholars who were working independently on different aspects of Locke's philosophy

(Anstey 2006: 5). Anstey cites the example of two conflicting interpretations, on Locke's view of the relationship between will and belief formation, as existing as parallel branches of Locke scholarship with no points of intersection. As he rightly remarks,[49] we should not be satisfied with simply examining Locke's texts, but should rather talk to each other, and read each other's writings, in order to resolve any inconsistencies that exist among ourselves. So we need today more scholarly exchanges and dialogues than we have had in the past. Fortunately, the situation seems to be improving now. The John Locke Society[50] has been founded, and it now oversees the online publication of the journal *Locke Studies*.[51] Since 2018, the John Locke Society has also officially begun to hold international John Locke conferences in different parts of the world. My hope is that the present collection of chapters will stimulate Locke scholarship and contribute to a greater cross-fertilization of ideas on a larger international scale.

Notes

1. Perhaps J. K. Numao may also count as an exception, as he is Japanese Canadian and writes on Locke primarily in English.
2. J. R. Milton and Philip Milton report that the original book was *Beschrivinghe [sic] van het Machtigh Conincrijck [sic] Iapan . . .* (1649). An English translation was published in 1663 as *A True Description of the Mighty Kingdoms of Japan and Siam*. Locke may not have read this translation, but this was included in other subsequent English books. See Locke (2006: 157).
3. For an account of the likely sources of Locke's passage about the Japanese persecution, see Locke (2006: 157–9).
4. Ibid.: 300.
5. Ibid.: 301.
6. A case in point is *Shimabara no Ran* (Shimabara Rebellion, 1637–8), which the Tokugawa government was ready to treat as a Christian uprising. Later historians often claim, however, that the rebellion combined a peasant uprising with elements of Christian resistance.
7. Takano is his family name while Choei is his given name. In this Introduction, I adopt the well-established convention of putting their family names first when I refer to Japanese historical figures, including those who published before the end of the Second World War (15 August 1945). When I refer to those who are alive and those who published after the Second World War, I put their given names first.
8. Takano (1978b: 190).
9. Takano (1978a).

10 The name of the incident, often mentioned in books on Japanese history, merely reflects the Tokugawa government's perception of it, and not that of the scholars involved.
11 It should also be noted that the long vowels 'ā', 'ō' and 'ū' are usually indicated in Romanized Japanese words, with the exception of the names already well known in the West (e.g. Tokyo and Kyoto). The name 'Choei', for instance, is often written as 'Chōei'. But I have removed the long-vowel symbol (i.e. horizontal bar) from the names of all Japanese authors that appear in this Introduction, in recognition of the fact this makes it easier to digitally search for proper names.
12 In writing the next two paragraphs, I have relied on Sonoko Yamada's survey of the Locke literature of the pre-war period in Yamada (2012), and on the historical account given in Otsuki (1968: 54–9).
13 Locke (1930).
14 Locke (1940).
15 See Fukuda (1910), Takahashi (1918a, 1918b), Takahashi (1919a, 1919b).
16 To see the output of Japanese scholars, the reader might consult John Attig's 'John Locke Bibliography' (https://openpublishing.psu.edu/locke/bib/index.html, accessed 25 September 2020), or Hall and Woolhouse (1983).
17 For the rise of the study of Locke's politics for the period of 1946–69, see Yamada (2016a: 5–6). Of the 202 publications on Locke (i.e. the books and articles, including translations) which appeared in this period, 55 discussed Locke's theory of politics, and more than 90 dealt with various topics from the 'Second Treatise'. By contrast, only twenty-eight of them discussed Locke's philosophy (narrowly defined), ibid.: 5.
18 The Constitution of the Empire of Japan (Meiji Constitution, 1889) states that the Empire of Japan shall be governed 'by a line of Emperors unbroken for ages eternal' (Article 1); that the emperor is 'sacred and inviolable' (Article 3); and that he is 'the head of the Empire, combining in Himself the rights of sovereignty' (Article 4). By contrast, the new Constitution of Japan (1946) states: 'The Emperor shall be the symbol of the State and of the unity of the People, deriving his position from the will of the people with whom resides sovereign power' (Article 1).
19 Kiyomiya (1948).
20 Locke (1948).
21 Locke (1955, 1968b, 1968c).
22 The situation was somewhat different in private universities such as Waseda University, Keio University and Chuo University, as they had a stronger tradition of teaching British and American philosophy as well as economic and legal thought.
23 See Ota (1953), Hattori (1974).
24 Locke (1977). This was preceded by his partial translation of the *Essay* contained in his edition of *Rokku, Hyūmu* (1968). Like the earlier translator Kato, Otsuki as

a student had attended the reading sessions organized by Professor Oshima at his house from the late 1920s onwards (Otsuki 1968: 59).

25 Locke (1962a).
26 As Bertrand Russell once remarked, the Japanese government held a theory 'closely similar to Filmer's', and treated the emperor's power as having a divine origin while also assimilating political power to a parental power over children (Russell 2004: 565).
27 By claiming that it was a 'non-religious' tradition, the government tried to argue that everyone's religious liberty could be made compatible with State Shintō, and that there could not be an infringement of religious liberty. Religious liberty was stipulated by the Constitution of the Empire of Japan. But its protection was not effective since it did not incorporate the principle of the separation of church and state.
28 For accounts of State Shintō, see Murakami (1970), Hardacre (1989) and Shimazono (2010).
29 The words quoted here are from the text of the Shintō Directive, found in appendix 2 of Hardacre (1989: 167–70).
30 See Locke (1962b and 1968a).
31 Locke (1970a).
32 Inoue (1978).
33 Locke (1974). 'Toleratio', included in Locke (1974: 47), was printed from Bodleian Library MS Locke d. 1, pp. 125–6. This fragment was later published in Locke (1997a: 276–7) as 'Toleration D', and in Locke (2010b: 172–3) as 'Toleration and Sincerity'.
34 Tanaka and Hirano (1980). This volume is part of a series of books published on major British thinkers, and its editors and many of its contributors were members of the Japanese Society for British Philosophy. This is the one major scholarly society which has continued to support Locke scholars.
35 Ichinose (1997).
36 Reviewed in Morimura (2001).
37 Reviewed in Shimokawa (2011b). Miura later published a revised English version of the Japanese book; see Miura (2013).
38 Locke (1997b).
39 Locke (2010a, 2015, 2018, 2019).
40 Filmer (2016).
41 The theme of Locke as a philosopher of moderation had appeared in the pre-war period, but it was taken up again by quite a few scholars in the post-war period. For this and the dissenting voice, see Yamada (2016b: 4–5, 10–11).
42 See Kihachiro Kanno's long-standing disagreement with the renowned constitutional scholar Toshiyoshi Miyazawa over the definition of the right of resistance, which is found in Kanno (2001: 1–62).

43 Tanaka (1968) treated Locke's theory as having both liberating and exploitative aspects. But like Macpherson, Tanaka stressed that Locke's labour theory was initially liberating for every labourer, but was later overshadowed by a justification of the production and exchange of commodities, of the unlimited accumulation of capital and of the subordination of wage-labourers to it. Yet not every scholar shared this view. One scholar was willing to treat Locke as a proto-socialist, suggesting that there was a link to Thomas Hodgskin's claim about labour and property. For this and a related disagreement, see Yamada (2016a: 14).
44 This critical response first appeared in Shimokawa (1999), and its shorter version was later incorporated in Shimokawa (2000: 93–105). The English version of this critical response is found in Shimokawa (2006: 196–201).
45 See Shimokawa (2006: 201, and also 204–6).
46 See Imamura (2011: 29–44, 179–212).
47 Miura attributes this argument to Locke, in Miura (2009: 56–9, 67–8).
48 Both my criticism and alternative account are briefly stated in Shimokawa (2011a: 162) and Shimokawa (2011b: 134). But they are fully developed in my English work. See Shimokawa (2013: 574–83) for a detailed discussion.
49 Anstey (2006: 6).
50 See https://thejohnlockesociety.com/.
51 See https://ojs.lib.uwo.ca/index.php/locke/index.

References

Aikyo, K. (2003), *Kindai Rikkenshugi Shisō no Genzō* (The Original Image of Modern Constitutionalist Thought), Tokyo: Hōritsubunkasha.

Anstey, P. R. (2006), 'General Introduction', in P. R. Anstey (ed.), *John Locke: Critical Assessments of Leading Philosophers*, series II, vol. 1, 1–7, London: Routledge.

Attig, J. C. (n.d.), 'John Locke Bibliography', https://openpublishing.psu.edu/locke/bib/index.html

Caron, F. (1649), *Beschrijvinge van het Machtigh Koninckrijcke Japan*, Amsterdam: Hartgers.

Caron, F. and J. Schorten (1663), *A True Description of the Mighty Kingdoms of Japan and Siam*, trans. Capt. R. Manley, London: Samuel Broun and John de l'Ecluse.

Filmer, R. (2016), *Firumā Chosakushū* (Filmer's Works), trans. H. Ito and H. Watanabe, Kyoto: Kyoto University Press.

Fukuda, T. (1910), 'Jon Rokku no Shiyūzaisan Seidoron' (John Locke's Theory of the Institution of Private Property), *Mitagakkai Zasshi*, 3 (2): 111–25.

Furuta, T. (2018), *Robāto Firumā no Seijishisō* (The Political Thought of Robert Filmer), Tokyo: Iwanami Shoten.

Hall, R. and R. S. Woolhouse (1983), *80 Years of Locke Scholarship: A Bibliographical Guide*, Edinburgh: Edinburgh University Press.

Hardacre, H. (1989), *Shintō and the State: 1868–1988*, Princeton: Princeton University Press.

Hattori, T. (1974), *Eikoku Keikenron to Rokku Tetsugaku* (British Empiricism and Locke's Philosophy), Tokyo: Sobunsha.

Humphrey, J. (1667), *A Proposition for the Safety and Happiness of King and Kingdom*, London, [s. n.].

Ichinose, M. (1997), *Jinkaku Chishikiron no Seisei: Jon Rokku no Shunkan* (The Rise of the Person-Knowledge Theory: The Moment of John Locke), Tokyo: Tokyo University Press.

Imamura, K. (2011), *Rōdō to Shoyū no Tetsugaku* (A Philosophy of Labour and Property), Kyoto: Showado.

Inoue, K. (1978), *Jon Rokku to sono Senkushatachi: Igirisu Kan'yōron Kenkyū Josetsu* (John Locke and His Forerunners: An Introduction to the Study of the Theories of Toleration in England), Tokyo: Ochanomizu Shobo.

Kanno, K. (2001), *Teikōkenron to Rokku, Hobbuzu* (The Theory of the Right of Resistance, and Locke and Hobbes), Tokyo: Shinzansha.

Kato, T. (1987), *Jon Rokku no Shisō Sekai* (The World of John Locke's Thought), Tokyo: Tokyo University Press.

Kiyomiya, S. (1948), 'Nihonkoku Kenpō to Rokku no Seijishisō' (The Constitution of Japan and Locke's Political Thought), *Kokkagakkai Zasshi*, 62 (9): 1–15.

Kobayashi, S, and K. Nishitani (1929), *Rokku no Tetsugaku to Kyōiku Shichō* (Locke's Philosophy and His Thought on Education), Tokyo: Dōbunsha.

Kujo, T. (2017), *Rokku Rinrigaku no Saisei* (Resurrecting Locke's Ethics), Kyoto: Koyo Shobo.

Locke, J. (1930), *Goseiron* (An Essay concerning Human Understanding), trans. S. Hatta, Tokyo: Shunjusha.

Locke, J. (1940), *Ningen Goseiron* (An Essay concerning Human Understanding), 2 vols, trans. U. Kato, Tokyo: Iwanami Shoten.

Locke, J. (1948), *Seijiron* (Two Treatises of Government), trans. K. Matsuura, Tokyo: Tozai Shuppansha.

Locke, J. (1955), *Tōchiron* (Second Treatise), trans. H. Suzuki, Tokyo: Kawade Shobo.

Locke, J. (1962a), 'Shizenhōron' (Essays on the Law of Nature), trans. M. Hamabayashi, in *Sekai Daishisō Zenshū: Shakai, Shūkyō, Kagaku 2*, Tokyo: Kawade Shobo Shinsha.

Locke, J. (1962b), 'Shūkyōteki Kan'yō ni kansuru Shokan' (A Letter Concerning Toleration), trans. M. Hamabayashi, in *Sekai Daishisō Zenshū: Shakai, Shūkyō, Kagaku 2*, Tokyo: Kawade Shobo Shinsha.

Locke, J. (1968a), 'Kan'yō ni tsuite no Shokan' (A Letter Concerning Toleration), trans. K. Ikimatsu, in H. Otsuki (ed.), *Rokku, Hyūmu*, 347–402, Sekai no Meicho, vol. 27, Tokyo: Chuokoronsha.

Locke, J. (1968b), *Shimin Seifuron* (Second Treatise), trans. N. Ukai, Tokyo: Iwanami Shoten.
Locke, J. (1968c), 'Tōchiron' (Second Treatise), trans. T. Miyagawa, in H. Otsuki (ed.), *Rokku, Hyūmu*, 189–346, Sekai no Meicho, vol. 27, Tokyo: Chuokoronsha.
Locke, J. (1970a), *Kan'yō ni tsuiteno Shokan, Epistola de Tolerantia* (A Letter Concerning Toleration, Epistola de Tolerantia), Intro. R. Klibansky, trans. A. Hirano, Tokyo: Asahi Shuppansha.
Locke, J. (1970b), *Kirisutokyō no Gōrisei, Kisekiron* (The Reasonableness of Christianity, A Discourse of Miracles), trans. T. Hattori, Tokyo: Misaki Shobo.
Locke, J. (1974), *An Essay Concerning Toleration and Toleratio*, ed. K. Inoue, Nara: The Society for the Study of Locke's Philosophy, Department of Philosophy, The Faculty of Letters at Nara Women's University.
Locke, J. (1977), *Ningen Chiseiron* (An Essay concerning Human Understanding), 4 vols, trans. H. Otsuki, Tokyo: Iwanami Shoten.
Locke, J. (1997a), *Political Essays*, ed. Mark Goldie, Cambridge: Cambridge University Press.
Locke, J. (1997b), *Zen'yaku Tōchiron* (An Unabridged Translation: Two Treatises of Government), trans. H. Ito, Tokyo: Kashiwa Shobo.
Locke, J. (2006), *An Essay Concerning Toleration and Other Writings on Law and Politics, 1667–1683*, eds J. R. Milton and P. Milton, Oxford: Clarendon Press.
Locke, J. (2010a), *Kan'yaku Tōchiniiron* (A Complete Translation: Two Treatises of Government), trans. T. Kato, Tokyo: Iwanami Shoten.
Locke, J. (2010b), *A Letter Concerning Toleration and Other Writings*, ed. M. Goldie, Indianapolis: Liberty Fund.
Locke, J. (2015), *Chisei no Tadashii Michibikikata* (Of the Conduct of the Understanding), revised edn, trans. K. Shimokawa, Tokyo: Chikuma Shobo.
Locke, J. (2018), *Kan'yō ni tuiteno Tegami* (A Letter Concerning Toleration), trans. T. Kato and J. Lee, Tokyo: Iwanami Shoten.
Locke, J. (2019), *Kirisutokyō no Gōrisei* (The Reasonableness of Christianity), trans. T. Kato, Tokyo: Iwanami Shoten.
Matsushita, K. (1959), *Shimin Seijiriron no Keisei* (The Making of the Political Theory of Citizens), Tokyo: Iwanami Shoten.
Miura, N. (2009), *Jon Rokku to Amerika Senjūmin: Jiyūshugi to Shokuminchi Shihai* (John Locke and the Native Americans: Liberalism and Colonialism), Tokyo: Ochanomizu Shobo.
Miura, N. (2013), *John Locke and the Native Americans: Early English Liberalism and Its Colonial Reality*, Newcastle upon Tyne: Cambridge Scholars.
Morimura, S. (1997), *Rokku Shoyūron no Saisei* (The Rebirth of a Lockean Theory of Property), Tokyo: Yuhikaku.
Morimura, S. (2001), 'Review of *John Locke no Jiyushugi Seijitetsugaku*' (John Locke's Liberal Political Philosophy), *Locke Studies*, 1: 276–80.
Murakami, S. (1970), *Kokka Shintō* (State Shintō), Tokyo: Iwanami Shoten.

Oshima, M. (1938), *Rokku* (Locke), Tokyo: Iwanimi Shoten.

Ota, Y. (1953), *Chikara nituite: Ningengoseiron dai nikan nijyūichishō no Kenkyū* (Of Power: A Study of vol. 2, ch. 21 of *An Essay concerning Human Understanding*), Tokyo: Josui Shobo.

Otsuki, H. (1968), 'Igirisu Kotenkeikenron to Kindai Shisō' (British Classical Empiricism and Modern Thought), in H. Otsuki (ed.), *Rokku, Hyūmu*, 7–60, Sekai no Meicho, vol. 27, Tokyo: Chuokoronsha.

Russell, B. (2004), *History of Western Philosophy*, London: Routledge. The 1st British edn 1946.

Sasaki, T. (2017), *Jon Rokku no Dōtoku Tetsugaku* (John Locke's Moral Philosophy), Tokyo: Maruzen Shuppan.

Seno, G (2005), *Rokku Shūkyōshisō no Tenkai* (The Development of Locke's Religious Thought), Osaka: Kansai University Press.

Shimazono, S. (2010), *Kokka Shintō to Nihonjin* (State Shintō and the Japanese), Tokyo: Iwanami Shoten.

Shimokawa, K. (1999), '"Jinkaku Chishikiron" to Jon Rokku no Tetsugaku' ('The Person-Knowledge Theory' and John Locke's Philosophy), *Chubu Daigaku Jinbun Kenkyū Ronshū*, 2: 123–54.

Shimokawa, K. (2000), *Jon Rokku no Jiyūshugi Seijitetsugaku* (The Liberal Political Philosophy of John Locke), Nagoya: The University of Nagoya Press.

Shimokawa, K. (2006), 'Locke's Concept of Property', in P. R. Anstey (ed.), *John Locke: Critical Assessments of Leading Philosophers*, Series II, vol. 1, 177–216, London: Routledge.

Shimokawa, K. (2011a), 'Shohyō: Jon Rokku to Amerika Senjūmin: Jiyūshugi to Shokuminchi Shihai' (Book Review: John Locke and the Native Americans: Liberalism and Colonialism), *Shakaishisōshi Kenkyū*, 35: 160–4.

Shimokawa, K. (2011b), 'Review: *Jon Rokku to Amerika Senjumin: Jiyushugi to Shokuminchi Shihai*' (John Locke and the Native Americans: Liberalism and Colonialism), *Locke Studies*, 11: 181–8.

Shimokawa, K. (2013), 'The Origin and Development of Property: Conventionalism, Unilateralism, and Colonialism', in P. R. Anstey (ed.), *The Oxford Handbook of British Philosophy in the Seventeenth Century*, 563–86, Oxford: Oxford University Press.

Takahashi, S. (1918a), 'Jon Rokku no Rishigakusetsu (jou)' (John Locke's Doctrine of Interest (I)), *Mitagakkai Zasshi*, 12 (8): 1–30.

Takahashi, S. (1918b), 'Jon Rokku no Rishigakusetsu (ge)' (John Locke's Doctrine of Interest (II)), *Mitagakkai Zasshi*, 12 (9): 27–67.

Takahashi, S. (1919a), 'Jon Rokku no Tetsugaku to sono Keizaigakusetsu to no Kōshō (I)' (Interactions between John Locke's Philosophy and his Economic Doctrine (I)), *Mitagakkai Zasshi*, 13 (8): 51–82.

Takahashi, S. (1919b), 'Jon Rokku no Tetsugaku to sono Keizaigakusetsu to no Kōshō (II)' (Interactions between John Locke's Philosophy and His Economic Doctrine (II)), *Mitagakkai Zasshi*, 13 (9): 21–56.

Takano, C. (1978a), 'Bojutsu Yumemonogatari' (The 1838 Tale of a Dream), in S. Sato (ed.), *Kazan Choei Ronshū* (The Selected Works of Kazan and Choei), 199–211, Tokyo: Iwanami Shoten.

Takano, C. (1978b), 'Seiyo Gakushi no Setsu' (Doctrines of Western Philosophers), in S. Sato (ed.), *Kazan Choei Ronshū* (The Selected Works of Kazan and Choei), 190–8, Tokyo: Iwanami Shoten.

Takei, K. (2016), *Kokka, Kyōkai, Kojin* (The State, Church and Individuals), Kyoto: Kyoto University Press.

Tanaka, S. (1968), *Jon Rokku Kenkyū* (John Locke Studies), Tokyo: Miraisha.

Tanaka, S. and A. Hirano, eds (1980), *Jon Rokku Kenkyū* (John Locke Studies), Tokyo: Ochanomizu Shobo.

Tomida, Y. (1991), *Rokku Tetsugaku no Kakusareta Ronri* (A Hidden Logic of Locke's Philosophy), Tokyo: Keiso Shobo.

Tomida, Y. (2006), *Kannensetsu no Nazotoki* (Solving the Puzzle of the Theory of Ideas), Kyoto: Sekaishisōsha.

Yamada, S. (2006), *Jon Rokku Kan'yōron no Kenkyū* (A Study of John Locke's *Essay Concerning Toleration*), Hiroshima: Keisuisha.

Yamada, S. (2012), 'Senzen Nihon no Rokku Kenkyū' (Locke Scholarship in Pre-war Japan), *Hiroshima Hōgaku*, 36 (1): 31–54.

Yamada, S. (2013), *Jon Rokku no Kyōkairon* (John Locke's Theory of Church), Hiroshima: Keisuisha.

Yamada, S. (2016a), 'Sengo Nihon ni okeru Jon Rokku Kenkyū (jou): 1946–1969nen' (Locke Scholarship in Post-war Japan (I): 1946–1969), *Hiroshima Hōgaku*, 39 (4): 1–18.

Yamada, S. (2016b), 'Sengo Nihon ni okeru Jon Rokku Kenkyū (ge): 1946–1969nen' (Locke Scholarship in Post-war Japan (II): 1946–1969), *Hiroshima Hōgaku*, 40 (1): 1–24.

Watanabe, Y. (2020), *Jon Rokku no Kenriron: Seizonken to sono Shatei* (John Locke's Theory of Rights: The Right of Subsistence and Its Scope), Kyoto: Koyo Shobo.

Part I

Knowledge and experimental method

1

Locke and non-propositional knowledge[1]

Peter R. Anstey

In *An Essay concerning Human Understanding* (hereafter *Essay*) Locke claims:

(1) *Knowledge* ... consists in the perception of the agreement or disagreement of *Ideas*. (*Essay* IV. vii. 2)[2]

He also speaks of

(2) our Knowledge, which all consists in Propositions. (*Essay* II. xxxiii. 19)

These two claims do not sit well together. How can the perception of a relation between ideas be some proposition? Needless to say, a wide range of interpretations have been proposed by scholars in order to explain how both of these claims can be true for Locke. The favoured strategy in the secondary literature is to interpret the first claim so that it conforms to the second.[3] Thus, it is argued that, for Locke, the perception of the agreement or disagreement of ideas just is the forming of a true proposition. As David Owen puts it, for Locke '[i]n knowledge, there is no distinction between perceiving the agreement or disagreement of ideas, forming the proposition, and knowing it to be true' (Owen 1999: 47).[4] This strategy is favoured because, to many scholars, the view that Locke believed that knowledge is fundamentally propositional seems very secure: if he believed anything about knowledge, it is claimed, he believed that all knowledge is propositional.

Yet this strategy is not without its problems. This is because it ties Locke's definition of knowledge to his theory of true propositions, and the theory of true propositions concerns not only the agreement and disagreement of ideas, as required by Locke's definition, but also the agreement and disagreement of the things signified by those ideas. As Locke puts it, propositions are the joining and separating of signs and the word 'truth' signifies 'nothing but *the joining or separating of Signs, as the Things signified by them, do agree or disagree one with another*' (*Essay* IV. v. 2). In response to this Ruth Mattern, a proponent of this orthodox, propositional interpretation, suggests that Locke had two senses of the terms 'agreement' and 'disagreement'; a stricter one referring only to ideas and a looser one for ideas and those things represented by the ideas in question.[5] Samuel Rickless, another proponent, responds in a diametrically opposed way, claiming that since 'agreement' and 'disagreement' are restricted to relations between ideas, Locke denies that we can have knowledge of contingent truths. On Rickless's view, all knowledge, for Locke, is of necessary truths (or falsehoods).[6]

Neither of these strategies is very satisfying. There is no clear evidence of a loose sense of 'agreement' in Locke's writings, and a theory of knowledge that precludes knowledge of contingent facts seems to undercut the prominent role of experience in Locke's overall project, doing away with what Locke calls sensitive knowledge altogether.

In this chapter I propose a different strategy: instead of forcing claim 1 to conform to claim 2, I shall argue that claims 1 and 2 are about different types of knowledge and that claim 1 should not be interpreted so as to conform to claim 2. In fact, I go further and argue that claim 1 is concerned with a form of non-propositional knowledge. Thus, I deny that, for Locke, all knowledge is propositional. I argue that what Locke means when he makes claims such as claim 1 is that the objects of knowledge in its most fundamental sense are ideas, and on the few occasions that he makes claim 2, he means that all the objects of knowledge, in the sense of 'all the things that we know', are propositions.

There is a more precise way of setting out what is at stake here. The orthodox view of Locke on knowledge, the view that I oppose, can be stated as a bi-conditional:

3. One perceives the agreement or disagreement of ideas *A* and *B* *if and only if* one perceives the truth of a proposition containing ideas *A* and *B*.

According to the interpretation offered in this chapter, it is true that if one perceives the truth of a proposition then one perceives the agreement or disagreement of its constituent ideas. This is because one perceives the truth of a proposition as a result of perceiving the agreement or disagreement of its constituent ideas.[7] However, I deny that Locke was committed to the second conditional, namely, that if one perceives the agreement or disagreement of ideas, then one perceives the truth of a proposition. The difference between these two conditionals is subtle but important. Many of Locke's discussions about perceiving the agreement or disagreement of ideas appear in the context of a discussion of how we come to know the truth of propositions; that is, they pertain to the first conditional. In my view, these need clearly to be demarcated from those discussions of the perception of the agreement or disagreement of ideas that have to do with the definition of knowledge and the exposition of Locke's three degrees of knowledge: intuitive, demonstrative and sensitive.

To put this another way, some of what Locke says concerning knowledge and propositions has to do with how we know the truth or falsity of propositions that we encounter by some means or other. But Locke also has things to say about acquiring knowledge directly with reference to ideas only and not to propositions. In the former case, if we encounter a proposition, through conversation, say, we know that it is true or false by perceiving the agreement or disagreement between its constituent ideas. By contrast, if in the absence of any proposition we perceive that two ideas agree or disagree, we are then able to form a proposition concerning that agreement or disagreement. It is important to the argument of this chapter that these two different contexts for the perception of the agreement or disagreement of ideas are not conflated.

The chapter proceeds as follows. It sets out an interpretation of Locke as holding a four-step theory of the acquisition of knowledge, culminating in knowledge of verbal propositions. The steps can be labelled as perceiving, affirming, assenting and verbalizing. Of course, Locke does not present his theory as comprising these four steps: this parsing of the theory is my own. However, I contend that the four-step interpretation is a very effective way of coming to grips with the content of his theory.

The most salient feature of these steps is that the first involves a form of non-propositional knowledge. Along the way I discuss the passages in which Locke claims that all our knowledge is of propositions, and I point out a number of weaknesses in some of the leading alternative interpretations of Locke on knowledge. However, this chapter does not provide a thorough and systematic critique of all the interpretations in the large secondary literature that conflict with my own. Instead, it is intended that the interpretation offered here should stand in its own right as a positive alternative to those who interpret Locke as holding that all knowledge is fundamentally propositional.

It should be said at the outset that Locke's views about ideas and about knowledge contain gaps and do not answer all of the questions that we like to ask of them.[8] Nevertheless, in my view, there are enough materials to construct a coherent theory, and that is what I propose to do here. The chapter concentrates on intuitive and demonstrative knowledge and has little to say about sensitive knowledge. This is not because this third form of knowledge does not fit the interpretation offered here, but because it is, in my view, more complicated, and offering an interpretation of the nature of sensitive knowledge would be a distraction from the chapter's main aim.[9] The main aim is to set out the four-step interpretation of Locke on knowledge with special reference to the fact that Locke is committed to a form of foundational, non-propositional knowledge. Each of the following four sections deals with one of the steps in Locke's view of knowledge. For ease of exposition all terms denoting ideas are in italics and all mentions of propositions are between angle brackets '< >'.

1 Step One: Perceiving the agreement or disagreement of two ideas

The first step in acquiring intuitive or demonstrative knowledge involves the perception of the relation of agreement or disagreement between two ideas.[10] Further, according to Locke, to acquire demonstrative knowledge is to perceive that two ideas agree or disagree with the assistance of a third, intermediate idea.[11] Locke calls intermediate ideas proofs,[12] but this can be confusing for modern interpreters, and I will restrict myself to calling them intermediate ideas. Locke also claims that more than one intermediate idea might be needed, but I will largely ignore this complication here.

Step One is the step that I claim is pre-propositional. It is simply perceiving the agreement. I suggest that we avoid expressing this as seeing *that* they agree, that is, seeing that the idea of *a* agrees with the idea of *F*. Here we need to rid ourselves of contemporary notions of propositions such as that nature has a propositional structure.[13] We also need to avoid being deceived by the manner in which I am expressing these thoughts. As Locke himself points out,[14] we can only discuss these matters using verbal propositions, but the point is that when, according to Locke, we acquire intuitive or demonstrative knowledge, we are simply perceiving the agreement of *a* and *F*. To perceive the relations of agreement and disagreement is not to perceive propositionally, even though what is perceived can only be expressed and communicated propositionally.

Here is textual evidence for this view. Locke claims:

> §1. SINCE *the Mind*, in all its Thoughts and Reasonings, hath no other immediate Object but its own *Ideas*, which it alone does or can contemplate, it is evident, that our Knowledge is only conversant about them.
> §2. *Knowledge* then seems to me to be nothing but *the perception of the connexion and agreement, or disagreement and repugnancy of any of our Ideas*. In this alone it consists. (*Essay* IV. i. 1–2)

In this quotation he does not mention *propositions*, or what philosophers call knowing *that*. Instead his view is that we have knowledge when we perceive the agreement or disagreement of ideas. To be sure, the nature of agreeing and disagreeing needs to be cashed out, but this is Locke's primitive notion of knowledge. Later, in the chapter on reason, Locke tells us:

> Though the deducing one Proposition from another, or making *Inferences in Words*, be a great part of Reason, and that which it is usually employ'd about: yet the principal Act of Ratiocination is the finding the Agreement, or Disagreement of two *Ideas* one with another, by the intervention of a third. (*Essay* IV. xvii. 18, underlining added)

The most natural reading of this passage is that it sets up a contrast between deducing one proposition from another and perceiving the agreement or disagreement of two ideas with the aid of a third. This is really quite an important contrast. Locke is saying that the 'principal act of ratiocination' is not making deductions from propositions or making inferences using words, but rather 'finding the Agreement, or Disagreement of two *Ideas* one with another'.[15] Elsewhere he says, 'to discover the Agreement or Disagreement . . . this is that which we call *Reasoning*' (*Essay* IV. ii. 2).[16]

Locke provides a clear example of how this works in his *Second Reply* to Bishop Stillingfleet. He asks: 'cannot the sides of a given triangle be known to be equal by the intervention of two circles, whereof one of these sides is a common radius?' (Locke 1823, 4: 232).

In this example one can perceive that the ideas of the three sides of the triangle do agree with the assistance of the two ideas of circles with the same radius and that the relevant sort of agreement is equivalence of length (see Figure 1.1).[17] We can, of course, express this propositionally, but the example aims to show that it is the 'seeing' that they agree with the help of the intermediate ideas – it is the moment that the penny drops – that is the moment one has acquired demonstrative knowledge for Locke.

It is not enough to say that our perceivings of the agreements of ideas in this example are not knowledge because if they were knowledge they would have to be true and perceptions cannot be true. For that is to beg the question: that is to start from the premise that knowledge is propositional, the very claim that this interpretation of Locke's view implicitly denies. And yet, a *modus tollens* is looming here because, as many are quick to point out, Locke does seem to claim in a number of places that all the things we know are propositions.

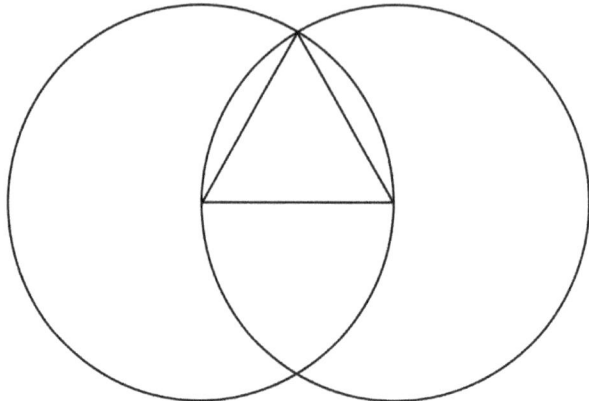

Figure 1.1 Two circles and an equilateral triangle.

1.1 Is *all* knowledge propositional?

Here are the passages in chronological order. In the very last sentence of Book Two of the *Essay* of 1690 Locke says:

> our abstract *Ideas*, and general Words, have so constant a relation one to another, that it is impossible to speak clearly and distinctly of <u>our Knowledge, which all consists in Propositions</u>, without considering, first, the Nature, Use, and Signification of Language; which therefore must be the business of the next Book. (*Essay* II. xxxiii. 19, underlining added)[18]

In his *Second Reply* to Stillingfleet of 1699 Locke says:

> Every thing which we either know or believe, is some proposition: now no proposition can be framed as <u>the object of our knowledge</u> or assent, wherein two ideas are not joined to, or separated from one another. (Locke 1823, 4: 357, underlining added)

Finally, in the posthumous *Elements of Natural Philosophy* it is claimed:

> Knowledge, which is the highest degree of the speculative faculties, <u>consists in the perception of the truth of affirmative or negative propositions</u>. (Locke 1823, 3: 329, underlining added)

Ostensibly, these three passages provide strong support for the view that, for Locke, all knowledge is propositional knowledge. The burden of proof, therefore, lies with those who would challenge this interpretation. And yet it is worth pausing to point out that none of these passages, on its own, is particularly persuasive.

The first passage from the end of Book Two of the *Essay* is clearly a segue into the next book, Book Three, which deals with words and language: this naturally follows on from Book Two, which is concerned with ideas. The passage is not about Locke's theory of knowledge. Nevertheless, the expression 'which all consists in Propositions' can be read in a way that is consonant with the orthodox interpretation if 'to consist in' means to have its essence or essential character in.[19] Moreover, Locke has a strong preference for using 'to consist in' in this essentialist sense. Ironically, we know this because far and away Locke's most common use of the term 'consist in' in the essentialist sense is in the claim that knowledge consists in the perception of the agreement or disagreement of ideas.[20] If Locke is using 'consists in' in this essentialist sense, then it is possible to interpret the passage, *contra* the orthodox view, as referring to that particular sort of 'Knowledge, which all consists in Propositions'.[21] However, 'to consist in' can also mean to be composed of,[22] and, I contend, on the basis of the context of the passage – irrespective of the persuasiveness of the interpretation of Locke on knowledge argued for in this chapter – that this is the sense here. It is far more natural to regard Locke as saying in this passage that all the knowledge we share through the use of words comprises propositions, and since words are the constituents of verbal propositions, they are the subject of the next book.

The second passage is concerned not with the definition of knowledge but its objects. The juxtaposition of knowledge and belief together with the claim that 'no proposition can <u>be framed</u> as the object of our knowledge or assent' suggests that Locke is thinking of propositions as constructed by the understanding. None of this precludes another sense of 'knowledge' that is pre-propositional, i.e. the perception of the agreement of ideas. Thus, this passage on its own does not provide a definitive proof text for the orthodox interpretation.

The third passage is more problematic still. For, it is now clear that some passages of the *Elements* were added after Locke's death and, as a result, the authorship of the entire work is in question. It may well not have been composed by Locke at all and it certainly does not carry any weight as a guide to the correct interpretation of the *Essay*.[23] In short, Locke may not have ever claimed that knowledge consists in 'the perception of the truth of affirmative, or negative Propositions'. He certainly never used the term 'speculative facultys' in any published work or in his correspondence, and this alone is enough to give us caution when approaching this passage. Nevertheless, given the combined weight of these three passages, the onus is on those who would deny that for Locke all knowledge is propositional, to put forward an alternative case.

1.2 Locke's perception of agreement or disagreement is akin to knowledge by acquaintance

The claim that not all knowledge is propositional should hardly surprise us. For there is another type of knowledge which, at least since Russell, we are all familiar with, namely, knowledge by acquaintance. For Russell:

> We shall say that we have *acquaintance* with anything of which we are directly aware, without the intermediary of any process of inference or any knowledge of truths. (Russell 1976: 25)

I contend that Locke's view that knowledge is the perception of the agreement or disagreement of ideas is best explicated as a form of knowledge by acquaintance.[24]

A preliminary consideration in favour of this interpretation is the fact that Locke claims that we can know individual ideas:

> Every one that has any Knowledge at all, has, as the Foundation of it, various and distinct *Ideas*: And it is the first act of the Mind, (without which, it can never be capable of any Knowledge,) to know every one of its *Ideas* by it self, and distinguish it from others. (*Essay* IV. vii. 4)

This passage clearly states that we know each one of the ideas in our mind. Locke goes on in this section to say, '[e]very one finds in himself, that he knows the *Ideas* he has . . . And that when more than one are there, he knows them distinctly and unconfusedly one from another.' There is no mention here of the agreement or disagreement of ideas and no mention of propositions. In fact, the parenthetical clause in the earlier part of the passage (cited earlier) suggests that the knowing of individual ideas is foundational in so far as it is a prerequisite for knowledge in some broader (perhaps propositional) sense: without knowing individual ideas we are 'never capable of any Knowledge'. The defender of the orthodox view might counter that, for Locke, to know an idea 'by it self' is just to perceive that it *agrees* with itself and is therefore propositional. But Locke never claims as much, and this interpretation commits Locke to the extreme view that, in every case, to have an idea is to know a proposition. Worse still, this interpretation is open to the following *reductio*:

(1) If S perceives one idea, then S knows (*Essay* IV. vii. 4).
(2) S knows IFF S perceives the agreement of two ideas (Orthodox interpretation).

(3) If S perceives the agreement of two ideas, then S perceives two ideas (Necessary truth).
(4) Therefore, if S perceives one idea, then S perceives two ideas.

It is clear, therefore, that this passage (and others like it[25]) presents a real problem for the orthodox view.

This brings us to consider what Russell says about knowledge by acquaintance:

> Knowledge of things, when it is of the kind we call knowledge by *acquaintance*, is essentially simpler than any knowledge of truths, and logically independent of knowledge of truths, though it would be rash to assume that human beings ever, in fact, have acquaintance with things without at the same time knowing some truth about them. (Russell 1976: 25)

For Russell, knowledge by acquaintance is independent of knowledge of truths (or falsehoods). It is a form of awareness that is of the highest epistemic standing and it is reflected in common language about knowledge. Likewise, for Locke, the objects with which the understanding is directly acquainted are our ideas, including the direct perception of relations between ideas, and this is independent of knowledge of truths.

Furthermore, for Locke, the perception of the agreement or disagreement of ideas is non-inferential. In the simplest form of knowledge, what he calls intuitive knowledge, this is obviously the case. Intuitive knowledge is 'the perception of the certain Agreement, or Disagreement of two *Ideas* immediately compared together' (*Essay* IV. xvii. 17). In the case of demonstrative knowledge, by contrast, the mind is not passively acquainted with the ideas. Locke describes the perception involved in demonstrative knowledge as 'not without pains and attention: There must be more than one transient view to find it. A steddy application and pursuit is required to this Discovery' (*Essay* IV. ii. 4).[26] Nevertheless, the perception of the holding of the relation of agreement or disagreement with the assistance of an intermediate idea is just that, a perception.

Of course, there are differences between Locke's view and Russell's view, and we need to be on guard against anachronism here. Locke, for example, takes ideas to be the direct objects of perception and many ideas, being concepts, are representational in nature. Russell, by contrast, in his early formulation, posits that we have immediate epistemic access to sense data. Among contemporary acquaintance theorists there is a variety of views as to the nature of the relata of the acquaintance relation.[27] Nevertheless, it does seem that Locke's notion of perception is closely analogous to Russell's acquaintance and a consequence of this is that when he claims that 'the principal Act of Ratiocination is the finding the Agreement, or Disagreement of two *Ideas* one with another', he has something akin to what we now call knowledge by acquaintance in view. By contrast, when Locke speaks of all of the things that we know or believe being propositions, he is referring to the objects of knowledge, that is, propositions.

Locke did not have the terminological distinction between 'knowledge by acquaintance' and 'propositional knowledge'. However, just as the determinate-determinable distinction in the theory of properties is clearly present in Locke's *Essay*, so too, I contend, is a latent form of our modern distinction between knowledge by acquaintance and propositional knowledge.

2 Step Two: Affirming and the construction of mental propositions

The second step in the acquisition of knowledge involves the construction of a mental proposition. For Locke, to perceive a simple idea is not to perceive a proposition; to perceive a complex idea is not to perceive a proposition; to perceive the joining or separating of two ideas is not to perceive a proposition; to perceive the three ideas *black*, *white* and *disagreement* is not to perceive a proposition. Why should we think, therefore, as the orthodox view demands, that to perceive the holding of a disagreement relation between *black* and *white* is the perceiving of a proposition? Is it plausible to think that there is something about the disagreement relation that changes the object of perception from three ideas to a proposition? And if Locke equates perceiving the disagreement here with perceiving a proposition, why does he never say that we perceive propositions or that propositions can be the objects of perception? In order to answer these questions we need to get clear on how, according to Locke, the understanding constructs propositions.

For Locke, a proposition is '[t]he *joining* or *separating* of signs' (*Essay* IV. v. 2) and in the case of mental propositions the signs are ideas.[28] However, it is not merely the joining or separating of signs that results in a proposition, because the construction of complex ideas also involves joining or separating and yet complex ideas are not propositions.[29] The difference between complex ideas and mental propositions lies in their mode of construction. In the case of the construction of complex ideas, the power involved is combining (or separating in the case of abstract ideas). In the case of a mental proposition, one of two powers of the understanding are involved in their construction, namely, affirming or negating.[30]

For example, in his discussion of the origin of maxims Locke says that there are no 'eternal truths', that is, 'Propositions in any ones Mind, till he, having got the abstract *Ideas*, joyn'd or separated them by affirmation or negation' (*Essay* IV. xi. 14). The powers of affirmation or negation applied to the ideas make those ideas the constituents of mental propositions. Ideas are affirmed or denied (negated) of each other in so far as these ideas are perceived to agree or disagree *in virtue of* the agreement or disagreement of the things signified. Furthermore, it is in virtue of this complex set of relations between both the signs themselves, and the signs and the things signified that propositions have truth-values: they are either true or false. For Locke, strictly speaking it is only propositions that are said to be true or false, though he does allow a derivative sense in which ideas may be true or false.[31]

The key feature of Step Two is that the construction of a mental proposition follows or is subsequent to the perception of the agreement or disagreement of two ideas. Once one is acquainted with the holding of the agreement relation between two ideas, say, then one can affirm that a is F or that $x = y$. To affirm in this context is to form or make a mental proposition from constituent ideas.[32] It is pre-linguistic in so far as it does not involve words: it merely involves the ideas a and F related by *co-existence*, or x and y related by *identity*.[33] And it is pre-propositional in so far as the creation of a mental proposition results from this act of affirmation.[34] Thus, when Locke speaks of knowing 'the truth of certain Propositions, that will arise from the Agreement or Disagreement, which he will perceive in his own *Ideas*. Such Propositions are therefore called *Eternal Truths*' (*Essay* IV. xi. 14),[35] I take it that it is the propositions that 'arise from' perceiving the agreement of ideas. Again, Locke speaks of *making* propositions when he says, '[t]he signs we chiefly use, are either *Ideas*, or Words, wherewith <u>we make</u> either mental, or verbal Propositions. *Truth* lies in so joining, or separating these Representatives, as the Things they stand for, do, in themselves, agree, or disagree' (*Essay* II. xxxii. 19, underlining added).[36]

For Locke, to affirm F of a is to join the constituent ideas by affirmation in order to construct the mental proposition <*a is F*>.[37] By parity of reasoning then (to fill in the details that Locke omits to provide) to negate is to affirm $\neg F$ of a, that is, to construct the mental proposition <*a is ¬F*>. The formation of the mental proposition involves the construction or bringing together of signs. The signs signify and the mental proposition has a truth-value: it is either true or false. Its truth-value is determined by the way the things signified are and not by the signs themselves.[38] If the mental proposition contains the idea of *This snow* and the idea of *white* related by *co-existence*, then the nature of snow in the world will be the truthmaker for the mental proposition <*This snow is white*>.[39]

Note here that affirming and negating are not propositional attitudes. To affirm F of *a* is not to believe or know <*a is F*>. It is simply to bind the ideas of *a*, F in virtue of the perception of their *co-existence*. Negation, by parity of reasoning (again filling in the details that Locke omits to provide[40]), is not unbinding but rather binding the ideas of *a*, F in virtue of the perception of their *in-co-existence*. Locke sometimes uses the word 'affirm' in the sense of believe, but that is not the sense in this context.[41] When it comes to propositions, to affirm is to construct an affirmative mental proposition and to negate is to construct a negative mental proposition. He also calls affirming *putting together* and negating *separating*. Here is how he expresses it in *Essay* IV. v. 6:

> Every one's Experience will satisfie him, that the Mind, either by perceiving or supposing the Agreement or Disagreement of any of its *Ideas*, does tacitly within it self put them into a kind of Proposition affirmative or negative, which I have endeavoured to express by the terms *Putting together* and *Separating*. But this Action of the Mind, which is so familiar to every thinking and reasoning Man, is easier to be conceived by reflecting on what passes in us, when we affirm or deny, than to be explained by Words.

2.1 David Owen's interpretation

David Owen claims that this is not a second step here but a description of the first step: that the act of perceiving the agreement or disagreement of two ideas is constitutive of the forming of the mental proposition. For Owen, perceiving that two ideas agree or disagree is the joining or separating of ideas to form a proposition.[42] Indeed, Owen uses the very extract just cited as his proof text, claiming '[t]his passage is unambiguous' (Owen 2007: 415).

However, there are problems with Owen's claims here. First, Locke's phrase 'by perceiving or supposing the agreement or disagreement' could mean 'in the very act of perceiving . . . [the mind puts] them into a kind of proposition'. This is Owen's reading. But equally, the preposition 'by' here could mean 'as a result of', thus, 'as a result of perceiving or supposing the agreement . . . he tacitly within itself put them into a kind of proposition'.[43] Moreover, as Benjamin Hill has pointed out, the fact that the proposition is formed tacitly reinforces this latter interpretation. If the processes were identical, namely, the perceiving the agreement and the construction of the proposition, the adverb 'tacitly' would not seem appropriate here.[44] 'Tacitly' here almost certainly means by implication or by way of consequence. Indeed, the OED cites *Essay* III. ii. 8 for this very meaning of the adjectival form 'tacit'.⁴⁵ Locke's sense, then, is that the mind, as a result of presuming that the two ideas agree, tacitly, that is, by way of consequence, constructs a mental proposition.

Furthermore, Owen wrongly takes Locke's talk here of affirming and denying as referring to propositional attitudes. Owen claims 'perceiving, or judging, of two ideas' agreement or disagreement just is knowing or believing something. So constructing a proposition is the very same mental act as knowing or believing' (Owen 2007: 414). But, to repeat the interpretation offered here, to affirm is not to know or to believe, but to put together ideas having perceived their agreement. For Locke, one perceives that the idea of *black* and the idea of *white* disagree and then one denies the idea of *black* of the idea of *white* by forming the mental proposition <Black is not white>. Locke does not speak of propositions as the objects of perception, because they are constructed out of the objects of perception.

3 Step Three: Assenting and knowing *that*

Once the understanding has constructed the mental proposition, it can then assent to or dissent from the proposition.⁴⁶ On this view, the proposition is the object of knowing, so it is not the product or outcome of an act of knowing. Thus, the mind can have or can apprehend a proposition without knowing it to be true or false.⁴⁷ This is not an idiosyncratic view on Locke's part, for as Gabriel Nuchelmans pointed out, the distinction between a proposition being present to, or entertained by, the understanding in the absence of a propositional attitude of assent or dissent was a familiar one in early modern logic.⁴⁸ The claim that affirming one idea of another is a distinct act from assenting to a proposition containing those very ideas is important because it absolves Locke of an accusation that has repeatedly been brought against his theory. This is the charge that he conflates the formation of a proposition with the having of a propositional attitude to that proposition.⁴⁹

It might be asked, however, whether it is appropriate to speak of assent in this context. A careful survey of Locke's use of the term reveals that it is. Take, for example, the following claim in his *Second Vindication of the Reasonableness of Christianity* which clearly distinguishes between affirmation and assent:

> The Question is about a Proposition to be believed, which must first necessarily be understood. For a Man cannot possibly give his assent to any Affirmation or

Negation, unless he understand the terms as they are joyn'd in that Proposition, and has a Conception of the thing affirm'd or deny'd, and also a Conception of the thing concerning which it is affirm'd or deny'd as they are there put together. (Locke 2012: 80)[50]

Now, while much of what Locke has to say about assent pertains to judgement and probable opinion,[51] he also speaks of assent in relation to intuitive and demonstrative knowledge. For example, Locke claims that in the case of demonstrative knowledge, 'though it be certain, yet the evidence of it is *not* altogether *so clear* and bright, <u>nor the assent so ready</u>, *as* in *intuitive* Knowledge' (*Essay* IV. ii. 4, underlining added). So, in the case of demonstrative knowledge we assent less readily to the proposition than we do in the case of intuitive knowledge. Likewise, when someone recalls from memory a proposition of which they previously perceived the agreement or disagreement of its constituent ideas, 'he, without doubt or hesitation, embraces the right side, <u>assents to</u>, and is certain of the Truth of it' (*Essay* IV. i. 8, underlining added).

Locke's reference to certainty in this last passage leads us to a further consideration that weighs heavily in favour of the view that knowledge for Locke is fundamentally non-propositional and this is his claim about the certainty of knowledge in the Stillingfleet correspondence. Stillingfleet had accused Locke of founding the certainty of knowledge on the way of ideas and not the way of reason. To found certainty on reason is, according to Stillingfleet, to found it on principles, that is, propositions that are self-evident. Locke objects that there must also be a foundation to the certainty of these principles and that foundation is the perception of the agreement or disagreement of their constituent ideas. If Locke had believed that this perception were propositional in form, he could simply and quickly have dealt with Stillingfleet's objection. For he could have claimed that they are really talking past each other: the perception of the agreement of ideas in a self-evident proposition just is a proposition. However, this, notoriously, is not the line that Locke takes. Instead Locke repeatedly makes the following sort of claim:

> Your lordship here contends, that my argument is not taken from the idea, but from true principles of reason. I do not say it is taken from any one idea, but from all the ideas concerned in it. But your lordship, if you herein oppose any thing I have said, must, I humbly conceive, say, not from ideas, but from true principles of reason; several whereof your lordship has here set down. And whence, I beseech your lordship, comes the certainty of any of those propositions, which your lordship calls true principles of reason, but from the perceivable agreement or disagreement of the ideas contained in them? Just as it is expressed in those

propositions, *v.g.* 'a man cannot doubt of his own perception', is a true principle of reason, or a true proposition, or a certain proposition: but to the certainty of it we arrive, only by perceiving the necessary agreement of the two ideas of perception and self-consciousness. (*Letter to Stillingfleet*, Locke 1823, 4: 61)[52]

4 Step Four: Verbalizing and the construction of verbal propositions

Once the mental proposition has been formed, the understanding normally moves very quickly to put it into verbal form: to name the ideas and to express the proposition as a sentence in a natural or symbolic language.

> To form a clear Notion of *Truth*, it is very necessary to consider *Truth* of Thought, and *Truth* of Words, distinctly one from another: but yet it is very difficult to treat of them asunder. Because it is unavoidable, in treating of mental Propositions, to make use of Words: and then the Instances given of *Mental Propositions*, cease immediately to be barely Mental, *and* become *Verbal*. For a *mental Proposition* being nothing but a bare consideration of the *Ideas*, as they are in our Minds stripp'd of Names, they lose the Nature of purely *mental Propositions*, as soon as they are put into Words. (*Essay* IV. v. 3)

As with the formation of mental propositions, the formation of verbal propositions involves affirmation and negation:

> *Verbal Propositions*, which *are Words* the signs of our *Ideas put together or separated in affirmative or negative Sentences*. By which way of affirming or denying, these Signs, made by Sounds, are as it were put together or separated one from another. (*Essay* IV. v. 5)

And once this step is taken, according to Locke, we can assent to or dissent from the verbal proposition. Much of our reasoning happens at this level after we have acquired language and a sufficient stock of ideas.[53] Assent and dissent are faculties that the mind applies, not only to mental propositions (as we saw above), but to verbal propositions: 'This Faculty of the Mind, when it is exercised ... about Truths delivered in Words, is most commonly called *Assent* or *Dissent*' (*Essay* IV. xiv. 3).

Now, it might be thought that this fourth step always follows the third step such that the formation of verbal propositions is subsequent to the asserting of a mental proposition. There is no reason, however, why the verbal proposition need be formed at all. Locke does not discuss the chronological sequence of the steps in any detail, and it is conceivable on his view that the formation of the verbal proposition normally occurs immediately after the formation of the mental proposition. In this case, the asserting of the mental proposition and the assenting to the verbal proposition would be experienced as virtually simultaneous. What is clear, however, is that the formation of the verbal proposition cannot precede the formation of the mental proposition.

We need not digress into the origins or the implications of Locke's view that words signify ideas for his philosophy of language. For the point at issue here is the tight link between our words, the ideas that they signify and the things that our ideas represent. The latter is of two sorts: ideas can refer to extra-mental entities, that is, things in the world, or they can refer to the operations and contents of the understanding. Thus, ideas can signify other ideas and, in the case of some modes, ideas can signify themselves.

For Locke, however, the salient point about the truth of verbal propositions is that they are founded on that which the signified ideas themselves signify. The verbal proposition <This snow is white> signifies the mental proposition <*This snow is white*> which is presumed to be true in virtue of the agreement of some particular snow and the secondary quality in the world that causes the idea of white. We have (sensitive) knowledge of this when we perceive the agreement of the sensory ideas *snow* and *white* with the idea of *actual existence*.[54] This perception is a form of non-propositional knowledge by acquaintance. Thus, just as Russell could claim that '[a]ll our knowledge, both knowledge of things and knowledge of truths, rests upon acquaintance as its foundation', so too, Locke claims that 'the principal Act of Ratiocination is the finding the Agreement, or Disagreement of two *Ideas* one with another' (Russell 1976: 26; *Essay* IV. xvii. 18).

5 Conclusion

This chapter has argued for a four-step interpretation of Locke on the acquisition of knowledge. The steps proceed from perceiving to affirming to assenting, and finally to verbalizing. Each step is a necessary condition for the one that follows it, but no step necessarily follows from the one that precedes it. Thus, for example, one can perceive the disagreement of *black* and *white* without forming the mental proposition <*Black is not white*> and one can assent to this mental proposition without forming the verbal proposition <Black is not white>.

Is this the most plausible interpretation of Locke on the acquisition of knowledge? As ever with Locke, one must find the interpretation of best fit. Some scholars may find independent grounds for endorsing the view that Locke accepted a form of non-propositional knowledge. For example, this interpretation harmonizes well with the view that Locke's critique of the syllogistic requires that rational demonstration be pre-propositional.[55] It may be argued that it is consistent with what Locke says about the role of the will in deliberation and belief. Again, it may be thought to be consistent with interpreting Locke as an imagist about the nature of ideas. These issues, however, are ultimately tangential to the interpretation offered here.

I believe that this interpretation is at least as good as its rivals. The orthodox view is based on a handful of proof texts, but the interpretation of the proof texts does not do justice to the full scope of what Locke has to say about knowledge. If we juxtapose those few proof texts with the numerous comments on knowledge as the perception of the agreement and disagreement of ideas and our knowledge of individual ideas in our minds, another interpretive possibility opens up, namely, that Locke's fundamental notion of knowledge is a form of knowledge by acquaintance. Moreover, if the four-step analysis is close to the mark, additional advantages accrue. The distinction between Steps Two and Three outlined earlier, that is, the affirming one idea of another and assenting to a proposition, undercuts the charge that Locke conflates the construction of a proposition with its assertion. And, above all, the four-step interpretation and the role of acquaintance therein better accommodate the variety of things that Locke has to say about knowledge. On this issue it is perhaps best to let Locke himself have the last word. Among his marginalia to John Sergeant's *Solid Philosophy Asserted* of 1697 there is an interesting response to Sergeant's claim that all knowledge is reducible to propositions of identity:

> Knowledg has its bottom only in the perception of the agreement or diversity of any two Ideas and is neither founded on nor can be reduced to Identical propositions.[56]

Notes

1 This chapter was read at the universities of Neuchâtel, Sydney, Melbourne, Bucharest, Gakushuin and Victoria Wellington. I would like to thank David Bronstein, Richard Glauser, Ed Mares, Jennifer Smalligan Marušić, Samuel Rickless, Laura Schroeter, Kiyoshi Shimokawa and J. C. Walmsley for helpful comments.

2 See, inter alia, '*Knowledge* then seems to me to be nothing but *the perception of the connexion and agreement, or disagreement and repugnancy of any of our Ideas*. In this alone it consists' (*Essay* IV. i. 2); 'All our Knowledge consisting, as I have said, in the view the Mind has of its own *Ideas*' (IV. ii. 1); and IV. xvii. 17.
3 See, for example, Mattern (1998), Soles (1985), Owen (2007) and Hill (2008).
4 See also Owen (2007: 414): 'constructing a proposition is the very same mental act as knowing'.
5 Mattern (1998: 234-9). Mattern's case for the additional sense of 'agree' and 'disagree' in Locke leans heavily on the possibility that Locke was influenced by the theory of propositions found in Arnauld and Nicole's earlier *Logic or The Art of Thinking* (Locke owned the 1674 printing of the 4th edition). However, the discontinuities between Locke's view of propositions and that of Arnauld and Nicole, together with the absence of any positive evidence of direct influence, count strongly against the connection. For example, Arnauld and Nicole call affirming and denying judging (Arnauld and Nicole 1996: 82), whereas Locke reserves the term 'judging' for just those cases where one does not perceive an agreement or disagreement between two ideas. Though see also Marušić (2014) for an attempt to bring Locke in line with the view of Arnauld and Nicole. For criticisms of Mattern's view from the perspective of his own view, see Rickless (2008: 86-90).
6 Rickless (2008: 93-7) and (2014: 152-9); see Rickless (2014: 152): 'Locke is a *necessitarian* about knowledge, in the sense that he takes all genuine knowledge to be of necessary truths.'
7 Of course, proponents of the orthodox view agree with this. See, for example, David Soles: 'the claim that knowledge consists in the perception of an agreement or disagreement of ideas . . . is a detailed statement of what is involved in perceiving that a proposition is true', Soles (1985: 20).
8 Claude Panaccio, for example, argues that the resources to develop a theory of reference for the constituents of mental propositions were available to Locke in Ockham's theory of signification, but Locke appears not to have been familiar with this theory. See Panaccio (2003).
9 The chapter also does not discuss the derivation of new knowledge by inferring from propositions.
10 Samuel Rickless has suggested, in correspondence, that this interpretation requires Locke to be a realist about relations. However, all of the relations perceived or presumed to hold seem to be internal relations.
11 *Essay* IV. ii. 2.
12 *Essay* IV. ii. 3.
13 This was the view of the Scots philosopher John Anderson. See Armstrong (1997: 3-4).
14 *Essay* IV. v. 3.
15 Compare it, for example, with the view of John Wilkins: 'The discerning of that connexion or dependance which there is betwixt several Propositions, whereby we

are enabled to infer one Proposition from another, which is called *Ratiocination*, or Discourse', Wilkins (1675: 56).

16 It is for this reason that Locke also calls demonstrative knowledge rational knowledge. See *Essay* IV. iii. 3 and IV. xvii. 17. See also *Second Reply*, Locke (1823, 4: 232).

17 This example, of course, has its origins in Proposition One of Euclid's *Elements*. See Euclid (1956: 241–2).

18 At *Essay* IV. vi. 2 Locke claims, 'All the Knowledge we have, being only of particular or *general Truths*'. That this is not a definition of knowledge is clear from the context. The chapter is entitled 'Of Universal Propositions, Their Truth and Certainty'. Its explicit focus is on propositions and Locke's claim here is that of all the objects of knowledge they are propositions either expressing particular truths or expressing general truths.

19 OED, Consist vb, meaning 6 b. Locke says, 'some have made the whole essence of *Body*, to consist in Extension' (*Essay* II. xiii. 24).

20 Locke uses locutions such as 'knowledge or certainty consists in the perception of the agreement or disagreement of ideas' in the *Second Reply* over thirty times. See Locke (1823, 4: 213–493 *passim*).

21 David Bronstein pointed this out to me.

22 OED, Consist vb, meaning 6 e. Locke says, 'Your lordship's first argument consists in these propositions', *Second Reply*, Locke (1823, 4: 357); and the nominal essence of triangle 'consists in a very few *Ideas*' (*Essay* II. xxxii. 24).

23 See Milton (2012).

24 Locke does use the term 'acquaintance' and its cognates to describe those ideas 'Mind is *first* and most easily acquainted with' (*Essay* IV. vii. 9). However, for Locke, 'acquaintance' is not a name for this type of knowledge. For the claim that Locke's intuitive knowledge is similar to Russell's knowledge by acquaintance, see van Woudenberg (2005: 22). René van Woudenberg, however, claims that Locke's demonstrative knowledge is propositional knowledge, Woudenberg (2005: 21).

25 See, for example, 'a Man cannot conceive himself capable of a greater Certainty, than to know that any *Idea* in his Mind is such, as he perceives it to be' (*Essay* IV. ii. 1).

26 See also *First Letter to Stillingfleet*, Locke (1823, 4: 54–5).

27 See Chalmers (2010: 291) for a brief discussion of the range of options over and above sense data that is open to acquaintance theorists.

28 See also *Essay* IV. v. 5.

29 See *Essay* II. xii. 1, 2, 8. Ayers and Marušić claim, wrongly in my view, that in Draft A of the *Essay* Locke viewed complex ideas as propositional, though he subsequently backed away from this position. See Ayers (1991, 1: 24–5) and Marušić (2014: 264 n. 27). The relevant passage is Draft A §1, Locke (1990: 4–6). Locke says there when discussing wrong and imperfect definitions of words 'the first affirmation or negation of our mindes are about these materiall objects [such as gold] in the frameing of our Ideas of them which is noe more but this that where

there are some of these simple Ideas there there are others v.g. gold is ductil'. I take it that here Locke means 'ductil' is affirmed of 'gold' and not that the inclusion of ductile in the complex idea of gold is an act of affirmation. According to Ayers's Locke, '[p]ropositional thought is paradigmatically the perception of such a relation [of agreement or disagreement of ideas]', Ayers (1997: 167).

30 Locke does speak of a form of 'direct Negation' when describing the construction of complex ideas, but the example he gives reveals that he conceives of this as a form of joining. See *Essay* II. xxxii. 18.
31 *Essay* II. xxxii. 1 and 26.
32 So Rickless (2008: 87).
33 Interestingly, Locke held this view as early as Draft A. However, it seems that at that time (1671) he did not have the notion of a mental proposition. Here is how he puts it: 'The next thing it [the understanding] doth is to joyne two of these Ideas considerd as destinct togeather or seperate them one from an other by way of affirmation or negation, which when it comes to be expressed in words is cald proposition & in this lies all truth & falshood', Locke (1990: 20).
34 Here I am in broad agreement with the spirit of Walter Ott's interpretation. See Ott (2004: 48): 'Locke . . . sees affirmation and negation as sub-propositional.' Locke allows an analogous form of affirmation and negation to verbal propositions. With regard to self-evident propositions he says: 'And therefore where-ever the mind with attention considers any proposition, so as to perceive the two *Ideas*, signified by the terms and affirmed or denyed one of the other, to be the same or different; it is presently and infallibly certain of the truth of such a proposition' (*Essay* IV. vii. 4).
35 See also Locke's *Second Reply*, where in his discussion of sensitive knowledge he claims in passing: 'the two ideas, that in this case are perceived to agree, and do thereby produce knowledge', Locke (1823, 4: 360).
36 See also *Essay* IV. xii. 14.
37 According to Locke, one can also affirm an idea of itself. See *Essay* IV. vii. 4, 10.
38 See *Essay* IV. v. 2, 5.
39 This is a case of sensitive knowledge; however, a number of features of sensitive knowledge are overlooked in this example.
40 For Leibniz's criticism of the incompleteness of Locke's discussion here, see Leibniz (1996: 396). Locke does discuss negation in the construction of verbal propositions. See *Essay* III. vii. 1.
41 See, for example, *Essay* II. xiii. 21; II. xxiii. 5.
42 Owen claims that for Locke, '[p]roposition formation, predication, assertion, and affirmation all come down to a single act of perceiving or presuming agreement of ideas' (2007: 416).
43 OED 'by' 36. a.: 'The sense of "means" sometimes approaches or passes into that of "cause" or "reason": Because of, on account of, in consequence of, through; in virtue of, on the ground of, by so, by that: therefore.'

44 Hill (2008: 189–90).
45 Locke says, 'common use, by a tacit Consent, appropriates certain Sounds to certain *Ideas* in all Languages' (*Essay* III. ii. 8).
46 My Step Three is equivalent to Lex Newman's third cognitive element in his three-element interpretation of Locke on the acquisition of knowledge. However, Newman, wrongly in my view, calls assent affirmation. See Newman (2007: 321 n. 14).
47 In his book-length study of the early modern theory of propositions Nuchelmans interprets *Essay* IV. v. 6 (discussed above) as describing affirming as a case of knowing or believing, an interpretation I deny. However, he goes on to say 'in many other passages [of the *Essay*] it is equally clear that the formation of the proposition precedes the act of assenting to it or taking it to be true', Nuchelmans (1983: 145).
48 See Nuchelmans (1998: 125). For a contemporary theory of entertaining as a type of propositional attitude, see Kreigel (2013).
49 For a recent accuser, see Owen (2007: 416). For discussion of this charge see Ott (2004, ch. 2). See also Marušić (2014) which defends the view that, for Locke, the formation of propositions is an act of judging.
50 Cited in Jaffro (2018: 176).
51 See especially 'Of the Degrees of Assent', *Essay* IV. xvi.
52 See also the protracted discussion of this very issue in Locke's *Second Reply*, Locke (1823, 4: 366–429).
53 See *Essay* IV. v. 4.
54 Locke says in the *Second Reply* to Stillingfleet that in the case of sensitive knowledge the ideas that agree are 'the idea of actual sensation . . . and the idea of actual existence of something without me that causes that sensation', Locke (1823, 4: 360).
55 See Anstey (2011, ch. 7) for a defence of this view of Locke on demonstration.
56 See *The Digital Locke Project* http://www.digitallockeproject.nl/cgi/t/text/text-idx?type=proximity;c=locke;cc=locke;search=advanced;sid=f9c319ab3abf61cecef8e602dcf29608;q1=agreement;cite1restrict=All;cite1extrarestrict=All;op2=near;cite2restrict=All;cite2extrarestrict=All;op3=near;cite3restrict=All;cite3extrarestrict=All;amt2=40;rgn=div1;view=text;subview=detail;sort=occur;idno=DLP-AFC;node=DLP-AFC%3A1.

References

Anstey, P. R. (2011), *John Locke and Natural Philosophy*, Oxford: Oxford University Press.
Armstrong, D. M. (1997), *A World of States of Affairs*, Cambridge: Cambridge University Press.
Arnauld, A. and P. Nicole (1996), *Logic or the Art of Thinking*, ed. J. V. Buroker, Cambridge: Cambridge University Press, 5th edn, 1683.

Ayers, M. (1991), *Locke: Epistemology and Ontology*, 2 vols, London: Routledge.
Ayers, M. (1997), 'Review of *The Cambridge Companion to Locke*, ed. V. Chappell, Cambridge: Cambridge University Press, 1994', *The Locke Newsletter*, 28: 157–88.
Chalmers, D. J. (2010), *The Character of Consciousness*, Oxford: Oxford University Press.
Euclid (1956), *The Thirteen Books of Euclid's Elements*, vol. 1, 2nd edn, trans. T. L. Heath, New York: Dover.
Hill, B. (2008), 'Locke on Propositions and Assertion', *The Modern Schoolman*, 85: 187–205.
Jaffro, L. (2018), 'Locke and Port-Royal on Affirmation, Negation, and Other Postures of the Mind', in P. Hamou and M. Pécharman (eds), *Locke and Cartesian Philosophy*, 172–85, Oxford: Oxford University Press.
Kreigel, U. (2013), 'Entertaining as a Propositional Attitude: A Nonreductive Characterization', *American Philosophical Quarterly*, 50: 1–22.
Leibniz, G. W. (1996), *New Essays on Human Understanding*, trans. P. Remnant and J. Bennett, Cambridge: Cambridge University Press.
Locke, J. (1823), *The Works of John Locke*, 10 vols, London: T. Tegg.
Locke, J. (1975), *An Essay concerning Human Understanding*, ed. P. H. Nidditch, Oxford: Clarendon Press, 1st edn, 1690; abbreviated as *Essay*.
Locke, J. (1990), *Drafts for the Essay Concerning Human Understanding and Other Philosophical Writings*, vol. 1, Drafts A and B., eds P. H. Nidditch and G. A. J. Rogers, Oxford: Clarendon Press.
Locke, J. (2012), *Vindications of the Reasonableness of Christianity*, ed. V. Nuovo, Oxford: Clarendon Press.
Marušić, J. S. (2014), 'Propositions and Judgments in Locke and Arnauld: A Monstrous and Unholy Union?', *Journal of the History of Philosophy*, 52 (2): 255–80.
Mattern, R. (1998), 'Locke: "Our Knowledge, Which All Consists in Propositions"', in V. Chappell (ed.), *Locke*, 226–41, Oxford: Oxford University Press. First published in *Canadian Journal of Philosophy*, 8 (4), 1978: 677–95.
Milton, J. R. (2012), 'Locke and the *Elements of Natural Philosophy*: Some Problems of Attribution', *Intellectual History Review*, 22: 199–219.
Newman, L. (2007), 'Locke on Knowledge', in L. Newman (ed.), *The Cambridge Companion to Locke's 'Essay Concerning Human Understanding'*, 313–51, Cambridge: Cambridge University Press.
Nuchelmans, G. (1983), *Judgment and Proposition from Descartes to Kant*, Amsterdam: North Holland Publishing Company.
Nuchelmans, G. (1998), 'Proposition and Judgement', in D. Garber and M. Ayers (eds), *The Cambridge History of Seventeenth-Century Philosophy*, vol. 1, 118–31, Cambridge: Cambridge University Press.
Ott, W. (2004), *Locke's Philosophy of Language*, Cambridge: Cambridge University Press.

Owen, D. (1999), *Hume's Reason*, Oxford: Oxford University Press.

Owen, D. (2007), 'Locke on Judgment', in L. Newman (ed.), *The Cambridge Companion to Locke's 'Essay Concerning Human Understanding'*, 406–35, Cambridge: Cambridge University Press.

Panaccio, C. (2003), 'Ockham and Locke on Mental Language', in R. L. Friedman and L. O. Nielsen (eds), *The Medieval Heritage in Early Modern Metaphysics and Modal Theory*, 37–51, Dordrecht: Kluwer.

Rickless, S. C. (2008), 'Is Locke's Theory of Knowledge Inconsistent?', *Philosophy and Phenomenological Research*, 77 (1): 83–104.

Rickless, S. C. (2014), *Locke*, Oxford: Wiley Blackwell.

Russell, B. (1976), *The Problems of Philosophy*, Oxford: Oxford University Press. First published in 1912.

Sergeant, J. (1697), *Solid Philosophy Asserted*, London: Roger Clavil.

Soles, D. (1985), 'Locke on Knowledge and Propositions', *Philosophical Topics*, 13 (2): 19–30.

Wilkins, J. (1675), *Of the Principles and Duties of Natural Religion*, London: A. Maxwell.

Woudenberg, R. van (2005), 'Intuitive Knowledge Reconsidered', in R. van Woudenberg, S. Roeser and R. Rood (eds), *Basic Belief and Basic Knowledge: Papers in Epistemology*, 15–40, Frankfurt: Verlag.

2

Boyle and Locke on primary and secondary qualities: A reappraisal

Shigeyuki Aoki

1 Introduction

Some distinction between two groups of qualities of bodies – primary qualities (PQs) and secondary qualities (SQs) – is fundamental to the modern conception of the natural world, both metaphysically and scientifically.[1] This distinction, as traditionally conceived, says that of all the qualities of bodies (solidity, bulk, figure, number, texture as well as colour, smell, taste, sound), the qualities solidity, bulk, figure, number and texture are real qualities of bodies themselves, while the qualities like colour, smell, taste and sound are just ideas or sensations in our minds, not the real qualities of external objects.

I say 'some distinction' here, since the nature of this PQ/SQ distinction and the qualities classified as primary and secondary do often change depending on the particular perspective adopted by a philosopher. A PQ/SQ distinction goes back to Aristotle's writings,[2] but there is a wide agreement in the philosophical literature that John Locke is the first philosopher who formulated the PQ/SQ distinction as we know it today in a philosophically satisfactory manner.[3] The Lockean PQ/SQ distinction was subsequently dismissed as 'out of date'[4] in response to George Berkeley's vigorous criticisms, but in the 1970s and 1980s, commentators on Locke tried to show he was 'neither foolish nor incompetent',[5] and placed Locke's PQ/SQ distinction side by side with the PQ/SQ distinction of Robert Boyle,[6] which was most fully developed in his work *The Origine of Formes and Qualities* published in 1666-7 (hereafter *Forms and Qualities*). And the story continues. Invaluable manuscript studies from the 1990s onwards[7] have proven that Locke took just one note from *Forms and Qualities*, which is quite unusual if we look at the tremendous number of other notes, which show Locke's systematic reading of other works of Boyle in the 1660s.[8] So the endeavours to understand Locke's own PQ/SQ distinction by way of Boyle's *Forms and Qualities* obviously face the minimum evidential problem, i.e. whether Locke really read or studied *Forms and Qualities* and incorporated Boyle's corpuscular philosophy in *Forms and Qualities* into his arguments for the PQ/SQ distinction.

The relation of Locke to Boyle raises, along with the evidential question, another broader question about the relation of philosophy to science. Given (for the sake of argument) that Locke inherited Boyle's version of PQ/SQ distinction, one may wonder where Locke's original contribution to the distinction actually lies. Was Locke just a popularizer of the Boylean corpuscular philosophy? Or did Locke produce his own unique philosophical, metaphysical or epistemological arguments in favour of the distinction? A famous phrase to remember in this connection is Locke's own self-acknowledgement to be an 'Under-Labourer' of master-builders, such as Boyle, Sydenham, Huygens and Newton, in the Epistle to the Reader of *An Essay concerning Human Understanding* (1690). The following passage has been quoted very often, but it deserves full quotation again to illustrate the orientation of this chapter:

> The Commonwealth of Learning, is not at this time without Master-Builders, whose mighty Designs, in advancing the Sciences, will leave lasting Monuments to the Admiration of Posterity; But every one must not hope to be a *Boyle* or a *Sydenham*; and in an Age that produces such Masters, as the Great – *Huygenius*, and the incomparable Mr. *Newton*, with some other of that Strain; 'tis Ambition enough to be employed as an Under-Labourer in clearing the Ground a little, and removing some of the Rubbish, that lies in the way to Knowledge; which certainly had been very much more advanced in the World, if the Endeavours of ingenious and industrious Men had not been much cumbred with the learned but frivolous use of uncouth, affected, or unintelligible Terms, introduced into the Sciences, and there made an Art of, to that Degree, that Philosophy, which is nothing but the true Knowledge of Things, was thought unfit, or uncapable to be brought into well-bred Company, and polite Conversation. (*Essay*: 9–10)

Locke's role as an under-labourer has been much discussed in the literature,[9] since the word 'Under-Labourer' is itself metaphorical and presumably excites our imaginations as to the true connotation Locke must have given to the word. However, if we look impartially at this passage, the meaning is very clear. Locke intended to remove the rubbish of unintelligible terms at his time, which he thought hindered the advancement of sciences by the master-builders. In short, he meant to clear scholastic jargon and so to open the way for experimental philosophy which those master-builders were advancing,[10] and then to replace such jargon with plain wordings which would be fit for the 'well-bred Company and polite Conversation'.

This chapter will address the following two interconnected questions. First, it will ask again the evidential question as to whether Boyle did influence Locke on the formulation of the PQ/SQ distinction, as assumed in the Locke literature in the 1970s and 1980s. It will turn out that although the striking *morphological* similarities are found between Boyle's and Locke's wordings, no direct evidence attests Locke's debt to Boyle's work, notably *Forms and Qualities*, for the formation of Locke's own PQ/SQ distinction. Nevertheless, a strong connection of *common nomenclature* can be established between Boyle and Locke, which allows us to make a historical connection between the two philosophers.

Second, given that Locke developed his own PQ/SQ distinction, as the recent Locke literature emphasizes, this chapter tries to assess what contribution, if any, Locke made to the understanding of the PQ/SQ distinction by comparing Locke's formulations with those of Boyle (or other contemporary writers). This task is *not* to establish the existing link between the two philosophers, but to offer an *interpretative reconstruction* of both Boyle and Locke, with a view to giving an evaluation of Locke's philosophical endeavours with hindsight, rather than through the eyes of Locke's contemporaries. But I think that Locke would be happy with this approach, since it fits well with his original intention, that is, the role of an under-labourer clearing the rubbish of unintelligible terms.

2 Boyle's distinction between primary affections and secondary qualities as part of his corpuscular philosophy

Among the works on qualities, the principal theoretical work in which Boyle developed his corpuscular philosophy in the fullest detail is *The Origine of Formes and Qualities* first published in 1666. Naturally, expositors of Boyle (sometimes with Lockean interests in view) have focused on this work, but recent studies on Boyle have had a rather different perspective. The focus on Boyle's writings on qualities once emphasized the similarities of Locke's and Boyle's doctrines of qualities, reading Boyle *backwards* from Locke – they approached Boyle's doctrine of qualities with Locke's PQ/SQ distinction in mind. Some recent studies on Boyle reject this *retrospective* temptation, and try to sever Boyle's doctrine from Locke's, seeing Boyle's doctrine of qualities in its own right.[11] As a result, it has been found that there are some important differences between Boyle's and Locke's doctrines of PQ/SQ, not least their different nomenclatures. Boyle's distinction is between[12] PAs and SQs, and Boyle emphasizes the metaphysical distinction between *absolute* and *relative* qualities of things. Boyle talks of *modes* or *accidents* of matter, words which Locke never uses. Also, the argumentation is apparently different. Boyle constructs his PA/SQ distinction *a priori*, while Locke's PQ/SQ distinction is arguably more *a posteriori*.[13]

Nonetheless, I would like to point out that Boyle and Locke shared an important core. They both rejected the unintelligible account of the scholastics, especially the heavy uses of scholastic jargon. Boyle says:

> Indeed the doctrines of Forms and Qualities, and Generation and Corruption, and Alteration, are wont to be treated of by Scholastical Philosophers, in so obscure, so perplex'd, and so unsatisfactory a way, and their Discourses upon these Subjects do consist so much more of Logical and Metaphysical Notions and Niceties, then of Physical Observations and Reasonings, that it is very difficult for any Reader of but an ordinary Capacity, to understand what they mean. (*Forms and Qualities* 289)

Thus, Boyle also faced the problem of obscure scholastic doctrines which ordinary people could not understand. This reminds us of Locke's intention to be an under-labourer removing the 'rubbish' of the Scholastics, which Locke thought prevented the advancement of sciences and talk of philosophy in polite conversation.

How, then, did Boyle draw the PA/SQ distinction? Did he successfully avoid scholastic jargon as he intended? Let us take a closer look at Boyle's corpuscularian explanation of the qualities developed in *Forms and Qualities*. Our discussion will deal with different passages of *Forms and Qualities*, till we come to find one where Boyle draws the PA/SQ distinction.

(1) As a first step, Boyle started with the assumption that there is 'one Catholic or Universal Matter common to all Bodies' (*Forms and Qualities* 305).[14] By *matter* he means 'a Substance extended, divisible, and impenetrable'. Boyle does not provide an argument or experimental evidence for taking matter as universal to all bodies; he just follows 'the generality of Philosophers'.

(2) Such *a priori* theorizing in Boyle's presentation is also obvious in the second step, where he introduces the *motion* of matter. Since all bodies are constituted by homogenous matter, the diversities which we find in nature *must* come from something else. Moreover, since matter is a divisible substance, it can be put into motion and be divided into several parts, resulting in various particles of matter.

(3) Boyle says that matter and motion are the 'two grand and most Catholick Principles of Bodies'. Once he introduces these two principles, he goes on to introduce two attributes of matter – *magnitude* or *size*, and *figure* or *shape*. Since a finite body is terminated it must have some size and figure. Boyle calls these two *inseparable accidents* (*Forms and Qualities* 307), since a finite body cannot be devoid of some determinate size and figure, while it just happens to have this or that size and shape.

Boyle first talks about 'primary affections' of bodies in this context. He says,

> Whether these Accidents may not conveniently enough to be call'd the Moods or primary affections of Bodies, to distinguish them from those lesse simple qualities, (as Colours, Tastes, and Odours,) that belong to Bodies upon their account, or whether with the Epicureans they may not be called the Conjuncts of the smallest parts of Matter, I shall not now stay to consider. (*Forms and Qualities* 308)

The contrast here between PAs and less simple qualities is clear. PAs are moods (modes) of bodies, while qualities such as colours or tastes are generated as a result of interacting bodies with PAs. Later, in 'An EXCURSION about the Relative Nature of Physical Qualities', Boyle explains how the bodies having only PAs produce so-called SQs with the illustration of locks and keys. Boyle says that locks and keys are in themselves considered only as pieces of iron, with certain figures and sizes. However, once these two pieces of iron are applied to one another, they 'now Obtain a new Capacity': keys now obtaining a faculty or power of opening and shutting the locks, while no changes are made in terms of their PAs. Boyle extends this analogy to sensible qualities, and introduces the notion of the *texture* of bodies.

> I do not see, why we may not conceive, That as to those Qualities, (for Instance) which we call Sensible, though by virtue of a certain Congruity or Incongruity in point of Figure or Texture, (or other Mechanical Attributes,) to our Sensories, the Portions of Matter they Modifie are enabled to produce various Effects, upon whose account we make Bodies to be Endow'd with Qualities; yet They are not in the Bodies that are Endow'd with them any Real or Distinct Entities, or differing from the Matter its self, furnish'd with such a Determinate Bigness, Shape, or other Mechanical Modifications. (*Forms and Qualities* 310)

For example, the fact that gold is soluble in *aqua regis* but not in *aqua fortis* is explained by its peculiar texture. *Texture* is an important word to which Boyle gave a new meaning and of which he made heavy use. And he explains texture in the next, fourth step.

(4) Boyle requires us to conceive that 'all the rest of the Universe were annihilated, except any of these entire and undivided Corpuscles' (*Forms and Qualities* 315). Here he means that we should make a thought experiment of considering corpuscles themselves, removing all other things surrounding the corpuscles. Then we would find, Boyle says, 'two new Accidents or Events' of bodies, i.e. *posture* and *order*. The postures of corpuscles are either 'Erected, Inclin'd, or Horizontal', while orders are the relations of corpuscles being placed in some specific ways, for example, AN or NA. Then, many corpuscles get together to make an ordinary gross object, such as a stone or a metal, and 'there doth emerge a certain Disposition or Contrivance of Parts in the whole' (*Forms and Qualities* 316). Boyle calls this the *texture* of an object.

(5) Considered in itself, a stone has only material essence and inseparable accidents. However, in the real world there are sentient humans, with organs of sense – the eye, the ear, etc. of a certain texture. External bodies affect our sense organs, and these operations of the objects are named light or colour, sound, or odour. In this way Boyle introduces *sensible* qualities, saying, 'a long Catalogue of such Things as, for their relating to our Senses, we call Sensible Qualities' (*Forms and Qualities* 316).

In the next step (6), where Boyle draws a distinction between the relative nature of sensible qualities and their absolute being (irrespective of us), we see Boyle introducing SQs, at last:

> I say not, that there are no other Accidents in Bodies then Colours, Odours, and the like; for I have already taught, that there are simpler and more Primitive Affections of Matter, from which these Secondary Qualities if I may so call them, do depend: and that the Operations of Bodies upon one another spring from the same, we shall see by and by. (*Forms and Qualities* 317)

Boyle here talks of so-called SQs (in Locke's terminology 'ideas' of SQs) in bodies,[15] alongside 'simpler and more Primitive Affections of Matter'. We also notice here that the distinction between PAs and SQs is not schematic (as we might anticipate from Lockean hindsight) and not so sharp, as this distinction is relative, i.e. 'more' primitive or 'less' simple. Thus, the PA/SQ distinction is *not* the main point Boyle himself made. The point for him is that bodies, considered in themselves, have material essences and inseparable accidents, and affect either our senses or other bodies. In this way, 'sensible qualities' is the main conceptual tool for Boyle, and he merely suggests 'secondary qualities' in the course of arguing for the relative nature of qualities.

Table 2.1 Boyle's Primary Affections and Secondary Qualities

Two Grand Principles[16]	Matter
	Motion
Inseparable Accidents or Primary Affections	Size
	Figure
New Accidents	Posture
	Order
Emergent Accident from New Accidents	Texture
Sensible Qualities Relating to our Sense	Colour
	Sound
	Odour

We have so far followed Boyle, while trying not to read Locke back into Boyle, and have seen how he introduced his PAs and SQs. Now we sum up Boyle's formulation of PA/SQ, in Table 2.1:

The steps leading up to the PA/SQ distinction are made *a priori*,[17] and there are numerous hints in this work, *Forms of Qualities*, and elsewhere, that show Boyle's extensive reading of ancient and modern writers of atomism or corpuscularianism, such as Epicurus, Descartes and Gassendi.[18] He probably had in his mind these figures when he mentioned 'the generality of philosophers' to introduce the catholic nature of matter in the first step. Motion, size and figure are *a priori* requisites for a corpuscularian explanation of nature. Thus, PAs are derived as *inseparable* accidents of bodies. Such *a priori* considerations are most manifest in his thought experiment of annihilation, by which Boyle derives the posture, order and texture of corpuscles. Sensible qualities are produced by corpuscles with their peculiar textures interacting, and this conceptualization is drawn from an analogy of locks and keys; since this is a conceptual issue, no empirical evidence is used to back up or prove the claim.

Having thus grasped the *a priori* character of Boyle's theory of qualities,[19] let us go back to Boyle's criticisms of scholasticism. As we found, according to Boyle the scholastic doctrines of qualities are 'obscure, perplexed, and unsatisfactory, and their doctrines consist of logical or metaphysical niceties, rather of physical observations and reasonings'. Was Boyle's theory faithful to his own criticism of scholasticism? Did he succeed in basing his theory of qualities on physical, not metaphysical, foundations? I think that Boyle was vulnerable to this very criticism in some key passages in *Forms and Qualities* and other works.

A first reader of Boyle's works may soon find out that Boyle's wordings are perplexing in a nontrivial way. We have already noted that Boyle used various technical terms, like *attributes, accidents, moods, affections, qualities* and *modifications*, on the one hand, and 'faculties', 'powers', 'dispositions' and 'textures' on the other. These terms have subtle meanings, but they may rather confuse the general reader. For example, the following is a passage from *An Introduction to the History of Particular Qualities* (1671), where Boyle introduces the primary *modes* of matter:

> And there are some other Attributes, namely *Size, Shape, Motion,* and *Rest*, that are wont to be reckon'd among Qualities, which may more conveniently be esteemed the *Primary Modes* of the parts of Matter; since from these simple Attributes, or Primordiall Affections, all the Qualities are deriv'd. But this consideration relating to Words and Names, I shall not insist upon it. (Boyle 1999–2000, 6: 267)

In this passage, such terms as *attributes, modes* and *affections* are used as if they were interchangeable.[20] To be sure, as we confirmed in *Forms and Qualities*, Boyle distinguishes between affections and qualities, the former being the attributes of matter and the latter being something emergent from PAs (in this passage 'primary modes') of matter. However, it is hard for ordinary people to distinguish such niceties, and moreover, the problem still remains as to how to distinguish among 'Attributes', 'Modes' (or 'Moods') and 'Affections'.

Why does this sort of rather confusing variety of wordings prevail in Boyle's writings? Here it is useful to know that Boyle himself was aware of redundant uses of several words, as he himself states that 'I sometimes imploy variety of Terms and Phrases to express the same Thing, I did it purposely . . . for the Advantage of *Pyrophilus*' (*Forms and Qualities*, 291). So he made use of several interchangeable terms on purpose, for the better understanding of readers. The first answer to the question above lies, therefore, in Boyle's recognition that uses of such scholastic niceties – 'essence/accident' dichotomy, 'modes', and 'moods' or 'affections' of substance as modifications of the same substance – would enhance the reader's understanding. The second, more important answer would be that Boyle was still working within the scholastic conceptual framework, notably the scholastic niceties. As we have seen Boyle was indifferent to the problem of ambiguous uses of words, and did not mind borrowing from diverse sources, both ancient and modern theorists of atomism or corpuscularianism, while meshing various technical terms into one piece of work. Boyle's *a priori* formation of his corpuscular philosophy (as we have seen Boyle using the scholastic 'accidents', or 'moods' of bodies, while accepting 'one Catholic or Universal Matter' following the generality of philosophers) exemplifies this aspect of Boyle's corpuscular philosophy.[21]

In the next section, we look at how Locke started his idea-empiricism and introduced the PQ/SQ distinction along the empiricist line. In hindsight, I mean, with the backward-looking reconstruction of intellectual history, Locke *can be said* to have taken one step forward towards removing the rubbish of unintelligible scholastic terms.

3 Boylean corpuscularianism in Locke's *Essay*

Just as Boyle has been studied in his own right (severed from Lockean interests), Locke's development of mechanism in Draft A, Draft B, the 'Epitome', *Abrégé*[22] and Draft C has been documented in the recent literature.[23] The common, or influential, claim among scholars is that Locke's PQ/SQ is a result of his own thinking over many years, and should be understood from the *epistemological* constraints like 'conceivability' (Walmsley) or the 'impulse principle' (Hill). Some scholars also seem to agree that Locke's PQ/SQ distinction is to be understood *separately* from Boyle's distinction, and in the case of Walmsley, he clearly denies the influence of Boyle on Locke, as had been strongly assumed in the Lockean literature in the 1970s and 1980s.[24] To be sure, these studies are invaluable in broadening our understanding of Locke's thought prior to the *Essay*. In my view, however, two questions remain: (1) Whether Locke's debt to Boyle was either *nothing* or trivial in the formulation of the PQ/SQ distinction, and (2) Whether Locke's thinking on the PQ/SQ distinction remained *unchanged* throughout the early *Drafts* (1671) and the many editions of the *Essay* from 1690. I would like to explore these two questions.

First, at the evidential level, it is true that although Locke owned a copy of the first edition of *Forms and Qualities* (1666), there is very little mention of *Forms and Qualities* in the 1660s (as noted before). From the manner of note taking (taking only factual memos) it is presumed that Locke, at this stage of his life, had little interest in corpuscular or mechanical philosophy.[25] There is no clear hint that Locke incorporated corpuscular or mechanical philosophy into his medical manuscripts or early *Drafts* (1671), either.[26] However, in Draft C (1685) we clearly see virtually the same corpuscularian line of argument for the PQ/SQ distinction. Thus we can infer that somewhere between Drafts A and B, and Draft C, Locke adopted the 'corpuscular hypothesis' which he explicitly endorses in the *Essay*. In the course of arguing for the PQ/SQ distinction in the *Essay* Locke admits that 'I have in what just goes before, been engaged in Physical Enquiries a little further than, perhaps, I intended' and goes on to say,

'I shall be pardoned this little Excursion into Natural Philosophy' (*Essay* II. viii. 22). This statement clearly shows that Locke himself thought that his arguments for the PQ/SQ distinction were made within the realm of natural philosophy.

Then, what natural philosophy did he have in mind as he argued for his PQ/SQ distinction? In spite of strong *morphological* similarities between Boyle's and Locke's wordings,[27] I suspect they come short of establishing the expected link between the two. After all, the wordings such as 'primary', 'secondary' and even 'tertiary' go back to Aristotle's writings, and the essential part of the distinction was established by ancient atomists. Locke also seriously read Descartes's natural philosophical writings, and made some notes from Gassendi, so he knew enough about mechanical or corpuscular philosophy before the intimate personal contacts with Boyle.[28] The linking by morphological evidence is always haunted by this kind of 'plural sources' problem.

In contrast, let us remember the philosophical use of 'idea' after Descartes. The mark to distinguish early modern philosophers into 'pre-Descartes' and 'post-Descartes' is the use of 'idea' in the Cartesian manner: we can identify the *link* between Descartes and a post-Descartes philosopher by checking whether he or she used that philosophical term. Since the Cartesian 'idea' is the unique invention of Descartes, it provides not only the morphological similarity but also the *linkage* of thoughts down the generations. We might call this a *common nomenclature* connection.

I suppose that the same can be said of Boyle's use of 'texture', to which Boyle gave a new meaning. 'Texture' in today's usage means something like 'feeling' with respect to touch, for example, 'the texture of this cloth is smooth'. However, in Boyle's use 'texture' means 'arrangement of corpuscles'. This is a unique invention of Boyle,[29] and OED's entry shows this.

> 4. In extended use: The constitution, structure, or substance of anything with regard to its constituents or formative elements. **a.** Of organic bodies and their parts. **1665** BOYLE *Occa. Medit.* IV, iv. The Leaves . . . of a Tree . . . are of a more solid Texture, and a more durable Nature than the Blossoms . . .
>
> **b.** Of inorganic substances, as stone, soil, etc.: Physical (not chemical) constitution; the structure or minute moulding (of a surface).
>
> **1660** BOYLE. *New Exp. Phys. Mech.* xxii. 165 Air is . . . endow'd with an Elastical power that probably proceeds from its Texture. (OED, 17: 854)

Thus, Locke's frequent uses of 'texture' in his treatments of the PQ/SQ distinction and in explaining the cases such as Manna, Porphyre and Almond[30] reveal that he made heavy use of Boyle's corpuscular philosophy as an integral part of his 'little Excursion into Natural Philosophy'. In this way we can establish the *linkage* between Boyle and Locke.[31]

Given that Locke was under the direct influence of Boylean corpuscularianism as he made this 'little excursion', his argument for the PQ/SQ distinction looks somewhat different from the way it is understood in the recent literature. As we have seen, recent studies emphasize the originality of Locke's epistemological considerations for the PQ/SQ distinction, and the focus on Locke's use of the 'impulse principle' highlights this reading of Locke. However, I would like to point out that, in spite of the philosophical merits of this interpretation,[32] Locke's own thought on the PQ/SQ distinction departed from this 'impulse principle' (hereafter IP).

The textual evidence in support of this IP interpretation, according to Hill (2009), comes from the first three editions of Locke's *Essay*. In contrast to the fourth or later editions of the *Essay* (with which we are now familiar from Nidditch's critical edition), in the first three editions the sections on IP appear *between* Locke's definitions of PQs and SQs. Hill takes this to be the evidence that '[H]ere too it is *in the light of the impulse principle* that secondary qualities are defined and the distinction between primary and secondary qualities is established' (Hill 2009: 93, Hill's emphasis).

We might wonder if the insertion of sections on IP between PQs and SQs is decisive for drawing the distinction between PQs and SQs. Let us read the relevant sections from the first edition:[33]

> §9. Concerning these *Qualities*, we may, I think, observe these *primary* ones in Bodies, that produce simple *Ideas* in us, viz. Solidity, Extension, Motion or Rest, Number and Figure.
> §10. These, which I call *original* or *primary Qualities* of Body, are wholly inseparable from it; and such as in all the alternations and changes it suffers, all the force can be used upon it, it constantly keeps; and such as Sense constantly finds in every particle of Matter, which has bulk enough to be perceived, and the Mind finds inseparable from every particle of Matter, though less than to make it self singly be perceived by our Senses. *v.g.* Take a grain of Wheat, divide it into two parts, each part has still *Solidity*, *Extension*, *Figure*, and *Mobility*; divide it again, . . .
> §11. The next thing to be considered, is, how Bodies operate one upon another, and this is manifestly by impulse, and nothing else. It being impossible to conceive, that Body should operate on what it does not touch, (which is all one as to imagine it can operate where it is not) or when it does touch, operate any other way than by Motion . . .

§14. What I said concerning *Colours* and *Smells*, may be understood also of *Tastes*, and *Sounds*, and *other the like sensible Qualities*; which, whatever reality we by mistake attribute to them, are in truth nothing in the Objects themselves, but Powers to produce various Sensations in us, and *depend on those primary Qualities*, viz. Bulk, Figure, Texture, and Motion of Parts; and therefore I call them *secondary Qualities*.

Thus, Hill is right insofar as he points out that in the earlier editions of *Essay* introduction of SQs comes after the IP.[34] Does this establish the claim that the distinction between PQs and SQs is drawn on the grounds of the IP?

I think that the insertion of the IP between PQs and SQs is not strong enough to establish that claim. As we can confirm from the first edition, the definitions[35] and listing of PQs are finished before the introduction of IP. In other words, Locke *defines PQs without the IP*. Then, *ex hypothesi*, the rest of the qualities being automatically defined to be secondary (without the help of the IP), the IP does not play any substantial role in demarcating qualities into primary or secondary. The point is that Locke does *not* argue in the way that the IP narrows down PQs.[36] Locke defines PQs first and then introduces the IP, and not vice versa. Locke says, '[T]he next thing to be considered' as he introduces the IP. Clearly, Locke thinks that the definition of PQs is independent of the IP. This fact leads us to doubt the status of the IP in Locke's argument for the PQ/SQ distinction.

As a proof of this, in the later editions Locke backs away from the IP. From the fourth edition of *Essay*, PQs and SQs are defined and introduced side by side before the IP. This change tells us not only that Locke thinks that the IP is concerned about *the way of production of ideas in us* and not about *the distinction of qualities in bodies*,[37] but also that the reader (like us) can understand the PQ/SQ distinction easily without the help of the IP.

We can also turn to another source than the *Essay*. In Wynne's *An Abridgement of Mr Locke's Essay*[38] (1700 edition), we find that the IP has completely *dropped out*. In this edition of the *Abridgement*, the arguments for the PQ/SQ distinction proceed from the distinction between ideas and qualities, the distinction between two qualities (primary and secondary), and the resemblance or non-resemblance theses. No mention is made of the IP. If Locke thought that the IP were so fundamental to drawing the PQ/SQ distinction, why would he have approved Wynne's *Abridgement* of 1700 edition, which contains no reference to the IP? I consider that Locke's approval of the *Abridgement* further confirms the view that Locke thought of IP as irrelevant to drawing and understanding the PQ/SQ distinction.

Table 2.2 The Primary and Secondary Quality Distinction in the First and Fourth Editions of the *Essay* and Wynne's *Abridgement* (1700)

1st edition, II. viii	4th edition, II. viii	*Abridgement* (1700), II. viii
9. *primary qualities*	9. wholly inseparable . . . original or <u>primary Qualities of Body</u>	These Qualities are of two Sorts; First, Original, or <u>Primary</u> . . . Secondly, <u>secondary Qualities</u> . . .
10. wholly inseparable . . .		
11. **The next thing to be considered** . . . [IP]	10. nothing but Powers . . . <u>secondary Qs</u>	
12. animal Spirits . . .	11. **The next thing to be considered** . . . [IP]	[no mention of IP]
13. Ideas of secondary Qualities . . .		
14. nothing but Powers . . . <u>secondary Qs</u>	12. animal Spirits . . .	
	13–14. Ideas of secondary Qualities . . .	The Ideas of Primary Qualities of Bodies, are Resemblances of them; . . .
15. Ideas of PQs are Resemblances . . .	15. Ideas of PQs are Resemblances . . .	

Now, it may be useful to show Locke's argumentation on the PQ/SQ distinction from the first edition (1690) to the fourth edition (1700) of the *Essay* and Wynne's *Abridgement* (1700), in a table like Table 2.2.

We conclude, therefore, that Locke's own thinking on the PQ/SQ distinction in the published *Essay* leans much more on the natural philosophy of his day, especially Boylean corpuscularianism, than recent studies suppose. We have to remember the plain fact that Locke himself admits his 'little Excursion into Natural Philosophy' and that his explanation of various cases were totally Boylean.[39]

4 Locke's empirical reconstruction of PQs and SQs

Given that Locke leans very much on natural philosophy of his day, especially Boylean corpuscularianism, in accounting for PQs and SQs, what is Locke's contribution to the PQ/SQ distinction? I hold that Locke departed from Boyle in two important respects, and correspondingly, I claim Locke's contribution is twofold. The first is his idea-empiricism and removal of scholastic jargon, through his 'Historical, plain Method' (*Essay* I. i. 2). So Locke offered the *empirical criterion of meaning* for the corpuscularian terms. The second is his rejection of scholastic framework, that is, *a priori*, essence-accident dichotomy, and Locke arguably adopted the empirical criterion for sorting out PQs. I would like to call this the *empirical criterion of conceptualization* for sorting out qualities. Let us look at these criteria in turn.

Before the discussions of the PQ/SQ distinction in *Essay* II. viii, Locke explains how simple ideas, the building blocks of all our reasoning and knowledge, come into our minds by experience. Experience is divided into sensation and reflection, and Locke repeatedly asks the reader to turn to experience to obtain such simple ideas as colours, sounds, tastes, smells[40] as well as solidity,[41] extension, figure, rest and motion.[42] Introspection and memory plainly show us that we obtain these ideas by experience. Now, remember that these simple ideas are exactly the building blocks of PQs and SQs. Why Locke discussed the PQ/SQ distinction at Book II, chapter viii (entitled 'Some farther Considerations concerning our simple Ideas') of the *Essay* is explained by the order of exposition in Book II as a whole – Locke first introduces simple ideas, explains how these simple ideas are distinguished from qualities in bodies and then moves on to explain the origins of complex ideas like modes, substances and relations. Locke's discussion of the PQ/SQ distinction is in the course of this general schema of idea-empiricism, and so the meaning of every term employed in corpuscularian explanations is plain to everyone.

For an illustration of this, let us focus on the simple idea of solidity. Solidity is the idea which always comes first in the list of PQs. Locke introduces this idea of solidity from everyday experience of things: 'Whether we move, or rest, in what Posture soever we are, we always feel something under us, that supports us ... That which thus hinders the approach of two Bodies, when they are moved one towards another, I call *Solidity*'. Having once got this idea from everyday experience, we can trace 'it farther' and consider it 'as well as Figure, in the minutest Particle of Matter, that can exist' (*Essay* II. iv. 1). So, the meanings of corpuscularian terms (even in the unobservable realm) have steady connections with grosser, observable things in everyday life. The same can be said of ideas other than the idea of solidity, such as those of extension, figure, motion or rest and number. They comprise the PQs.

Locke can thus be understood to have offered *an empirical*, plain *reconstruction* of the existing natural philosophy of his day so that it would be cleared of 'the Rubbish' and be thought to fit with the 'well-bred Company and polite Conversation'.

Lockean idea-empiricism of the corpuscularian type has another aspect: the *arguments* for the PQ/SQ distinction are (in important respects) *a posteriori*, or *experimental* in his contemporary terminology. As I have argued elsewhere,[43] Locke's three conditions for sorting out PQs well remind us of the preceding arguments of Locke in the chapter dealing with solidity (*Essay* II. iv). In this chapter on solidity, Locke explains how the idea of solidity, obtained from the sense of touch, is to be distinguished from pure space or hardness, by resorting to everyday sense experience and 'The Experiment at Florence'. Set side by side, the similarities between the passages in chapter iv and chapter viii are striking (Table 2.3):

Table 2.3 *Essay* II. iv and viii Compared

Essay II. iv.	*Essay* II. viii. 9
There is <u>no *Idea*, which we receive more constantly from Sensation</u>, than Solidity.	Qualities thus considered in Bodies are, First such as are <u>utterly inseparable from the Body, in what estate soever it be</u>; such as in all the alternations and changes it suffers, <u>all the force can be used upon it</u>, it constantly keeps; and such as <u>Sense constantly finds</u> in every particle of Matter, which has bulk enough to be perceived, and <u>the Mind finds inseparable from every particle of Matter</u>, though less than to make it self singly perceived by our Senses.
though our Senses take no notice of it, but in masses of matter, of a bulk sufficient to cause a Sensation in us; Yet <u>the Mind</u>, having once got this Idea from such grosser sensible Bodies, traces it farther, and considers it, as well as Figure, in the minutest Particle of Matter, that can exist; and <u>finds it inseparably inherent in Body, where-ever, or however modified</u>.	
The Experiment … at Florence, with a hollow Globe of Gold fill'd with Water, and exactly closed, father shews the solidity of so soft a body as Water. For the golden Globe thus filled, being put into a Press, which was driven <u>by the extreme force of skrews</u>, the water made it self way through the pores of that very close metal, …	

Thus, Locke's arguments for the PQ/SQ distinction are already anticipated by the preceding chapter on solidity, where Locke repeatedly resorted to daily experience and a scientific experiment to show that solidity is 'most intimately connected with, and essential to Body' (*Essay* II. iv. 1). Locke, in his discussions of PQs and SQs in *Essay* II. viii, always lists solidity first in his lists of PQs. This, taken together with the striking similarities of passages above, well establishes the claim that Locke considers solidity as the paradigm primary quality.[44]

5 Conclusion

In this chapter, I have argued that (1) Boylean influence on Locke's treatment of PQs and SQs is much stronger than some recent commentators have supposed, on the grounds of the *common nomenclature* connection (i.e. Locke inherited the term 'texture' of Boyle's unique invention), and (2) Locke can be *interpreted* to have removed the scholastic jargon inherent in Boyle's formulation, and made the twofold *empirical reconstruction* of the corpuscular philosophy.[45] Indeed, Locke was not entirely free from the scholastic jargon or framework, but he can be understood to have taken a big step forward in intellectual history, so that many readers today learn the PQ/SQ distinction by reading his *Essay*, without being tormented by the scholastic jargon like 'attributes', 'modes', 'moods' and 'affections'.

Gilbert Ryle once remarked that Locke completely changed the intellectual atmosphere from the 1600s to 1700s.[46] If we invented a time machine and travelled to the 1600s, like a fish out of water we would not be able to breathe. However, in the 1700s we could breathe the fresh air just as we do today. I think this is a fair evaluation of Locke's philosophical enterprise, and becomes all the more obvious if we compare Locke's formulation with the contemporary ones.

Notes

1 Many historians and theorists of philosophy discuss the PQ/SQ distinction. For a classic treatment by historians of philosophy, especially on Boyle and Locke, who have argued for the distinction, see Mandelbaum (1964), Alexander (1974), Alexander (1985). 'Fair' expositions of Locke's view, which aimed at releasing Locke from Berkeley's traditional charges by way of Boyle's corpuscular philosophy, have raised chain reactions from Berkeley's expositors who questioned whether Berkeley

'misunderstood' the Lockean PQ/SQ distinction. Recent literature on the PQ/SQ distinction (or more broadly on Locke's natural philosophy) focuses on Locke's own development of mechanism, trying to trace Locke's thought in its own light. See Milton (2001), Walmsley (2003), Allen (2008) and Hill (2009).

2 The uses of words 'firstly', 'secondly' and even 'thirdly' appear in his natural philosophical writings, in Book II of *De Generatione et Corruptione* (*On Generation and Corruption*). See Aristotle (1941: 509). Note that when Aristotle talks of 'primary' or 'originative' qualities such as hot-cold or dry-moist, he means them to be potential *forms*, not actual or sensible qualities of things.

3 Locke's PQ/SQ distinction is by many expositors considered to be fairly defensible and also serves as a philosophical gem, providing various insights into the problem. However, it is not quite clear why Galilean, Cartesian or Boylean versions of PQ/SQ distinction (which respectively deserve serious study) receive less attention than Lockean version, and I imagine the reason would be rather institutional or pedagogical than philosophical. For a comprehensive account of material qualities in seventeenth-century Britain from Hobbes and Charleton to Boyle and Locke, see Anstey (2013).

4 For Russell's influential account, see Russell (1993: 585).

5 These words are from Peter Alexander's influential paper. See Alexander (1974: 51).

6 Strictly, Boyle never uses the term 'primary quality'. See Section 2 of this chapter.

7 As far as I can see, serious manuscript studies on Locke's natural philosophy began in the 1960s by Dewhurst, followed by Romanell, Meynell in the 1970s and 1980s. From the 1990s onwards, Milton, Walmsley and Anstey drastically increased our knowledge of Locke's medical and philosophical activities prior to the publication of *Essay*.

8 Those works from which Locke made extensive notes include *Physiologicall Essays* (1661), *Scepticall Chymist* (1661) and *Of the Usefulness of Experimentall Natural Philosophy* (1663). The original title of the work is 'Physiological', but in Locke's hand we read 'Physiologicall'. The same is true of 'Scepticall' and 'Experientall'. See Bodleian Library MS Locke d. 11: 280, 281, 282–3.

9 Alexander (1985: 6–7) enumerates five roles of Locke as an under-labourer, while Jolley (1999: 56–8) says there are two main targets for Locke: Cartesian dogmatism and the scholastic doctrine of substantial forms. More recently, Anstey (2011a: 224), after a comprehensive investigation of Locke's natural philosophy, claims that 'the *Essay* is a genuine attempt at a natural history of the understanding'.

10 We just need to remember that Boyle and Newton were active members of the Royal Society of London established in 1660 for the promotion of experimental learning. For an influential account of experimental versus speculative natural philosophy in the seventeenth century, see Anstey (2005). Although Sydenham was not a fellow of the Royal Society, he was an ardent exponent of experimental medicine in England, having had strong influence on Locke's agnosticism. I

documented Locke's debt to Sydenham through early medical notebooks and Drafts A and B of the *Essay* in Aoki (2008a). For the view that Locke influenced Sydenham on natural historical method rather than Sydenham influencing Locke, see Anstey (2011b). It is also helpful to remember that, prior to this Epistle to the Reader, at the front page of his *Essay* Locke dedicated this philosophical work to Lord Herbert, then the president of the Royal Society. These facts help us understand the intellectual context in which the *Essay* was written and dedicated, and set the proper interpretive framework to evaluate Locke's original philosophical contribution, including the discussion of the PQ/SQ distinction.

11 See Keating (1993) and Anstey (2000). Keating (1993: 305) says, 'The mistaken interpretations are the result of the commentators reading their account of Locke back into Boyle in order to use Boyle to further clarify Locke. By un-Lock-ing Boyle, significant differences can be seen between them'. Anstey (2000) is an in-depth treatment of Boyle's philosophy per se, and argues for a systematization of Boyle's works on philosophy, including matter, qualities, laws of nature and mind/body interaction.

12 As Anstey points out, Boyle never uses the term 'primary quality'. That is because so-called PQs – such as shape, size, motion and texture – are affections of matter, from which all the qualities arise. See Anstey (2013: 254).

13 I will argue for this *a priori/a posteriori* difference later in Section 4.

14 Earlier in *Certain Physiological Essays* (1661), Boyle likewise talked of 'the more primitive and Catholick Affections of Matter, namely bulk, shape, and motion'. See Boyle (1999–2000, 2: 21).

15 Boyle sometimes mentions 'impressions' or 'ideas' in mind, in a similar way to the Cartesian or Lockean treatment of ideas. However, Boyle is not quite clear, and sometimes ambivalent on the ontological status of secondary qualities.

16 In his later work, *About the Excellency and Grounds of the Mechanical Hypothesis* (1674), Boyle stresses these two principles again and says that 'none can be more *few*, . . . or more *primary* than *Matter* and *Motion*' (Boyle 1999–2000, 8: 115).

17 M. A. Stewart (1979: xix), in his introduction to *Selected Philosophical Papers of Robert Boyle*, says, with regard to *An Introduction to the History of Particular Qualities* (1671), 'The largely *a priori* character of the concept of matter developed here, and indeed the existence of an Introduction without the Histories, suggests that, at the time of writing, Boyle's theory was still some way ahead of his practice.' Anstey (2000: 46) talks of Boyle's *a priori* criterion, saying, 'it is a necessary condition of something being matter that it have shape, size, and motion (or rest).'

18 Also in *Certain Physiological Essays* (1661), Boyle mentions 'the Learned Gassendus' and 'that most ingenious Gentleman Mons' Des-Cartes' (Boyle 1999–2000, 2: 12).

19 Boyle also emphasizes the importance of the historical part of *Forms and Qualities*, which is to 'set down some Observations of what Nature does, . . . as well as some Experiments wherein Nature is guided, . . . that so she may be made to attest the

Truth of our Doctrine' (*Forms and Qualities*: 381). I owe this observation to Peter Anstey.

20. See also Boyle's subsequent work, *Mechanical Origine or Production of divers particular Qualities* (1675/6), in which Boyle introduces 'mechanical principles', in Boyle (1999–2000, vol. 8).
21. As we know, Boyle writes so prodigiously on historical or experimental parts in his corpuscularian or mechanical writings, but it does not follow that his conceptual scheme was also historical or experimental.
22. Hill and Milton (2003: 16) argue that this abrégé dated from 1683 to 1685, that is, before Draft C (1685).
23. See Walmsley (2003) and Hill (2009).
24. Walmsley (1998: 243–4). James Hill takes a more eclectic position between scientific and epistemological interpretation. He says, 'Locke's preference for corpuscularian explanations should not, however, be taken to be merely the expression of a defence of natural science. He thought corpuscularianism exploited a fundamental fact about our ability to understand physical causation, which we might call "impulse principle"' (Hill (2010: 210).
25. Milton (2001) shows that Locke also had little interest in first philosophy at this stage of his life. However, Milton argues that through reading Descartes, Locke was well familiar with mechanism, at least in 1662.
26. For the view that Locke already used some corpuscularianism in Draft A and B, although with a qualification that he did not show 'a blanket acceptance of corpuscularian doctrines', see Downing (2001). I owe this reference to Peter Anstey.
27. For example, Boyle used 'primary affections' and 'secondary qualities', while Locke drew a distinction between 'primary qualities' and 'secondary qualities' in bodies. The lists of PQs and SQs are virtually the same between the two philosophers.
28. See footnote 25.
29. Boyle's use of 'texture' and Locke's adoption were first pointed out in Alexander (1974).
30. *Essay* II. viii. 18–20.
31. For a detailed account of the relationship of Boyle and Locke and of the former's influence on the latter, see Anstey (2020).
32. For example, the PQ/SQ distinction based on this impulse principle is no less vulnerable to Berkeley's charges than the scientific interpretation. Berkeley's charges were once interpreted to rest on 'relativity argument', but fairer interpretations in the 1980s showed that Berkeley was well aware that Locke's distinction had drawn on explanatory powers of corpuscularianism. See, for example, Wilson (1982: 109–10).
33. The first edition which I turned to is the one preserved at the British Library. Draft C (1685) has basically the same structure of arguments for the PQ/SQ distinction, that is, IP being inserted between PQs and SQs, with minor differences in section numbers. I am thankful to Professor G. A. J. Rogers for the reference of Draft C in the typescript.
34. Hill (2009) acknowledges that Keith Allen pointed out this fact to him.

35 Locke mentions the three conditions to sort out PQs. This stance was kept unchanged from the first to later editions throughout.
36 I think that Locke could have done so if he had really wanted to, but he did not.
37 Hill gives a different explanation of the change. He says, 'The author may forget that the original version had its own internal logic, which can be disrupted by later changes. This, I believe, is precisely what happened in the present case.' Granting that Locke did 'forget' the original, internal logic, one may also suspect that the role of IP is not so essential as Hill argues.
38 Although the first edition of Wynne's *Abridgement* (1696) was based on the first edition of *Essay* (1690), the *Abridgement* continued to incorporate the changes of the later editions of *Essay*, and sold very well through various editions from 1696 to 1700, 1721, 1731, 1737, 1744, 1752, 1770 and 1803. See Rogers (1990) for the circumstances of Wynne's *Abridgement*.
39 I am not saying that Locke's *arguments* for the PQ/SQ distinction were totally Boylean. But certainly Locke thinks that the merits of corpuscularianism are its explanatory power (in dealing with various cases, such as manna, porphyry and almond as well as the well-known hot and cold water) and its intelligibility. Locke appraises corpuscularianism elsewhere in *Essay* and also in *Some Thoughts Concerning Education*, Locke (1989: 247–8).
40 *Essay* II. iii. 1.
41 *Essay* II. iv. 1.
42 *Essay* II. v.
43 Aoki (2008b).
44 Locke explicitly says: 'There is no *Idea*, which we receive more constantly from Sensation than *Solidity*. . . . This of all other, seems the *Idea* most intimately connected with, and essential to Body, so as no where else to be found or imagin'd, but only in matter' (*Essay* II. iv. 1).
45 I am not saying that Locke accepted Boyle's arguments for the PQ/SQ distinction. Locke accepted the terminologies and explanatory framework of Boyle's corpuscularianism (probably together with other mechanical or corpuscular philosophies), and then revised it to the advantage of his philosophical system. Thus I argue for his *reconstruction* of the corpuscular philosophy.
46 Ryle (1990: 318).

References

Alexander, P. (1974), 'Boyle and Locke on Primary and Secondary Qualities', *Ratio*, 16: 51–67.
Alexander, P. (1985), *Ideas, Qualities and Corpuscles: Locke and Boyle on the External World*, Cambridge: Cambridge University Press.

Allen, K. (2008), 'Mechanism, Resemblance and Secondary Qualities: From Descartes to Locke', *British Journal for the History of Philosophy*, 16: 273–91.

Anstey, P. R. (2000), *The Philosophy of Robert Boyle*, London: Routledge.

Anstey, P. R. (2005), 'Experimental versus Speculative Natural Philosophy', in P. R. Anstey and J. A. Schuster (eds), *The Science of Nature in the Seventeenth Century: Patterns of Change in Early Modern Natural Philosophy*, 215–42, Dordrecht: Springer.

Anstey, P. R. (2011a), *John Locke and Natural Philosophy*, Oxford: Oxford University Press.

Anstey, P. R. (2011b), 'The Creation of the English Hippocrates', *Medical History*, 55: 457–78.

Anstey, P. R. (2013), 'The Theory of Material Qualities', in P. R. Anstey (ed.), *The Oxford Handbook of British Philosophy in the Seventeenth Century*, 240–60, Oxford: Oxford University Press.

Anstey, P. R. (2020), 'Boyle's Influence on Locke', in J.-E. Jones (ed.), *The Bloomsbury Companion to Robert Boyle*, 39–63, London: Bloomsbury.

Aoki, S. (2008a), 'Sydenham and Locke on the Historical Method [in Japanese]', *Studies in British Philosophy*, 31: 13–33.

Aoki, S. (2008b), 'Descartes and Locke on the Nature of Matter: A Note', in S. Hutton and P. Schuurman (eds), *Studies on Locke: Sources, Contemporaries, and Legacy*, 75–88, Dordrecht: Springer.

Aristotle (1941), *The Basic Works of Aristotle*, ed. R. McKeon, New York: Random House.

Boyle, R. (1999–2000), *The Works of Robert Boyle*, 14 vols, eds M. Hunter and E. B. Davis, London: Pickering and Chatto.

Downing, L. (2001), 'The Uses of Mechanism: Corpuscularianism in Drafts A and B of Locke's *Essay*', in C. Lüthy, J. E. Murdoch and W. R. Newman (eds), *Late Medieval and Early Modern Corpuscular Matter Theories*, 515–34, Leiden: Brill.

Hill, J. (2009), 'Primary Qualities, Secondary Qualities, and Locke's Impulse Principle', *British Journal for the History of Philosophy*, 17: 85–98.

Hill, J. (2010), 'Primary and Secondary Qualities', in S.-J. Savonius-Wroth, P. Schuurman and J. C. Walmsley (eds), *The Continuum Companion to Locke*, 199–201, London: Continuum.

Jolley, N. (1999), *Locke: His Philosophical Thought*, New York: Oxford University Press.

Keating, L. (1993), 'Un-Locking Boyle: Boyle on Primary and Secondary Qualities', *History of Philosophy Quarterly*, 10: 305–23.

Locke, J. (1700), *An Abridgement of Mr Locke's Essay Concerning Human Understanding*, 2nd edn, London: A. and F. Churchill.

Locke, J. (1975), *An Essay concerning Human Understanding*, ed. P. H. Nidditch, Oxford: Clarendon Press. 1st edn, 1690; abbreviated as *Essay*.

Locke, J. (1989), *Some Thoughts Concerning Education*, eds J. W. Yolton and J. S. Yolton, Oxford: Clarendon Press.

Mandelbaum, M. (1964), *Philosophy, Science and Sense Perception: Historical and Critical Studies*, Baltimore: Johns Hopkins University Press.

Milton, J. R. (2001), 'Locke, Medicine and the Mechanical Philosophy', *British Journal for the History of Philosophy*, 9: 221–43.

Milton, J. R. and J. Hill (2003), 'The Epitome (*Abrégé*) of Locke's *Essay*', in P. R. Anstey (ed.), *The Philosophy of John Locke: New Perspectives*, 3–25, London: Routledge.

Rogers, G. A. J. (1990), 'Introduction', in *An Abridgement of Mr Locke's Essay Concerning Human Understanding*, 4th edn, London, Bristol: Thoemmes Press.

Russell, B. (1993), *A History of Western Philosophy*, London: Routledge, 1st British edn, 1946.

Ryle, G. (1990), 'John Locke', in J. S. Yolton (ed.), *A Locke Miscellany: Locke Biography and Criticisms for All*, 318–31, Bristol: Thoemmes Press. First published in 1967.

Stewart, M. A. (1979), 'Introduction', in *Selected Philosophical Papers of Robert Boyle*, ed. M. A. Stewart, xi–xxxi, Manchester: Manchester University Press.

Walmsley, J. C. (1998), *John Locke's Natural Philosophy (1632–1671)*, PhD diss., King's College London.

Walmsley, J. C. (2003), 'The Development of Locke's Mechanism in the Drafts of the *Essay*', *British Journal for the History of Philosophy*, 11: 417–49.

Wilson, M. D. (1982), 'Did Berkeley Completely Misunderstand the Basis of the Primary-Secondary Qualities Distinction in Locke?', in C. M. Turbayne (ed.), *Berkeley: Critical and Interpretive Essays*, 108–23, Manchester: Manchester University Press.

3

Berkeley's experimental method in *An Essay Towards a New Theory of Vision*

Yasuaki Nakano

1 Introduction

In a seminal study of the emergence of Western scientific culture, Stephen Gaukroger gives Locke a central place in the transformation of natural philosophy in Britain and France in the first half of the eighteenth century. Gaukroger's narrative of 'the collapse of mechanism', the shift of natural philosophy away from the Cartesian type of systematic matter theory in the early eighteenth century, highlights Locke's vindication of 'experimental philosophy'.[1] According to Gaukroger, Locke's *Essay* has 'thoroughly natural philosophical origins'. Locke's primary concern in the *Essay* is to provide a philosophical defence of experimental philosophy as practised by members of the Royal Society, in particular by Boyle and Newton. From this interpretive perspective, Locke is seen as less enthusiastic about corpuscularianism than it has often been supposed: he rejects the universal validity of reductive explanation of phenomena in terms of the hypothesized micro-corpuscular structure.[2] Rather, Locke's concern is to defend the autonomy of 'horizontal' or phenomenal explanation, that is, the explanation which identifies the systematic connections at the phenomenal level.

Now what is remarkable about Gaukroger's narrative is that he consistently excludes Berkeley from his story of the eighteenth-century development of experimental philosophy after Locke. Indeed, it is his opinion that 'there is no continuous "empiricist" tradition in British thought' (Gaukroger 2010: 187). The historiographical story of 'British empiricism' according to which Lockean premises are concluded with Hume's scepticism via Berkeley's immaterialism distorts Locke's true status in the eighteenth century. This picture obscures Locke's place as the starting point for a distinctive natural philosophical tradition: the historical significance of Locke's *Essay* consists in that it provided a subtle defence of 'experimental philosophy' and thereby determined the general direction of natural philosophical practice in the early eighteenth century. In Gaukroger's judgement, however, Berkeley's philosophy is at odds with Locke's 'naturalistic' agenda, and he actually 'owed far more to that arch-Cartesian Malebranche than he did to Locke' (Gaukroger 2010: 157).[3] While it was the legitimatization of experimental study of nature that concerned Locke, Berkeley did not share this concern.

But it is not clear why Berkeley cannot be seen as taking part in the experimental philosophical movement of the early eighteenth century. I agree that 'experimental philosophy' is more useful category to capture the movement Locke created in the early eighteenth century. But was Berkeley an outsider to this movement? In fact, there was a gentlemen's society in Dublin that aimed to promote experimental natural philosophy immediately before Berkeley started his philosophical career. This society, the Dublin Philosophical Society (DPS), was established in 1683 by the initiative of William Molyneux, Locke's friend and correspondent, and continued to exist until 1708.[4] The DPS took as its model the Royal Society of London, and regularly corresponded with it. Berkeley not only had acquaintance with some of the original members of this society, such as Thomas Molyneux, William's younger brother, and St George Ashe,[5] but read a paper to the DPS, reconstituted in 1707 by William's son, Samuel, who became his pupil and a close friend.[6]

This chapter explores Berkeley's experimental philosophy in his first philosophical work, *An Essay Towards a New Theory of Vision* (hereafter the *New Theory*). Berkeley published the *New Theory* in 1709 and *A Treatise Concerning the Principles of Human Knowledge* (hereafter the *Principles*) in 1710. It would not be unreasonable to suppose that he was strongly influenced by the intellectual atmosphere surrounding him when these works were in preparation. Indeed, Berkeley's notebooks, called the *Philosophical Commentaries*, which he composed in preparation for the *New Theory* and the *Principles*, are believed to have been written between the summer of 1707 and the autumn of 1708,[7] and this overlaps with the period during which the DPS was revived. What I want to show in the following part of this chapter is, therefore, that in his early philosophy Berkeley was committed to the method of experimental philosophy, and that his first philosophical work, the *New Theory*, represents his experimental philosophical practice.

Berkeley's philosophy has been primarily interpreted in terms of the immaterialism expressed in the *Principles*. But it would be a serious mistake to see Berkeley solely as a metaphysician who had little concern with contemporary natural philosophy. He had keen interest in natural history throughout his life,[8] and his last major work *Siris*, published in 1744, testifies to his enduring concern to keep up with the current developments in natural philosophy. The psychology of vision developed in the *New Theory* owes much to William Molyneux's studies in the *Dioptrica Nova*. Berkeley not only learned technical knowledge from this book but took from Molyneux three test cases for visual theory, the Barrovian case, the moon illusion, the inverted retinal image,[9] not to mention the case of the man born blind. Molyneux's *Dioptrica Nova* is the most significant product from the activities of the DPS, and Berkeley's study of vision is clearly linked to the DPS via Molyneux.

However, the experimental tradition of the DPS and the debt to William Molyneux will not be sufficient for an understanding of Berkeley's experimental philosophy in the *New Theory*. It is also important to take into consideration the significant impact Newton had on natural philosophy. The experimental philosophy of the early Royal Society, and accordingly of the DPS, was primarily concerned, after the Baconian manner, to compile natural histories by experiments and observations.[10] Boyle's experimental study of the air using the air-pump provided a paradigmatic example of this. Newton's natural philosophy represented by the *Principia* of 1687, however, changed the general current of natural philosophical practice.[11] In this chapter, I will not explore Berkeley's connection with the DPS and Molyneux's study of vision, though it is no doubt of great interest. Instead, I look at Berkeley's discussion of natural philosophy in order to identify his conception of experimental philosophy in the post-Newtonian current of natural philosophy and then clarify how he can be seen as constructing his theory of vision according to the experimental method.

In Section 2, we will see Berkeley's remarks on natural philosophy in the early notebooks and then interpret his discussion of natural philosophy in the *Principles* in terms of these remarks. Berkeley's notebook remarks unambiguously suggest his preference for the experimental natural philosophy over the speculative. It will be argued that his critical remarks on Newton's theory of attraction in the *Principles* should be seen as only directed at the speculative side of that theory and not at experimental philosophy itself. In Sections 3 and 4, we turn to Berkeley's practice of experimental philosophy in the *New Theory*. In Section 3, we start by looking at the methodological remarks in *The Theory of Vision Vindicated* published twenty-four years after the *New Theory*, and two points from this later work are highlighted. First, Berkeley's theory of vision is independent of metaphysical causal enquiry. Second, Berkeley aimed to identify the explanatory principles of vision, as distinguished from metaphysical causes, by the method of analysis, and he understood this method as it was expressed by Newton in the *Opticks*. In Section 4, we will go deeper into the analytic procedure Berkeley takes in the *New Theory* to explain visual phenomena and clarify in what manner his analytic method can be regarded as particularly experimental.

2 Berkeley and the experimental/speculative distinction of natural philosophy

Berkeley's private notebooks, the *Philosophical Commentaries*, contain important background information that illuminates the arguments of the *New Theory* and the *Principles*.[12] The number of notebook entries concerning natural philosophy is not large, but they provide us, as we will see, with a significant clue to Berkeley's view of natural philosophy in the published writings. At the beginning of Notebook A, the second part of the notebooks, we find the following remark:

> I know there is a mighty Sect of Men will oppose me. but yet I may expect to be Supported by those whose minds are not so far overgrown with madness, these are far the greatest part of mankind. Especially Moralists, Divines, Politicians, in a word all but Mathematicians & Natural Philosophers (I mean only the Hypothetical Gentlemen). Experimental Philosophers have nothing whereat to be offended in me. (PC 406)

Here Berkeley identifies the opponents of his philosophical project in 'Mathematicians & Natural Philosophers', whom he calls 'Hypothetical Gentlemen'. But in spite of his critical attitude to natural philosophers expressed in the above, he thinks 'experimental philosophers' will support him. More interestingly, some twenty folios further into Notebook A, we find Berkeley stating not just that he will be supported by experimental philosophers but that he supports them.

> N Mem. much to Recommend & approve of Experimental Philosophy. (PC 498)

Since the marginal letter 'N' is used by Berkeley to signify 'Natural Philosophy',[13] this leaves no doubt that when he mentions 'experimental philosophy' what he has in mind is experimental *natural philosophy*. Taken together, the aforementioned two quoted remarks suggest Berkeley's unambiguous approval of the experimental natural philosophy in opposition to the speculative.

The notebook entries we have just seen show that Berkeley draws a clear line between two ways of practising natural philosophy: the *experimental* and the *speculative*. As Peter Anstey has revealed, the distinction between these two types of natural philosophical practice constituted '*the* fundamental dichotomy in discussions of natural philosophical methodology' (Anstey 2005: 216) from the late 1650s to the early eighteenth century. The distinction came to be invoked in Boyle's methodological writings of the 1650s to express the different approaches to *natural philosophy*, and was subsequently referred to in the apologetic writings of the Royal Society.[14] The dichotomy is roughly characterized as follows. *Experimental philosophy* aims at the construction of natural histories by observation and experiment, considering theories and hypotheses about the underlying causes to be approved only after sufficient collections of observational facts; whereas *speculative philosophy* directly turned to general theories and explanations in terms of the underlying causes and indulges in hypotheses without natural historical foundations. And in the methodological discourses on natural philosophy which refer to this distinction, it was experimental philosophy that was always recommended.[15]

Now it is clear that Berkeley was well acquainted with the experimental/speculative distinction of natural philosophy and that he preferred the experimental side of the distinction. In another entry of Notebook A, he goes so far as to say that speculative natural philosophy is 'absurd':

N Absurd to study Astronomy & other the like Doctrines as Speculative Sciences. (PC 434)[16]

In his philosophical works in the early and middle periods, Berkeley remained consistently critical of natural philosophers' pretention to explaining natural phenomena by the underlying physical causes, whether they are mechanical or non-mechanical, and his rejection of the speculative approach to natural philosophy can be understood from this perspective.

On the other hand, however, it seems unclear how he conceived of the experimental philosophy of which he approved. Since he wrote several pieces of natural history, he was certainly *not* critical of the construction of natural histories. But it is unlikely that Berkeley considered the Baconian natural histories to be the primary aim of natural philosophical practice. Newton's *Principia* had impressively shown that we could advance our natural knowledge far beyond the provisional gatherings of natural historical facts as had been practised in the early Royal Society and the DPS. In order to clarify Berkeley's conception of experimental philosophy, we should now look at sections 101–9 of the *Principles*, which may well be an elaboration of the notebook remarks we saw earlier. In these sections, Berkeley does not explicitly use the term 'experimental philosophy', but the experimental/speculative divide is implicit in his discussion.

In section 101, Berkeley starts his critical comments on natural philosophy with this statement: 'The two great provinces of speculative science, conversant about ideas received from sense, are *natural philosophy* and *mathematics*' (1st edn). Natural philosophy was traditionally considered speculative since it aimed to explain phenomena by their underlying causes. But the examples Berkeley takes up for critical examination in sections 101–9 are taken from the *modern* philosophy: mechanistic corpuscularianism and the theory of attraction. Since these are usually associated with two representative experimental philosophers, Boyle and Newton, it may appear that Berkeley wants to attack experimental philosophy. This is, however, not quite true.

We concentrate here on Berkeley's discussion of attraction. He starts his discussion by pointing out that the term 'attraction' actually does not refer to any causal powers in bodies nor to the ways of their operation in the production of phenomena, such as the falling of bodies, sea tides and cohesion of the parts of steel: 'in this, as in the other instances, I do not perceive that any thing is signified besides the effect it self; for as to the manner of the action whereby it is produced, or the cause which produces it, these are not so much as aimed at' (PHK 103). In fact, Newton warned in the *Principia* that he is not providing *physical* explanations, as distinguished from *mathematical* explanations, when he uses the term 'attraction' or its cognates.[17] And it is likely that Berkeley took hints from Newton when he observes that explanation by 'attraction' clarifies nothing of 'the manner of the action' of attractive power. Newton stated that he used 'interchangeably and indiscriminately words signifying attraction, impulse, or any sort of propensity toward a center' (Newton 1999: 408). But, in Berkeley's analysis, if 'attraction' does not refer to any definite modes of operation or to its physical basis, the purported explanation of phenomena by attraction is reduced to circularity and therefore uninstructive: it does not say anything more than 'stones fall by attraction because stones fall by attraction'.[18]

It is important to note, however, that Berkeley never suggests Newton's concept of attraction is useless for natural philosophical explanations. While pointing out its uselessness as it is deployed as a *causal* explanation, Berkeley gives an alternative view of Newton's achievement. As Berkeley sees it, 'attraction' refers to nothing other than the *phenomena* of the mutual tendency of bodies. Then how is Newton's explanation to be interpreted? According to Berkeley, natural philosophical explanation proceeds by identification of the *similarities* of phenomena through diligent observation and comparison of them. What

Newton really achieved in the *Principia*, therefore, is that he has successfully collected diverse phenomena of very extensive scope to subsume under 'the general name *attraction*', based on their *observable similarity*. For Berkeley, this amounts to subsuming them under a formulated general law, that is, the law of gravitation. Explanation in natural philosophy does not consist in explaining phenomena by an underlying physical cause, but in pointing out similarities between familiar phenomena and unfamiliar ones, say, between falling bodies and tidal movements, and thereby reducing what initially appeared anomalous, tidal movements, to 'a particular example of a general rule or law of Nature' (PHK 104), that is, the law of gravity.[19]

Throughout these critical comments on Newton's natural philosophy, Berkeley has no intention to undermine *experimental* natural philosophy. Corresponding to his remark in the notebook (PC 498), we find this statement in the conclusion of his discussion on the theory of attraction:

> from what hath been premised no reason can be drawn, why the history of Nature should not still be studied, and observations and experiments made, which, that they are of use to mankind, and enable us to draw any general conclusions, is . . . the result . . . only of God's goodness and kindness to men in the administration of the world. (PHK 107)

To be sure, the same section starts with the statement that 'philosophers amuse themselves in vain, when they inquire for any natural efficient cause, distinct from a *mind* or *spirit*'. This represents his metaphysical standpoint. But Berkeley does not think his immaterialist metaphysics, which denies causal power to physical things, is incompatible with experimental natural philosophy. Rather, according to his own assessment, '*hypotheses* and speculations are left out' and thereby 'the study of Nature is abridged' by his doctrine of immaterialism (PHK 102). Thus, although he takes up the 'moderns' rather than the scholastics in his discussion of speculative natural philosophy, and although he dares to choose Newton's theory of attraction for his target, we should not overlook the point that he never means to extend his criticism to the practice of experimental philosophy itself.

Concerning Berkeley's discussion of natural philosophy, one thing deserves special attention here. Although Berkeley approves of experimental philosophy, he does not endorse the view, prevalent in the early Royal Society and in the DPS too, that the primary task of natural philosophy consists in the construction of natural histories by experiments and observations. This reflects his awareness of a significant change that occurred to the methodological ideal of natural philosophy after Newton. The task of Newton's *Principia* was to establish 'the system of the world' in which phenomena ranging from the Earth to the heavens were integrated under the single principle of gravitation. The attraction or gravitation formulated by Newton as a law is the *general and comprehensive principle* which explains phenomena of the whole natural world, and this, as is well known, is successfully achieved by the construction of a mathematical system. Accordingly, Berkeley characterizes the task of natural philosophy as 'the grammar of nature' (PHK 108; 1st edn), which aims at the discovery of the general laws of nature: 'by a diligent observation of the phenomena within our view, we may discover the general laws of Nature, and from them deduce the other phenomena' (PHK 107).[20] Here the central role of 'general laws' as the principles and the reasoning from those laws to phenomena are clearly appreciated, and observations and experiments are not conceived merely in terms of natural histories but in terms of a general theory.

3 The explanatory principles and the method of analysis in the *New Theory*

Berkeley's *New Theory of Vision* has long been interpreted in light of his next, predominantly metaphysical work, the *Principles*. From this viewpoint, the *New Theory* has usually been regarded as primarily intended by Berkeley to be subservient to the immaterialist metaphysics of the *Principles*.[21] The reading I suggest herein, however, is that the *New Theory* represents Berkeley's experimental philosophy. We have seen earlier that he approves of experimental philosophy in his critical review of speculative natural philosophy. Our concern in this and the next section is to explore Berkeley's *actual practice* of experimental philosophy in the *New Theory*.

Reading the *New Theory* as a work of experimental philosophy will not be incompatible with the view that it has some metaphysical implications. The concluding statement that 'the proper objects of vision constitute the universal language of nature' (NTV 147; 1st edn) steps into the realm of metaphysics. In the third edition of 1732, 'nature' in this statement was replaced by '*the Author of nature*'. This alteration is coordinated with the fact that the third edition of the *New Theory* was attached to *Alciphron*, whose Dialogue IV contained the demonstration of God's existence based on the thesis that vision constitutes a language. Earlier in the *Principles*, giving a brief summary of the *New Theory*, Berkeley had already declared that 'visible ideas are the language whereby the governing spirit . . . informs us what tangible ideas he is about to imprint upon us' in harmony with our actions (PHK 44). Thus, there is no doubt that Berkeley intended the arguments of the *New Theory* ultimately to take us to metaphysics and theology. But my suggestion is that the *New Theory*, taken by itself, is a work of experimental philosophy and that it consciously adopts the experimental method.

In order to substantiate this interpretive standpoint, it will be convenient to begin with Berkeley's own assessment of the *New Theory* made twenty-four years later. In 1733, Berkeley published *The Theory of Vision or Visual Language . . . Vindicated and Explained* (hereafter the *Theory of Vision*) in response to an anonymous critic. This later work, in which Berkeley provides 'a commentary' on the *New Theory* (NTV 70), contains a number of observations about the method of the earlier work. In the following passage, Berkeley defines the aim and the subject matter of his study of vision.

> In treating of vision, it was my purpose to consider the effects and appearances, the objects perceived by my senses, the ideas of sight as connected with those of touch; to inquire how one idea comes to suggest another belonging to a different sense, how things visible suggest things tangible. (TVV 14)

Berkeley says his treatment of vision was restricted to considerations of 'the effects and appearances', that is, *sensible ideas* (visible and tangible ideas) and their *connections*. As he goes on to observe, the reasoning about 'the external, unseen Cause of our ideas' was entirely out of the scope of his discussion on vision (TVV 17). And the 'cause' here is used in the *metaphysical* sense: it refers to the unperceivable 'substance' which is distinct from sensible ideas and which produces ideas by its powers, whether it is corporeal or spiritual (TVV 19, 20). We may set out for such causal enquiry *after* we have achieved an exact understanding of the nature of vision, but

> in order to understand and comprehend this theory [of vision], and discover the true principles thereof, we should consider the likeliest way is not to attend to unknown substances, external causes, agents, or powers, nor to reason or infer any thing about or from things obscure, unperceived, and altogether unknown. (TVV 17)

The *New Theory*, then, is concerned to study the faculty of vision at the phenomenal level, that is, by concentrating on ideas as the objects of sense, without bothering to infer or reason about the nature of their causes. Berkeley acknowledges that the external cause of ideas may be the subject of enquiry in 'a treatise on some other science', but strongly insists on the distinction of visual theory he is concerned to establish from such a metaphysical kind of enquiry (TVV 19).

It is important to note, however, that Berkeley is not merely concerned to *describe* sensible ideas which constitute our visual experience. As is indicated in the title *An Essay Towards a New Theory of Vision*, Berkeley is striving to arrive at a *theory*. And he repeatedly states that his goal was to understand the *nature* of vision. Berkeley aims to discover 'the true principles' by which the nature of vision is explained. But he thinks the best method to achieve this is to ignore the 'causes' of visual phenomena and look for the explanatory principles in phenomena themselves (TVV 16–18). But then what does he mean by the discovery of 'the true principles'?

We can start to answer this question by looking at another important methodological remark in the *Theory of Vision*. After answering the critic, Berkeley proceeds to restate his arguments developed in the *New Theory*, but he says he now adopts the different method, 'the synthetical method', in which 'the conclusions in the analysis being assumed as principles'. The conclusion Berkeley points to here is '*Vision is the Language of the Author of Nature*'. Taking this proposition as the principle he now explains the nature of vision by 'deducing theoremes and solutions of phaenomena' from it (TVV 38). It seems clear, then, that one of the explanatory principles, and no doubt the fundamental principle, of his theory of vision for Berkeley is the proposition that vision is the language of the author of nature. From this methodological remark, we learn that in the *New Theory* Berkeley observed the method of 'analysis', starting from 'phenomena' which require explanation and arguing towards establishing the general principle that vision is a language as the conclusion.[22]

Now analysis and synthesis are the ancient methods of scientific enquiry which were frequently talked of by philosophers of the early modern period. Generally speaking, analysis is the method of discovering the principles of a certain particular problem or phenomenon which requires a solution or an explanation. Synthesis is the method of presenting a scientific system by deduction from the already discovered general principles. While analysis is the method of discovery in search for a science, synthesis delivers the already discovered science. It is difficult to identify the source for Berkeley's reference to the analytic method,[23] but he may well have been familiar with Newton's famous methodological remark in Query 31 of the second English edition of the *Opticks*.

> in Natural Philosophy, the Investigation of difficult Things by the Method of Analysis, ought ever to precede the Method of Composition. This Analysis

consists in making Experiments and Observations, <and in drawing general Conclusions from them by Induction... By this way of Analysis> we may proceed from Compounds to Ingredients, and from Motions to the Forces producing them; and in general, from Effects to their Causes, and from particular Causes to more general ones, till the Argument end in the most general. (Newton 1952: 404)[24]

For Newton, the starting point of analysis in natural philosophy is 'Experiments and Observations'. This is an important difference from Cartesian natural philosophy. Thus, according to Newton, natural philosophical investigation in the *Principia* proceeded by analysis to identify natural forces from observable motions; the *Opticks* involved the analytic process of decomposing white light into heterogeneous rays of light by experiments. Starting from experiments and observations, the method of analysis reduces compound phenomena to their elements and ascends 'from effects to their Causes, and from particular Causes to more general ones'.[25]

In the *New Theory*, Berkeley adopts an analytic method similar to the one expressed by Newton in the aforementioned passage. His discussion proceeds by reduction of compounds into ingredients: he argues that our visual experience of space, which appears uniform and uncompounded, is actually composed of two elements, visible and tangible ideas. The resolution of visual experience into two distinct ideas of sight and touch provides the general framework of the *New Theory*, and within this framework Berkeley explains vision by customary connections of visible and tangible ideas. The next section provides an overview of this analytic procedure and reveals how it is experimentally conducted.

4 Berkeley's experimental method in the *New Theory*

The cornerstone of Berkeley's *New Theory* is the distinction between immediate and mediate perception. Berkeley argues that distance, size and situation are *not immediately* perceived by sight. These spatial properties are in truth perceived only by touch. But they are perceived by sight *mediately*, by 'means' or cues that accompany vision and which are observed to be regularly correlated with those spatial properties perceived by touch. By analysis, then, our visual experience is resolved into two components: visible ideas, which are immediately perceived; and tangible ideas, which are perceived by means of the visibles. These two elements of our spatial experience are ultimately shown to be 'heterogeneous':

ideas of sight, which are only light and colours with their modifications, and ideas of touch, which contain spatial properties, are of entirely distinct kind. Their connection is based on 'custom', and it is only experience that teaches us their connection.

The analysis of compounds into ingredients, that is, the distinction between what is immediately perceived and what is not, provides the framework in which *causal* explanation of visual phenomena is to be given *without transcending the phenomenal level*. In the preceding section we saw Berkeley excluded metaphysical causes from the proper subject of the theory of vision. But this does not mean that he excluded all kinds of causal enquiry. In fact, in the *New Theory*, Berkeley uses 'cause' and the related terms, 'occasion' and 'coexistence' (NTV 25, 28, 36, 38, 70, 77), and they are used *in the phenomenal sense*, that is, in the sense of *observable causes*.[26] By the analytic procedure, our visual experience of a three-dimensional landscape, which is presented to us as an uncompounded appearance, is explained in terms of the combination of the phenomenal causes which can be identified in observable phenomena themselves.

In developing his explanation of vision, Berkeley can be seen as specifying three distinguishable things as the phenomenal causes which bring about our visual perception. Corresponding to the immediate/mediate distinction, these three phenomenal causes can be classified as follows:

(1) the cause of *immediate* perception: the optical condition, i.e. light rays and the retinal image
(2) the cause of *mediate* perception: visible ideas which function as 'signs' signifying tangible ideas
(3) the cause of *mediate* perception: the customary connection of ideas (and the function of 'suggestion') which transfers our perception from visible signs to tangible ideas of space.

The study of (1) properly belongs to optics, but it is also relevant to Berkeley's theory of vision. Berkeley makes an important use of it to draw the line between what is immediately perceived and what is not.[27] The study of (2) and (3), the causes of *mediate* visual perception, and the explanation of vision in their terms, is the central concern of the *New Theory*. Here we concentrate on Berkeley's treatment of *distance* perception and see how his arguments proceed in this part of analysis.[28]

Berkeley constructs the overall arguments in the way in which two different kinds of principles are in competition with each other: the principle of custom, which is his own, and the geometric principles. According to one of the latter, which he calls 'the received' principle (NTV 4; 1st edn), when an object is relatively near to us, we see distance by calculating the optic angles formed at the object when we turn the eyes towards it (NTV 4–5). This account conceives distance perception to depend upon geometrical reasoning based on a 'necessary connection'. By contrast, the alternative principle Berkeley gives in his account is the sensation we feel when we turn the eyes towards the object (NTV 17). This sensation has no necessary connection with the object's distance, but we learn by experience the regular connections between certain sensations and the correlated distances perceived by touch. Thus Berkeley puts forward 'customary connection' as the new principle which explains visual distance perception.

What Berkeley is trying to achieve by setting up such a competition is to specify the means (i.e. the cause) of distance perception in *a particular case*. And his discussion of the perception of distance, size and situation proceeds by specifying the means (the causes) by which those spatial properties are mediately perceived in each particular case. Accumulating such observations about particular cases of visual space perception, Berkeley ascends *by induction* to the identification of a general cause of mediate perception of space, namely, the customary connection of ideas. In the case we have just seen, the problem is to explain distance perception when we see a closely located object with both eyes. And this problem is solved by identifying *a particular cause*, i.e. sensation of the eye turning. But at the same time, *a more general cause* is introduced along with this particular cause.

> [B]ecause the mind has by constant experience found the different *sensations* corresponding to the different dispositions of the eyes to be attended each with a different degree of *distance* in the object, there has grown *an habitual or customary connexion between those two sorts of ideas*, so that the mind no sooner perceives the sensation arising from the different turn it gives the eyes, in order to bring the pupils nearer or farther asunder, but it withal perceives the different idea of distance which was wont to be connected with that sensation; just as upon hearing a certain sound, the idea is immediately suggested to the understanding which *custom* had united with it. (NTV 17; my italics)

Berkeley proceeds similarly in his treatment of another case of distance perception in which we see a very near object with one eye. According to the geometric principle which applies to this case, it is by 'the greater or lesser divergency of the rays' falling on the pupil that we see distance (NTV 6). In opposition to this, Berkeley's own solution begins with identifying the *particular* means or cause of distance perception, the confusion of appearance. But the *general* cause, customary connection, is also introduced. When we learn by experience the constant and regular correlation between nearer distance and confused appearances, 'there ariseth in the mind an habitual connexion between the several degrees of confusion and distance; the greater confusion still implying the lesser distance, and the lesser confusion the greater distance of the object' (NTV 21).

With this broad sketch of the analytic procedure Berkeley takes in the *New Theory*, let us now consider what it is that makes his method of analysis particularly *experimental*. Berkeley regards those who explain vision by optic angles as 'speculative men' (NTV 4; 3rd edn) and the geometric principles deployed by them as *hypothetical*: 'those lines and angles have no real existence in nature, being only an hypothesis framed by the mathematicians, and by them introduced into optics, that they might treat of that science in a geometrical way' (NTV 14). As he sees it, the geometric principles of visual perception are only fictional entities that are introduced for the systematic treatment of vision by mathematics. But Berkeley's aim in the *New Theory* is not simply to upset the currently received theory but to pave the way for an alternative *theory* by discovery of the new principles. By what criteria, then, are his own principles exempted from being merely fictional?

The first criterion Berkeley appeals to is that the means of mediate perception should be available to *consciousness*. If distance is perceived by some means, it is necessary that they should be accessible to the perceiver. For instance, when we perceive someone feeling shame by the redness of his face, it is necessary that we perceive the colour of the man's face (NTV 9). But optical angles are not accessible to us, for we are never aware of perceiving such things in visual perception (NTV 12). The means of distance perception Berkeley gives, on the other hand, is available to the perceiver. It is true that we are usually not aware that we make use of the sensation of the eye turning in perceiving distance, but we can bring it before consciousness as soon as we direct attention to it. Thus there is observational evidence which supports Berkeley's principles; whereas there is no such evidence for the explanation that distance perception occurs by geometric means.

The appeal to consciousness is one important feature of Berkeley's experimental method in the *New Theory*. It is by this criterion that the *particular* causes of mediate perception, that is, the means by which we perceive space, are identified in the phenomena of vision. But the consciousness criterion is not all that Berkeley has recourse to in order to establish his principles on the experimental methodological ground. Berkeley introduced *a general cause*, the principle of customary connection, when he identified a particular cause of distance perception, sensation of the turning of the eyes. But how is this general cause of mediate perception experimentally justified?

It would be helpful here to remember Berkeley's discussion of the theory of attraction we saw in Section 2. Indeed, there is an interesting parallel between Newton's 'attraction' as he understood it and the customary connection of his theory of vision. According to Berkeley, 'attraction' refers not to the unobservable physical causes inherent in bodies but to the *phenomenon* that bodies regularly tend to approach each other. In a similar way, 'customary connection' refers to the *phenomenon* that one idea regularly tends to follow another. But if 'customary connection' means nothing more than the regularity of phenomena, how can it serve as the general explanatory principle? According to Berkeley, Newton's achievement in the *Principia* consisted in the integration of diverse phenomena under the gravitational law by identification of their *similarities* through observation and comparison. Similarly, Berkeley's aim in the *New Theory* is to comprehend the diverse visual phenomena under the principle of customary connection by identification of the *similarities* between them: by observation and comparison of the visual phenomena of distance, size and situation, they are discovered to follow the same kind of order, that is, the connection which is based on custom, as opposed to necessary connection of the received geometric theory.

The principle of customary connection is experimentally justified because it is identified in phenomena themselves: it is justified by discovering the *observable similarity* of the phenomena collected from various cases of visual perception. Here the explanation of visual phenomena, as is the case with Newton's explanation of natural phenomena by attraction or gravitation, is achieved by *inductive generalization*. In Berkeley's theory of vision, our mediate visual perception of distance, size and situation, in the various instances considered in the *New Theory*, is inductively subsumed under the same law of custom and suggestion.

But Berkeley's analytic procedure in the construction of his theory of vision is not strictly inductive. It is an essential feature of the *New Theory* that the principle of customary connection is illustrated and amplified by the use of *analogy*: we see space just as we understand language. To put it more precisely, visible ideas *signify* tangible ideas of space by their customary connection learned through experience, just as words signify meanings by the convention we learn through experience. The analogy of vision with language would seem as hypothetical as the geometric lines and angles, for it is not founded on observation and experience. But Berkeley thinks it is justified by the *heuristic role* it plays in the explanation of vision. The fact that we are usually unaware of the compound nature of visual perception is illustrated by the linguistic phenomenon that in reading a book we are only aware of the meanings signified without paying attention to the words (NTV 51). The language analogy is also invoked to explain the context dependence of the function of 'suggestion', and this is effectively used in the explanation of the moon illusion (NTV 73). The introduction of the language analogy is useful because it enables us to solve the problems of visual phenomena by drawing analogies from the familiar phenomena of language. Through successful applications of the language analogy to various instances of visual phenomena, Berkeley thinks it justified to conclude his discussion with 'the most general' principle of his theory that 'vision is the language of the Author nature'.

5 Conclusion

We began this chapter with Gaukroger's reading of Locke's *Essay* as a vindication of English experimental natural philosophy. According to Gaukroger, the historical origin of Lockean empiricism is closely tied with a distinctive form of natural philosophical practice, that is, the newly emerged experimental methodology of natural philosophy represented by the Royal Society and its prominent members such as Boyle and Newton. The historical significance of Locke's *Essay* lies in his philosophical defence of experimental natural philosophy, which effectively paved the way to the flourishing of the non-systematic, experience-based study of natural phenomena in the first half of the eighteenth century. From this renewed perspective of Locke's place in the history of philosophy, Gaukroger considered Berkeley to be standing outside the experimental philosophical movement practised in the aftermath of Locke's *Essay*. But our discussion of Berkeley's experimental method earlier has given enough, I believe, for a correction of this judgement.

We have noticed that Gaukroger does not believe in the continuous British empiricist tradition as has been commonly conceived. Particularly, he does not believe Berkeley shared Locke's concern. As for Hume, however, Gaukroger seems to be willing to affirm continuity of the Lockean project. On the title page of the *Treatise of Human Nature*, Hume famously defined his work as 'an attempt to introduce the experimental method of reasoning into moral subjects'; in the Abstract of the *Treatise*, he observed that it is 'worth while to try if the science of *man* will not admit of the same accuracy which several parts of natural philosophy are found susceptible of' (*Treatise*, Abstract 1). These and similar remarks in Hume's writings, according to Gaukroger, exhibit 'a thoroughly Lockean appraisal' (Gaukroger 2014: 33).[29] Thus, Gaukroger thinks the Locke-Hume line of development is still worth maintaining in his alternative story.

I myself think it fruitful to reconsider Locke's *Essay* and its influence in the context of the emergence and development of experimental philosophy from the late seventeenth to the early eighteenth century. But I do not find this approach confirms Berkeley's long suspected heresy in the Locke-Berkeley-Hume trio. Rather, if we consider Gaukroger's conception of experimental philosophy, it is hard to deny Berkeley's standing as an experimental philosopher of the early eighteenth century. As Gaukroger explains, Locke rejected the Cartesians' ambition of the universal reduction of observable phenomena in terms of the underlying micro-corpuscles, which he calls vertical explanation as opposed to horizontal explanation. Locke was the first philosopher who had cogently argued that natural philosophical explanation need not be given by reference to a single fundamental system, like that of the Cartesian mechanistic matter theory which accommodates nothing other than extension and motion by impulse;[30] that the best method available to us is to discover connections between phenomena within local subjects of investigation,[31] without venturing to give an explanation of those natural phenomena by the all-encompassing principle. He defended, in Gaukroger's view, the autonomy of horizontal or phenomenal explanation.

It is clear from our discussion that Berkeley would have no reason to oppose the Lockean project of defending experimental philosophy thus conceived. Indeed, not only did he approve of experimental natural philosophy, but in the *New Theory* he actually engaged in the experimental philosophical practice, giving explanations of visual phenomena without transcending the phenomenal realm. For Berkeley, as we have seen in his methodological discussion in the *Theory of Vision*, successful explanation of the nature of vision does not depend on the discovery of metaphysical causes distinct from sensible ideas, 'the external, unseen Cause of our ideas'. It is within the realm of sensible ideas that we should discover the explanatory principles or causes of visual phenomena. Thus, according to Berkeley, the construction of a visual theory is possible within the phenomenal level, concentrating on sensible ideas and their connections which are the phenomenal causes of our visual space. It is a visual theory founded on phenomenal principles or causes that he pursues in the *New Theory*. It is true that the ultimate goal of Berkeley's philosophical endeavour is a theistic metaphysics, according to which only God and finite spirits can be efficient causes of phenomena. But this is irrelevant to his status as an experimental philosopher. The important point here is that he considered a science of vision, the subject of the *New Theory*, to constitute an independent field of phenomenal enquiry standing without any metaphysical support. What Berkeley aimed to do in the *New Theory* was to explain the visual perception of space by the principles or causes identifiable within the visual phenomena.[32]

Notes

1 'Reading Locke as a natural philosopher yields an image of him very much at odds with prevailing ones, but it is a reading that enables us to understand the decisive role that his thought played in the first half of the eighteenth century. Moreover, it allows a form of "empiricism" to come to light – namely empiricism as a successor to, and philosophical refinement of, seventeenth-century "experimental" natural philosophy – which is intimately tied up with natural-philosophical practice, and is quite distinct from the speculative epistemology to which it is reduced in the "rationalism/empiricism" debates'; Gaukroger (2010: 98). See also Gaukroger (2014: 15–16).
2 Discussions of Locke's scientific background up to the 1980s tended to emphasize Locke's debt to Boyle's mechanistic corpuscularianism and affirm his positive commitment to the use of hypothesis in scientific practice. A brief review of discussions of the Locke–Boyle relationship in the literature is given by Shigeyuki Aoki in Chapter 2 of this volume. There Aoki argues that Locke provides his own original arguments for the distinction of primary and secondary qualities in the *Essay* and that they are a rather *a posteriori* or 'experimental' justification of the distinction than a direct application of Boyle's corpuscular hypothesis. In recent studies of Locke on natural philosophy, Peter Anstey resurrects John Yolton's interpretation (Yolton 1970) and underlines Locke's commitment to Baconian natural histories. For the interpretation of Locke as committed to the Baconian type of experimental natural philosophy, see Anstey (2011, esp. ch. 3). While Anstey reconsiders Locke's debt to Boyle from the Baconian natural historical perspective, unlike Gaukroger he does not go so far as to deny the significant role of reductive corpuscular explanation in Locke; Anstey (2011: 155–7.).
3 Gaukroger's reaction to the standard story of empiricism seems to have been partly inspired by Luis Loeb's attack on 'the standard theory'. Loeb judged that Berkeley's metaphysics is 'a "trivial variant" of Malebranche's'. See Loeb (1981: 227). For criticisms of Loeb's view, see Ayers (1984, 2005).
4 For an excellent study of the DPS, see Hoppen (1970). For its prehistory, see Barnard (1972, 1974). The papers and minutes of the DPS are collected in Hoppen (2008). Recent studies include Breuninger (2014), Hemmens (2015) and Hunter (2015).

5   St George Ashe, Molyneux's college friend, was Donegal lecturer and professor of Mathematics at Trinity College and later became Provost. It was he who decided to introduce Locke's *Essay* into the undergraduate course of Trinity College after reading it on Molyneux's recommendation. He was the second secretary of the DPS succeeding Molyneux, but was absent from Dublin when the DPS was revived. See Hoppen (1970: 36–7, 174; 2008, 2: 797, 799, 936–7). Berkeley was ordained in February 1709 by Ashe, and later became tutor to Ashe's son George, accompanying him on a continental tour from 1716 to 1720. See Luce (1949: 43, 75–80).

6   The paper, 'Of Infinites', was read to the DPS on 19 November 1707. Interestingly, there are groups of entries in Berkeley's notebooks (351–6, 392–8) which appear to be closely related to this presentation. In 396, Berkeley mentions the approval he received from 'P' at a meeting. According to Luce, this 'P' is Lord Pembroke, who was then Lord Lieutenant of Ireland and the president of the DPS. If we remember that Pembroke was the man to whom Locke dedicated the *Essay* and that Berkeley, too, dedicated the *Principles* to him later, Berkeley's statement in the same entry, 'engagements to P. on account of the treatise that grew under his Eye', which clearly refers to Locke's words in the Epistle Dedicatory, is suggestive. See Luce's note to 396, Berkeley (1989: 226–9).

7   For a detailed discussion, see the Editor's Introduction to Berkeley (1989).

8   Berkeley's first writing was an essay on natural history, *Description of the Cave of Dunmore*, which was presumably read in January 1706 to a student philosophical society of Trinity College, in which he played a leading part with Samuel Molyneux; Luce (1949: 35). Thomas Molyneux sent this essay to the Royal Society's president Hans Sloane, recommending it for inclusion in the *Philosophical Transactions*; Hoppen (2008, 2: 721). While this first piece of natural historical practice did not appear in the *Transactions*, observations of the eruption of Mount Vesuvius, which Berkeley composed in 1717 while travelling in Italy and was communicated by John Arbuthnot to the Royal Society, appeared in the *Transactions* (vol. 30: 708–13). See Luce (1949: 60, 78), Berkeley (1948–57, 4: 247–50).

9   Molyneux's discussion of the Barrovian case and the inverted retinal image are in the *Dioptrica Nova*; see Molyneux (1692, Part 1: 105–6, 113–21 and Part 2: 211–13). Molyneux discussed the moon illusion and the difficulties of the existing explanations of this phenomenon in the inaugural meeting of the DPS on 15 October 1683, and this was subsequently published in the *Philosophical Transactions*; Molyneux (1688). See also Hoppen (2008, 1: 381–8). William King, who later criticized Berkeley's treatment of the moon illusion, responded to Molyneux's call for a satisfactory explanation with his own solution in the meeting of 31 October 1683, which, according to the minutes, was judged unsatisfactory by the members; Hoppen (2008, 1: 11).

10 For discussion of Baconianism in the DPS, see Hoppen (2008, 1: xxix–xxxv).

11 Anstey discusses the demise of Baconian natural history and the emergence of a new 'mathematical' experimental philosophy after Newton in Anstey (2014, 2015).
12 In this chapter the following abbreviations are used to refer to Berkeley's works: PC = *Philosophical Commentaries*; NTV = *An Essay Towards a New Theory of Vision*; PHK = *A Treatise Concerning the Principles of Human Knowledge*; TVV = *The Theory of Vision or Visual Language Vindicated and Explained*. All citations from the *Principles*, the *New Theory* and the *Theory of Vision* are from Berkeley (1948–57). Section numbers follow the abbreviation NTV, PHK or TVV in citations. I use Berkeley (1989) to refer to the *Philosophical Commentaries*. The entry numbers assigned by Luce follow the abbreviation 'PC' in citations.
13 For the meaning of marginal letters, see Luce's discussion in Berkeley (1989: 229–33).
14 Anstey and Vanzo (2012) discuss the historical origins of the experimental/speculative distinction. In the Irish context, this dichotomy is amplified in Molyneux's dedicatory letter to the Royal Society in the *Dioptrica Nova*. It is anticipated by Myles Symner, a correspondent of Hartlib and the first Donegal professor of Mathematics at Trinity College, who contrasts 'experimental learning' with 'idle speculations of ye schools'. See Barnard (1974: 62) and Hoppen (2008, 1: xix).
15 Anstey (2005: 216–20). As Anstey argues, some prominent experimental philosophers like Boyle and Hooke appreciated a role for hypothesis and speculation about causes in natural philosophy.
16 It may be the case that Berkeley's emphasis in this statement is on the impossibility of speculative natural 'sciences'. Berkeley refers to Newton's *Principia* as a 'grammar of Nature' in section 108 of the first edition of the *Principles*. But he is willing to call it a 'natural science' in section 110 of the second edition.
17 In definition 8, defining 'motive quantity of centripetal force', Newton claims: '[t]his concept is purely mathematical, for I am not now considering the physical causes and sites of forces', Newton (1999: 407).
18 A similar criticism of the explanation of gravity as circular appears in the *Three Dialogues Between Hylas and Philonous*; Berkeley (1948–57, 2: 241–2).
19 As Lisa Downing points out, in *De Motu* of 1721 Berkeley's notion of laws of nature undergoes significant revisions: particularly referring to Newton's fundamental laws of motion, Berkeley in *De Motu* does not see laws of nature as empirical generalizations by induction but as something *transcending* observable phenomena. See Downing (2005: 249–51). Thus, he states in section 38: 'In mechanics . . . notions are premised (praemittuntur notiones), i.e. definitions and first and general statements about motion from which afterwards by mathematical method conclusions more remote and less general are deduced.' This development in the notion of laws in mechanics led Berkeley, I think, to the clear distinction between

the 'experimental' and the 'mechanical' principles as is discussed in sections 36 and 71 of *De Motu*; Berkeley (1948–57, 4: 40, 51).

20 In the sentence immediately following this, Berkeley distinguishes 'deduce' and 'demonstrate'. The laws of nature discovered from observable phenomena are the 'principles' from which unobserved phenomena can be *deduced*, but this does not amount to *demonstration*; for, he says, demonstration rests upon 'a supposition that the Author of Nature always operates uniformly, and in a constant observance of those rules we take for principles: which we cannot evidently know' (PHK 107). Thus, while accepting the central role of the 'principles' in natural philosophy, Berkeley does not think Newton's *Principia* has provided us with a *demonstrative* science of nature.

21 A. A. Luce saw the *New Theory* as 'an *ad interim* statement of part, and part only, of Berkeley's case against matter; . . . it prepares the way for the *Principles*'; Berkeley (1948–57, 1: 148). Commentators after Luce, however, tended to point out that Berkeley's attempt to put the *New Theory* in service of immaterialism was a failure. See Armstrong (1960: 26–32) and Pitcher (1977: 25–33). For criticisms of Luce, Armstrong and Pitcher, see Atherton (1990).

22 Two recent papers, Atherton (2008) and Flage (2011), draw attention to and discuss the analytic method of the *New Theory*. Atherton interprets Berkeley's analytic procedure as consisting in the process of resolving our ordinary, three-dimensional visual field into a visual array of light and colours, taking away step-by-step such spatial meanings as distance, size and situation. I agree that Berkeley's analysis in the *New Theory* involves this kind of analytic reduction, and I consider my discussion in this chapter to be compatible with her interpretation.

23 Daniel Flage explores the possible sources of Berkeley's reference to the analysis/synthesis in Flage (2011).

24 The same passage, except the parts in angle brackets, had already appeared earlier in the Latin edition of 1706 in Query 23; Newton (1706: 347). In the draft of Query 23 of the Latin edition, Newton used 'experimental philosophy' instead of 'natural philosophy' in the first line of the quoted passage. In the second English edition, Newton uses the term 'experimental philosophy' in the sentence omitted from this quotation: 'Hypotheses are not to be regarded in experimental Philosophy.' According to Shapiro, Newton did not use 'experimental philosophy' before the draft for the Latin edition of the *Opticks*. The first *published* use of the term is in the General Scholium of the *Principia* of 1713. See Shapiro (2004: 189).

25 For discussion of Newton's application of the method of analysis/synthesis in natural philosophy, see Guicciardini (2009: 315–27).

26 Bertil Belfrage emphasizes the importance of the distinction between the 'empirical or scientific' sense of cause and the 'metaphysical' sense of cause for the interpretation of Berkeley's theory of vision; see Belfrage (2006: 205). I would say

'experimental or phenomenal' is more appropriate for what Belfrage calls 'empirical or scientific'.

27 This point is elaborately argued by Margaret Atherton; see Atherton (1990: 68–77, 144–8).
28 Although I am not prepared to discuss it here, Berkeley's treatment of the Barrovian case in sections 29–40 will be essential for understanding his experimental method. In these sections Berkeley applies his principles of the earlier sections to the solution of the singular phenomenon which Barrow considered to be 'founded in the peculiar nature of a certain odd and particular case'. By application of Berkeley's principles, the case which has been considered singular is shown to be a particular case which is to be assimilated to the regular phenomena of distance perception.
29 For a detailed discussion of Hume's experimental philosophy, see Demeter (2012, 2014).
30 In Gaukroger's account, Locke's defence of the autonomy of phenomenal explanation developed in opposition to Malebranche who expounded the Cartesian ideal of natural science by universal reduction to the underlying micro-corpuscular structure: 'One of the principal aims of the Lockean project was to come to terms with a question inherited from Boyle, namely that of how one can treat the establishment of connections, including causal connections, between the phenomena under investigation as having genuine explanatory power, in need of no supplementation, while at the same time maintaining that there is a micro-corpuscularian causal structure underlying the physical realm . . . [Malebranche's] *De la recherche de la vérité* . . . offered a detailed argument that there could be no causal relations between phenomena, and that all explanation must take the form of establishing the relations between those "primary qualities" – shape, speed, direction of motion, and bulk/volume/mass – identified by those in the tradition of Cartesian mechanism as the (quantifiable) sole qualities of micro-corpuscles from which material bodies are considered to be constituted. *De la recherche* offered a vision of a systematic ordering of knowledge on first principles, on a par with the systems of Spinoza and Leibniz . . . For Malebranche, the phenomenal level cannot be described in its own terms, but must be accounted for in terms of an underlying micro-corpuscularian structure'; Gaukroger (2014: 29). See also Gaukroger (2010: 171, 183).
31 Gaukroger (2010: 155; 2014: 28–33).
32 The original version of this chapter was presented at the John Locke Conference at Gakushuin (Tokyo, 10–11 December 2016). I am indebted to the editors of this volume, Kiyoshi Shimokawa and Peter Anstey, for their careful reading, corrections and helpful suggestions on the earlier draft of this chapter. I wish also to thank Tom Stoneham for helpful comments on the earlier draft.

References

Anstey, P. R. (2005), 'Experimental versus Speculative Natural Philosophy', in P. R. Anstey and J. A. Schuster (eds), *The Science of Nature in the Seventeenth Century: Patterns of Change in Early Modern Natural Philosophy*, 215–42, Dordrecht: Springer.

Anstey, P. R. (2011), *John Locke and Natural Philosophy*, Oxford: Oxford University Press.

Anstey, P. R. (2014), 'Philosophy of Experiment in Early Modern England: The Case of Bacon, Boyle and Hooke', *Early Science and Medicine*, 19 (1): 103–32.

Anstey, P. R. (2015), 'Experimental Pedagogy and the Eclipse of Robert Boyle in England', *Intellectual History Review*, 25 (1): 115–31.

Anstey, P. R. and A. Vanzo (2012), 'The Origins of Early Modern Experimental Philosophy', *Intellectual History Review*, 22 (4): 499–518.

Armstrong, D. M. (1960), *Berkeley's Theory of Vision: A Critical Examination of Bishop Berkeley's Essay Towards a New Theory of Vision*, Melbourne: Melbourne University Press.

Atherton, M. (1990), *Berkeley's Revolution in Vision*, Ithaca, NY: Cornell University Press.

Atherton, M. (2008), 'What Have We Learned When We Learn to See?: Lessons Learned from the Theory of Vision Vindicated', in P. Hoffman, D. Owen and G. Yaffe (eds), *Contemporary Perspectives on Early Modern Philosophy: Essays in Honor of Vere Chappell*, 273–87, Peterborough: Broadview Press.

Ayers, M. (1984), 'Berkeley and Hume: A Question of Influence', in R. Rorty et al. (eds), *Philosophy in History: Essays on the Historiography of Philosophy*, 303–27, Cambridge: Cambridge University Press.

Ayers, M. (2005), 'Was Berkeley an Empiricist or a Rationalist?' in K. P. Winkler (ed.), *The Cambridge Companion to Berkeley*, 34–62, Cambridge: Cambridge University Press.

Belfrage, B. (2006), 'The Scientific Background of George Berkeley's Idealism', in S. Gersh and D. Moran (eds), *Eriugena, Berkeley, and the Idealist Tradition*, 202–23, Indiana: The University of Notre Dame Press.

Barnard, T. C. (1972), 'Miles Symner and the New Learning in Seventeenth-Century Ireland', *The Journal of the Royal Society of Antiquaries of Ireland*, 102 (2): 129–42.

Barnard, T. C. (1974), 'The Hartlib Circle and the Origins of the Dublin Philosophical Society', *Irish Historical Studies*, 19 (73): 56–71.

Berkeley, G. (1948–57), *The Works of George Berkeley, Bishop of Cloyne*, 9 vols, eds A. A. Luce and T. E. Jessop, London: Thomas Nelson and Sons.

Berkeley, G. (1989), *Philosophical Commentaries: Transcribed from the Manuscript and Edited with an Introduction and Index by George H. Thomas; Explanatory Notes by A. A. Luce*, New York: Garland Publishing, 1st edn, 1976.

Breuninger, S. (2014), 'The Social Networks of the Irish Enlightenment: The Dublin Philosophical Society and the Royal Dublin Society', in I. Baird (ed.), *Social Networks in the Long Eighteenth Century: Clubs, Literary Salons, Textual Coteries*, 55–75, Newcastle upon Tyne: Cambridge Scholars Publishing.

Demeter, T. (2012), 'Hume's Experimental Method', *British Journal for the History of Philosophy*, 20 (3): 577–99.

Demeter, T. (2014), 'Enlarging the Bounds of Moral Philosophy: Newton's Method and Hume's Science of Man', in Z. Biener and E. Schliesser (eds), *Newton and Empiricism*, 171–204, Oxford: Oxford University Press.

Downing, L. (2005), 'Berkeley's Natural Philosophy and Philosophy of Science', in K. P. Winkler (ed.), *The Cambridge Companion to Berkeley*, 230–65, Cambridge: Cambridge University Press.

Flage, D. E. (2011), 'Analysis in Berkeley's Theory of Vision', in T. Airaksinen and B. Belfrage (eds), *Berkeley's Lasting Legacy: 300 Hundred Years Later*, 35–53, Newcastle: Cambridge Scholars Publishing.

Gaukroger, S. (2010), *The Collapse of Mechanism and the Rise of Sensibility: Science and the Shaping of Modernity 1680–1760*, Oxford: Clarendon Press.

Gaukroger, S. (2014), 'Empiricism as a Development of Experimental Natural Philosophy', in Z. Biener and E. Schliesser (eds), *Newton and Empiricism*, 15–38, Oxford: Oxford University Press.

Guicciardini, N. (2009), *Isaac Newton on Mathematical Certainty and Method*, Cambridge, MA: The MIT Press.

Hoppen, K. T. (1970), *The Common Scientist in the Seventeenth Century: A Study of the Dublin Philosophical Society 1683–1708*, London: Routledge and Kegan Paul.

Hoppen, K. T. (2008), *Papers of the Dublin Philosophical Society 1683–1709*, 2 vols, Dublin: Irish Manuscripts Commission.

Hume, D. (2007), *A Treatise of Human Nature*, vol. 1, eds D. F. Norton and M. J. Norton, Oxford: Clarendon Press; its Abstract is cited by paragraph number.

Hunter, M. (2015), 'Boyle, Narcissus Marsh and the Anglo-Irish Scene in the Late Seventeenth Century', in *Boyle Studies: Aspects of the Life and Thought of Robert Boyle (1627–91)*, 81–106, Aldershot: Ashgate.

Locke, J. (1975), *An Essay concerning Human Understanding*, ed. P. H. Nidditch, Oxford: Clarendon Press, 1st edn, 1690; abbreviated as *Essay*.

Loeb, L. (1981), *From Descartes to Hume*, Ithaca, NY: Cornell University Press.

Luce, A. A. (1949), *The Life of George Berkeley Bishop of Cloyne*, London: Thomas Nelson and Sons.

Memmens, S. (2015), 'Crow's Nest and Beyond: Chymistry in the Dublin Philosophical Society, 1683–1709', *Intellectual History Review*, 25 (1): 59–80.

Molyneux, W. (1688), 'Concerning the Apparent Magnitude of the Sun and Moon, or the Apparent Distance of Two Stars, When Nigh the Horizon and When Higher Elevated', *Philosophical Transactions of the Royal Society of London*, 16: 314–23.

Molyneux, W. (1692), *Dioptrica Nova (2 parts)*, London: Printed for Benjamin Tooke.

Newton, I. (1706), *Optice: sive de Reflexionibus, Refractionibus, Inflexionibus & Coloribus Lucis Libri Tres, Authore Isaaco Newton, Latine Reddidit Samuel Clarke*,

Accedunt Tractatus duo ejusdem Authoris de Speciebus & Magnitudine Figurarum Curvilinearum, Latine Scripti, London: Samuel Smith & Benjamin Walford.

Newton, I. (1952), *Opticks; or, A Treatise of the Reflections, Refractions, Inflections and Colours of Light, Based on the Fourth Edition London, 1730, with a Preface by I. Bernard Cohen, a Forward by Albert Einstein, an Introduction by E. T. Whittaker, and an Analytical Table of Contents by Duane H. D. Roller*, New York: Dover Publications.

Newton, I. (1999), *The Principia: Mathematical Principles of Natural Philosophy*, trans. I. B. Cohen and A. Whitman, Berkeley: University of California Press, 3rd edn, 1726.

Pitcher, G. (1977), *Berkeley*, London: Routledge and Kegan Paul.

Shapiro, A. E. (2004), 'Newton's "Experimental Philosophy"', *Early Science and Medicine*, 9 (3): 185–217.

Yolton, J. W. (1970), *Locke and the Compass of Human Understanding: A Selective Commentary on the 'Essay'*, Cambridge: Cambridge University Press.

Part II

Law and politics

4

A defence of Locke's consent theory against Hume's critique[1]

Takumichi Kojo

The question of why we ought to obey the government is known as the problem of political obligation.[2] This problem has a long history in ethics and political philosophy. As is well known, it is discussed in Plato's *Crito* and constitutes an important theme in Sophocles's tragedy *Antigone*. From ancient Greek times until now, scholars have suggested many different answers to this problem. Some of the simplest answers that have been offered make use of one version or another of contract theory. John Locke famously argues in his *Two Treatises of Government* (1690), for instance, that political obligation rests on the consent of individuals.

Although Locke's consent theory has had a significant influence on politics in Western societies, it seems to have lost its influence in the fields of ethics and political philosophy due to the many criticisms that have been raised against it.[3] Especially significant among them is David Hume's critique in his essay 'Of the Original Contract', which may be regarded as the most important of all existing critiques of social contract theory. Many philosophers seem to agree on this. John Rawls, who developed a new contract theory after the Second World War, states in his *Lectures on the History of Political Philosophy*:

> I think it may be said that Hume's essay ['Of the original contract'] (and Bentham's later essay, although Bentham says essentially the same thing that Hume does) was historically very influential in weakening the social contract view. There tend to be, at least in England, no successors to a doctrine like Locke's. On that evidence, Hume's essay was historically very effective. (Rawls 2007: 170)

According to Rawls, Hume's critique is not only effective but also pioneering.[4] Many may believe that Hume's critique successfully demolished Locke's consent theory.

That said, we may still ask whether Hume's critique is really valid. Even if it is valid, how appropriate is it as a critique of Locke's consent theory? In this chapter, I re-examine the plausibility of Locke's consent theory through consideration of Hume's critique, and try to offer a counter-argument to Hume from Locke's point of view. Since Locke himself cannot object to Hume's critique, I try to offer a Lockean response to it on his behalf, presenting the kind of argument which I believe can be reconstructed from Locke's own text and can counter Hume's critique. For this purpose, I divide the chapter into three sections. In the first section, I briefly explain Locke's consent theory. In the second, I summarize the main points of Hume's critique as we find them in his essay 'Of the Original Contract' and his book *A Treatise of Human Nature*. In the third and final section, I examine Hume's critique and provide a Lockean response to rebut some of his arguments.

1 Locke's consent theory

In the beginning of the 'Second Treatise', Locke defines political power in the following manner:

> *Political Power* then I take to be *a Right* of making Laws with Penalties of Death, and consequently all less Penalties, for the Regulating and Preserving of Property, and of employing the force of the Community, in the Execution of such Laws, and in the defence of the Common-wealth from Foreign Injury, and all this only for the Publick Good. (TT II. 3)

Locke begins his explanation of consent theory with a description of the state of nature, which is a state without any government. In the state of nature, there is the law of nature, according to which all individuals are naturally free, equal and have natural rights to their own lives, liberties and possessions (II. 4, 6). Additionally, the law of nature states that all individuals in the state of nature ought to refrain from harming others, or violating the natural rights of others. Locke says:

> The *State of Nature* has a Law of Nature to govern it, which obliges every one: And Reason, which is that Law, teaches all Mankind, who will but consult it, that being all equal and independent, no one ought to harm another in his Life, Health, Liberty, or Possessions. (TT II. 6)

If everyone observes the law of nature, the state of nature is perfectly peaceful. If, however, there is a conflict that causes violations of the rights of one or more individuals, each can exercise the natural right to judge the violations. Furthermore, each is given a natural right of punishment for the purpose of restraining those violations. Of the right of punishment, Locke states:

> And that all Men may be restrained from invading others Rights, and from doing hurt to one another, and the Law of Nature be observed, which willeth the Peace and *Preservation of all Mankind*, the *Execution* of the Law of Nature is in that State, put into every Mans hands, whereby every one has a right to punish the transgressors of that Law to such a Degree, as may hinder its Violation. (TT II. 7)

Thus everyone can legitimately punish criminals, and he or she can require them to compensate their victims for their loss in line with the law of nature (II. 10).

However, the state of nature tends to be unstable and inconvenient because there is no government, that is, there is neither a known positive law nor an impartial judge that serves to protect the natural rights of individuals (TT II. 123–5). Therefore, in the state of nature they make a 'compact' or 'agreement' with each other to establish a government in order to provide an effective protection of their natural rights (II. 97, 243). We should pause for a moment, and ask why an individual's consent is needed here. Locke claims:

> Men being, as has been said, by Nature, all free, equal and independent, no one can be put out of this Estate, and subjected to the Political Power of another, without his own *Consent*. (TT II. 95)

According to Locke, since all individuals are naturally free and equal, no one can be *forced* to leave the state of nature. This implies that nobody can be made to submit to the government, without his or her own consent. This is the consent which each individual gives when he or she leaves the state of nature and enters into the conditional circumstance of being a subject of a government. The government makes laws to protect them. But to justify each individual's obligation to obey the laws, each individual must agree, feely and voluntarily, to assume their obligations. This is how Locke justifies political obligation through the idea of a consent.

Strictly speaking, however, it is important that individuals come to have obligations to the government only indirectly, for there are two stages in Locke's consent theory. In the first stage, individuals make a society (or a community) by consent prior to the formation of a government. Individuals in the state of nature consent to two things. First, they consent to renounce some part of their rights to liberty. Second, they consent to renounce totally their power (i.e. right) of punishment. Now they give up the latter power wholly to the majority of the society, while they give up a part of the former only to the extent that 'the good, prosperity, and safety of the Society shall require' (TT II. 130, see also 128–9). We should note that they do not lose their rights, but they only transfer them to the majority of the society (II. 99). Once they have transferred them, they put themselves under the obligation of obedience to the majority of the society, that is, the collective entity which has one will and acts as one body (II. 95–9). Speaking of the community which is an equivalent of the society, Locke states:

> For when any number of Men have, by the consent of every individual, made a *Community*, they have thereby made that *Community* one Body, with a Power to Act as one Body, which is only by the will and determination of the *majority*. (TT II. 96)

Thus, all members of the society ought to obey the will of the majority, which passes for the will of the entire society.

In the second stage, the majority of the society forms a government which is composed of the legislative and executive powers.[5] The majority establishes the legislative power by placing it in the hands of a particular section of the society as it thinks fit. The transfer of the power from the society to the legislative agent involves what Locke calls trust (TT II. 136). The task of the legislative is to make laws in order to protect the lives, liberties and estates of the people (II. 134–5). It is the executive that rules the people by executing laws (II. 144, 147, 153). Although both the legislative and the executive govern by laws, the executive remains subordinate to the legislative (II. 153).

Locke considers the two different manners in which a consent may be given, and distinguishes between express consent and tacit consent (TT II. 119). Although Locke does not clearly explain express consent in detail, this type of consent must be given through a verbal declaration or statement.[6] In fact, Locke uses the expression '*Oaths of Allegiance* and Fealty' (II. 151). On the other hand, according to Locke, tacit consent is more difficult to explain than express consent (II. 119). However, since express consent is given verbally, tacit consent is presumably given in silence.[7] Actually, Locke uses the term 'acquiesce' (II. 164–5, 176, 227). Furthermore, he insists:

> And to this [i.e. tacit consent] I say, that every Man, that hath any Possession, or Enjoyment, of any part of the Dominions of any Government, doth thereby give his *tacit Consent*, and is as far forth obliged to Obedience to the Laws of that Government, during such Enjoyment, as any one under it; whether this his Possession be of Land, to him and his Heirs for ever, or a Lodging only for a Week; or whether it be barely travelling freely on the Highway; and in

Effect, it reaches as far as the very being of any one within the Territories of that Government. (TT II. 119)

Here Locke infers tacit consent from the fact that one lives under the government. Thus he seems to think that all individuals under the government assume political obligation through their own tacit consent.

2 Hume's critique

In this section, I summarize Hume's critique of Locke's consent theory. In my opinion, there are two kinds of critique found in Hume. The first is descriptive, and the second is normative.

Within the descriptive critique, Hume provides two specific criticisms. The first relates to Locke's idea of the state of nature. The existence of the state of nature forms an important premise for Locke's consent theory. However, Hume denies its historical existence. In his *A Treatise of Human Nature* Hume says:

> we may conclude, that 'tis utterly impossible for men to remain any considerable time in that savage condition, which precedes society; but that his very first state and situation may justly be esteem'd social. This, however, hinders not, but that philosophers may, if they please, extend their reasoning to the suppos'd *state of nature*; provided they allow it to be a mere philosophical fiction, which never had, and never cou'd have any reality. (*Treatise* 3.2.2.14)

For Hume, the idea of the state of nature is just a fiction. Although Locke, like many other contractarians, presupposes the existence of the state of nature, Hume points out that there was, in actuality, no such state that existed prior to the establishment of a government. Many of our contemporary scholars share the same view. For instance, Will Kymlicka explains the weakness of social contract arguments as follows:

> Why are social contract arguments thought to be weak? Because they seem to rely on very implausible assumptions. They ask us to imagine a state of nature before there is any political authority. (Kymlicka 2002: 60)

Thus, the first point Hume makes is that the theory based on the state of nature is historically false.[8]

The second descriptive criticism relates to the idea of an original contract. Hume argues:

> Almost all the governments, which exist at present, or of which there remains any record in story, have been founded originally, either on usurpation or conquest, or both, without any pretence of a fair consent, or voluntary subjection of the people. (Hume 1987: 471)

Like the idea of the state of nature, the idea of the original contract is just fiction. According to Hume, Locke's consent theory rests on an historically, unverifiable premise. Hume's descriptive critique has been so influential that even scholars of Locke's philosophy tend to agree with Hume. Aaron, for instance, claims that Locke's consent theory is actually based on 'bad history' (Aaron 1971: 273).

Now Hume presents three specific, normative criticisms. The first one relates to the necessity of a consent to justify the political obligation. In developing a new argument for the duty of allegiance, Hume claims:

> What necessity, therefore, is there to found the duty of *allegiance* or obedience to magistrates on that of *fidelity* or a regard to promises, and to suppose, that it is the consent of each individual, which subjects him to government; when it appears, that both allegiance and fidelity stand precisely on the same foundation, and are both submitted to by mankind, on account of the apparent interests and necessities of human society? . . . The general interests or necessities of society are sufficient to establish both. (Hume 1987: 480–1)

Since we can sufficiently justify our political obligation and fidelity by reference to 'general interests or necessities of human society', we no longer need a consent. Consent is irrelevant. In this way, Hume denies the necessity of consent as a device to justify political obligation.

The second and third criticisms relate to the idea of tacit consent. The second one is that tacit consent is not really free consent. In general, consent must be freely given if it is to justify any promissory obligation at all. However, tacit consent cannot be classified as a freely given consent. In a famous paragraph Hume argues:

> Can we seriously say, that a poor peasant or artizan has a free choice to leave his country, when he knows no foreign language or manners, and lives from day to day, by the small wages which he acquires? We may as well assert, that a man, by remaining in a vessel, freely consents to the dominion of the master; though he was carried on board while asleep, and must leap into the ocean, and perish, the moment he leaves her. (Hume 1987: 475)

According to Hume, living under a government, for many people, is not a result of their own choice. Tacit consent, or a consent that is inferred from the fact of living under a government, is not really a free consent.

The third criticism relates to the consequence of tacit consent. In providing the example of a usurper, Hume says:

> Can it be asserted, that the people, who in their hearts abhor his treason, have tacitly consented to his authority, and promised him allegiance, merely because, from necessity, they live under his dominion? (Hume 1987: 477)

Hume argues that if we assume that there was a tacit consent given in the situation in which one lives, from necessity, under the dominion of a usurper, we can justify any sort of government. However unlawful it may be, people who live under any government will be seen as having an obligation to obey it because they have tacitly consented. Thus, tacit consent justifies all governments, including unlawful ones, which Locke clearly cannot accept. Therefore, according to Hume, Locke's consent theory must be rejected.

3 A Lockean response

3.1 A counter-argument against Hume's descriptive critique

In this section, I examine Hume's critique, and try to rebut it from the perspective of Locke's consent theory. As I pointed out, in his descriptive and historical critique, Hume argues that Locke's consent theory is based on a false history. He holds that it rests on the idea of the state of nature and that of the original contract. In my opinion, however, this critique is based on a misunderstanding of Locke's theory, because neither of the ideas which he used in his consent theory should be treated as an historical description.

First, Locke does not claim that the state of nature is intended to be a device for an historical account. Locke himself emphasizes this many times. He defines the state of nature as one in which specific normative relationships hold among those human beings who share no common government:

> *Want of a common Judge with Authority, puts all Men in a State of Nature.* (TT II. 19)

Moreover, Locke says:

> those who have no such common Appeal, I mean on Earth, are still in the state of Nature, each being, where there is no other, Judge for himself, and Executioner; which is, as I have before shew'd it, the perfect *state of Nature*. (TT II. 87)

In short, the want of a common government places all individuals in the state of nature. It is not surprising that Locke points out that all rulers of independent governments all over the world are in the state of nature:

> 'Tis often asked as a mighty Objection, *Where are*, or ever were, there any *Men in such a State of Nature*? To which it may suffice as an answer at present; That since all *Princes* and Rulers of *Independent* Governments all through the World, are in a State of Nature, 'tis plain the World never was, nor ever will be, without Numbers of Men in that State. (TT II. 14)

So the idea of the state of nature is not an historical description. It is not the state that existed before the establishment of a government. It is a state which embodies normative relationships.[9]

If we understand the state of nature in terms of the definition provided above, it becomes clear that there is a state of nature even when one lives under a government. In fact, all individuals are born and brought up in the state of nature until they reach adulthood, and for this reason, all children can be said to be in the state of nature insofar as they have not given their consent and remain under their parental care. In order to demonstrate this, we must understand that individuals in the state of nature are not only free but also equal.

> A *State* also *of Equality*, wherein all the Power and Jurisdiction is reciprocal, no one having more than another: there being nothing more evident, than that Creatures of the same species and rank promiscuously born to all the same advantages of Nature, and the use of the same faculties, should also be equal one amongst another without Subordination or Subjection, unless the Lord and Master of them all, should by any manifest Declaration of his Will set one above another, and confer on him by an evident and clear appointment an undoubted Right to Dominion and Sovereignty. (TT II. 4)

Therefore, there obtains no subjection among individuals in the state of nature (II. 6). To be a subject of any government, a free and equal individual needs to give his or her own consent. Locke says:

> *Every Man* being, as has been shewed, *naturally free*, and nothing being able to put him into subjection to any Earthly Power, but only his own Consent. (TT II. 119)

And it is important that not only in establishing a new government but also in becoming a subject of the existing government, all individuals, especially all children who grow up under the government, need to give their own consent when they come of age. Locke writes:

> 'Tis plain then, by the Practice of Governments themselves, as well as by the Law of right Reason, that *a Child is born a Subject of no Country or Government*. He is under his Fathers Tuition and Authority, till he come to Age of Discretion; and then he is a Free-man, at liberty what Government he will put himself under; what Body Politick he will unite himself to. (TT II. 118)

Since all children are free and equal in the state of nature, they are not subjects of any government before becoming adults. In other words, the actual existence of a government has nothing to do with children's freedom or equality in the state of nature. Even if their fathers have consented to be subjects of their government, their consent cannot bind their children (II. 116). For a father and his child are independent human beings, and the child is free from the contract which the father has made. Locke continues to claim:

> Common-wealths themselves take notice of, and allow that there is *a time when Men* are to *begin to act like Free Men*, and therefore till that time require not Oaths of Fealty, or Allegiance, or other publick owning of, or Submission to the Government of their Countreys. (TT II. 62)

When all children reach adulthood, all governments must give them an opportunity to make a contract. At that time, children must decide whether they will become subjects of any particular government or not. Until that time, children enjoy their own natural liberty. Locke says:

> Nor is it now any more hindrance to the freedom of Mankind, that they are *born under constituted and ancient Polities*, that have established Laws and set Forms of Government, than if they were born in the Woods, amongst the unconfined Inhabitants that ran loose in them. (TT II. 116)

Therefore, the state of nature can exist not only in the past, but also in the present and future.[10] So Hume's claim about the false historicity of the state of nature is not a valid one.

How should we view the concept of the original contract? From Locke's point of view, we must not interpret the original contract as an historical device. Rather, the original contract is what justifies the transition from the state of nature to the civil or political state in which one remains a subject of a government. In fact, Locke declares:

> But I moreover affirm, That all Men are naturally in that State [of Nature], and remain so, till by their own Consents they make themselves Members of some Politick Society. (TT II. 15)

In order to become a subject of any government, any individual must consent. Without a consent, individuals are bound to continue in the state of nature.

Thus, the concept of the original contract is not an historical one; it is rather a normative one which serves to justify the transition to a political society.

Finally, Hume's criticism of consent theory from an historical point of view is irrelevant or unpersuasive. Locke says:

> an Argument from what has been, to what should of right be, has no great force. (TT II. 103)

Locke repeats the claim that what happened in the past should not be our norm (II. 57–9). We can also understand Locke's view if we look at his essay known as 'Some Thoughts Concerning Reading and Study for a Gentleman' (1703).[11] In this essay, Locke talks about politics, and states that there are two areas or branches of politics. The first one concerns 'the original of societies, and the rise and extent of political power', while the second relates to 'the art of governing men in society' (Locke 1997: 351). Locke then recommends his own *Two Treatises of Government* for study of the first branch. Conversely, he recommends history books to support an examination of the second branch. It is significant that Locke himself regards *Two Treatises of Government* not as a history book but as a normative one. In other words, Locke makes a distinction between a normative inquiry and an historical or descriptive one. Given Locke's classification, we may affirm that Hume's historical critique is irrelevant.

3.2 A counter-argument against Hume's normative critique

How should we view Hume's normative critique? As I pointed out, Hume provides three normative criticisms. The first one involves the claim that in order to justify a political obligation, we do not need a contract, but only need to appeal to the general interests or necessities of human society. As Hume insists, governments exist for the general interests or necessities of human society. Locke might agree to this, given his definition of political power. Yet he might also argue that the mere general interests or necessities of human society cannot justify one's political obligation to a *particular* government. In other words, Locke might claim that the general interests or necessities of human society are not sufficient to justify the political obligation to obey any one particular government. For Locke says:

> 'Tis in vain then to talk of Subjection and Obedience, without telling us whom we are to obey. For were I never so fully perswaded, that there ought to be Magistracy and Rule in the World, yet I am nevertheless at Liberty still, till it appears who is the Person that hath Right to my Obedience: since if there be

no Marks to know him by, and distinguish him, that hath Right to Rule from other Men, it may be my self, as well as any other. . . . To settle therefore Mens Consciences under an Obligation to Obedience, 'tis necessary that they know not only that there is a Power somewhere in the World, but the Person who by Right is vested with this Power over them. (TT I. 81)

However, one might wonder why such a theory is not enough. Locke continues to say:

> The great Question which in all Ages has disturbed Mankind, and brought on them the greatest part of those Mischiefs which have ruin'd Cities, depopulated Countries, and disordered the Peace of the World, has been, Not whether there be Power in the World, nor whence it came, but who should have it. (TT I. 106)

Therefore, it is fairly clear that Locke thinks it is not sufficient for political theory to make an appeal to the necessity of government alone. It must also explain which particular government ought to be obeyed. Without this explanation, we cannot judge which government we ought to obey. Beran criticizes Hume on a contractarian basis, and claims the following:

> [I]t may well be the case that we have the institution of the state because of its utility – because the state is necessary for civilized life. But, on the face of it, the utility of the state cannot in itself explain why a particular state stands in an authority relation to some particular individuals. Hence, both the question of utility (Is the state worth having?) and the question of fidelity (Do the members of a particular state owe it obedience?) have to be asked and answered. (Beran 1977: 265)[12]

From Locke's point of view, political theory must explain not only why we ought to obey the government of one kind or another, but also which particular government we ought to obey. But it is precisely this that Hume's political theory fails to explain.

Here one might object that Hume does acknowledge the problem of determining the political obligation to a particular government. It is true that he explicitly states the following:

> The general obligation, which binds us to government, is the interest and necessities of society; and this obligation is very strong. The determination of it to this or that particular prince or form of government is frequently more uncertain and dubious. Present possession has considerable authority in these cases, and greater than in private property; because of the disorders which attend all revolutions and changes of government. (Hume 1987: 486)

As shown in this quotation, Hume holds that in order to decide which government we must obey, we adopt the criterion of 'present possession', or the standard of who possesses political power at present. Hume does not inquire how the government begins. Instead, he introduces five standards or rules by which we can determine the political obligation to a particular government, that is, 'long possession', 'present possession', 'conquest', 'succession' and 'positive laws' (*Treatise* 3.2.10.4–14). However, if these rules conflict with each other, how can we decide? Hume's answer is by 'swords of the soldiery' (*Treatise* 3.2.10.15). In this way, Hume's political theory can justify all de facto governments. Locke criticized Filmer for justifying all de facto governments, and the same criticism applies to Hume as well.

Since Hume's second and third criticisms focus on tacit consent, I consider them together. To put them together, we can treat Hume as claiming that tacit consent is not a freely given consent, and that it could even be used to justify an unlawful government. In my opinion, there is an invalid or misleading argument which is implicit in or associated with Hume's critique. Hume's critique is too strong to be warranted in every respect. To be sure, Locke infers consent from the situation in which one is living under a government, but he does not infer it solely from that fact. To begin with, we should note that for Locke, two conditions must be met in order for consent to be valid. The first is that consent must conform to the law of nature. Locke argues:

> It remains only to be considered, whether *Promises, extorted by Force*, without Right, can be thought Consent, and *how far they bind*. To which I shall say, they *bind not at all*; because whatsoever another gets from me by force, I still retain the Right of, and he is obliged presently to restore. He that forces my Horse from me, ought presently to restore him, and I have still a right to retake him. . . . For the Law of Nature laying an Obligation on me, only by the Rules she prescribes, cannot oblige me by the violation of her Rules. (TT II. 186)

According to Locke, the only promises that are binding are those which conform to the law of nature. In other words, the law of nature requires that promises ought not to be extracted by force. In addition, Locke says:

> a Man can no more justly make use of another's necessity, to force him to become his Vassal, by with-holding that Relief, God requires him to afford to the wants of his Brother, than he that has more strength can seize upon a weaker, master him to his Obedience, and with a Dagger at his Throat offer him Death or Slavery. (TT I. 42)

This passage clearly shows that God prohibits anyone from taking advantage of another's weakness. So it follows that nobody should be justly compelled by another to make a contract to form a political society. Contracts extracted by force are not valid, for they are not free contracts in accordance with the law of nature.

Now, let us examine Hume's criticisms in more detail. Here we use the example of a man on a vessel, and that of a usurper, which I cited in the second section of this chapter. In the first example, Hume compares those who give tacit consent under a government with the man who is carried on board while asleep. As Steinberger argues, this identification is misleading because the man is kidnapped while asleep.[13] It goes without saying that the man has no intention to ride on the vessel. So in this case, the master of the vessel forces that man to be subject to his dominion, and since the master breaks the law of nature, the man has no obligation to obey him. From Locke's viewpoint, then, no political obligation arises from the vessel example.

The same holds true of the second example, that is, the case of a usurper. From the start, the act of usurping itself does not count as legitimate, for it is not a way of obtaining political power in accordance with the law of nature. Moreover, one who is in the position of a ruler is not allowed to make use of a subject's necessity. Subjects who live under the rule of a usurper, therefore, have no political obligation. Although Hume insists that Locke's account even justifies the obligation to obey a usurper, we can reject Hume's charge and affirm that Locke denies obedience to a usurper.

The second condition of a valid consent is an institutional one. Here we need to focus on the role of a consent of the people, rather than a consent of each individual. Locke points out that Greeks have a right of resistance against the unlawful Turkish government, and puts forward the following argument:

> For no Government can have a right to obedience from a people who have not freely consented to it: which they can never be supposed to do, till either they are put in a full state of Liberty to chuse their Government and Governors, or at least till they have such standing Laws, to which they have by themselves or their Representatives, given their free consent. (TT II. 192)

This statement suggests that in order to infer consent from the fact of living under a government, we should be able to assume in the first instance that the people freely choose their government, or freely consent to install their legislative power. But one might wonder why Locke takes such a view.

At this point, we should recall that members of a society have the duty to obey the will of its majority. Then, what is it like to consent to obey the will of the majority? Probably this sentence might drop a hint:

> [T]he Members ow[e] no *Obedience* but to the publick Will of the Society. (TT II. 151)

Then what is the public will of the society? To answer this question, we must consider Locke's account of the legislative power. Locke says:

> The great end of Mens entring into Society, being the enjoyment of their Properties in Peace and Safety, and the great instrument and means of that being the Laws establish'd in that Society; the *first and fundamental positive Law* of all Common-wealths, *is the establishing of the Legislative* Power. (TT II. 134)

This shows how important the legislative power is for Locke. Moreover, it is the people who decide the locus of the legislative power, or whose hands it should be placed in (II. 141). According to Josephson, Locke himself recommends members of the legislative to be elected by the people.[14] In short, Locke supports and encourages democracy (II. 132). He actually emphasizes that the legislative members are to be elected by the people (II. 141–2, 154, 212, 220, 222, 243). Locke further claims:

> For without this [sanction from legislative] the Law could not have that, which is absolutely necessary to its being a *Law, the consent of the Society*, over whom no Body can have a power to make Laws, but by their own consent, and by Authority received from them. (TT II. 134)

All the laws made in the society need its consent, and since members of the legislature are elected by the people, the consent of the people is the basis of the legislative power. Thus, the laws made by the legislature represent the will of the people or the society (II. 151). Now we come to understand what it means to consent to obey the will of the majority of the society. This is equivalent to the consent to observe the laws. As I said earlier, there are two conditions for a valid consent. Since the laws rest on the consent of the people, they must also be based on the law of nature and need to be made by a democratically elected legislature.[15]

It is now clear that Hume's normative criticisms contain some misunderstandings of Locke's consent theory. Locke's consent theory is not completely defeated by Hume's critique.

4 Conclusion

I now summarize the argument of this chapter. Although Locke's consent theory has had a significant influence on political thought in the Western world, it has lost much of its influence due to many subsequent criticisms. The most important critique is Hume's. It contains two kinds of critique. The first is descriptive or historical, while the second is normative.

Hume provides two specific, descriptive criticisms, and both of them deny the existence of the state of nature and that of the original contract. In discussing those criticisms, I have first pointed out that the state of nature, for Locke, is not an historical state in the sense that it is not the state which existed before the establishment of a government. The state of nature is, or rather embodies, a set of those human relations which lack a common authority or a common judge. So the state of nature can even exist under a government. In fact, all children are considered to be born and grow up in the state of nature because they are not subject to any common governmental authority. Secondly, I have argued that the original contract is not historical, either. In order to be a subject, every individual must make a contract because of his or her natural freedom and equality. Locke's consent is not historical but normative. Furthermore, the kind of historical criticism which Hume launches is irrelevant to Locke's consent theory because it seeks to explain how a government ought to be created, rather than how it has actually been created.

Hume also provides three normative criticisms. The first one is that it is not necessary for us to use the device of a contract to justify any political obligation, for the general interests or necessities of human society serve that purpose. The idea of consent, being closely linked to any contract, is thus rendered redundant. With respect to this criticism, I claim that on Hume's theory, it is difficult to determine which particular government we ought to obey, when there are several governments around us. Hume also admits that the 'swords of the soldiery' solve this problem, which leads to the suspicion that he might justify all de facto governments. Therefore, we need the idea of consent as a better alternative. Hume's theory turns out to be not a satisfactory normative theory, if we see it from Locke's point of view.

Hume's second and third, normative criticisms focus on Locke's tacit consent. The second criticism says that tacit consent is not free consent because living under a government is not a result of one's choice. The third says that tacit consent serves to justify even an unlawful government, which Locke himself cannot possibly accept. In my opinion, those criticisms are too strong to be accepted, and they involve some misunderstandings. For there are two conditions for any valid tacit consent. The first condition is that tacit consent should conform to the law of nature. For any individual, tacit consent is an inferred consent such that it conforms to the law of nature. Given the law of nature, nobody ought to compel other individuals to make a contract. And no government ought to injure the rights of the people. If a government injures those rights, it violates the law of nature. From Locke's point of view, it is impossible to justify any such government. The second condition of a valid tacit consent is that a democratically elected legislature needs to be established. By this kind of legislature we can protect our rights from arbitrary power. Once we have seen that the two conditions need to be met if tacit consent is to count as valid, Hume's third normative criticism need not worry us. Locke's tacit consent cannot be said to justify an unlawful government.

Thus in the end, we can adopt Locke's point of view and reject Hume's critique. Even now, Locke's consent theory still offers an attractive perspective on the problem of political obligation.

Notes

1 The argument of this chapter is based on chapters 2 and 7 of my book, Kojo 2017. This work was supported by JSPS KAKENHI Grant Number JP19K12941 and JP19H01203.
2 For an overview of this problem, see Klosko (2012), Dagger and Lefkowitz (2014).
3 As Simmons points out (Simmons 1993: 69), Locke does not make a clear distinction among the terms 'consent', 'contract' and 'promise'. So, in this chapter I use these terms interchangeably.
4 Rawls himself generally acknowledges the validity of Hume's critique; Rawls (1999: 296 n. 2).
5 Strictly speaking, there is a federative power in executive power (TT II. 145–8).
6 See Waldman (1957: 45–6), Russell (1986: 292–6), Simmons (1993: 84) and Josephson (2002: 149).
7 See Bennett (1979: 227) and Simmons (1979: 79–80).
8 This interpretation is commonly shared with Japanese Hume scholars, for example, Izumiya (1996: 159).
9 Simmons (1993: 15–16).
10 Simmons (1993: 21–2).
11 Locke (1997: 348–55).
12 Kiyoshi Shimokawa has the same view. See Shimokawa (2000: 223).
13 Steinberger (2002: 460 n. 10).
14 Josephson (2002: 205–25).
15 Locke points out that in the first ages of the world, the father of a family became a political ruler by the express or tacit consent of his children, without having

a legislative (TT II. 74 and 75). This might be taken to imply the denial of my interpretation. But this is primarily an historical description of the government. Thus, we can still maintain that as far as normative theory is concerned, Locke holds that civil society must have a legislative.

References

Aaron, R. (1971), *John Locke*, 3rd edn, Oxford: Oxford University Press.
Beran, H. (1977), 'In Defense of the Consent Theory of Political Obligation and Authority', *Ethics*, 87 (3): 260–71.
Bennett, J. G. (1979), 'A Note on Locke's Theory of Tacit Consent', *Philosophical Review*, 88 (2): 224–34.
Dagger, R. and D. Lefkowitz (2014), 'Political Obligation', *The Stanford Encyclopedia of Philosophy* (Fall 2014 Edition), Edward N. Zalta (ed.). https://plato.stanford.edu/archives/fall2014/entries/political-obligation/ (accessed 28 September 20).
Hume, D. (1987), 'Of the Original Contract', in *Essays Moral, Political, and Literary*, revised edn, ed. F. M. Eugene, Indianapolis: Liberty Fund.
Hume, D. (2007), *A Treatise of Human Nature*, vol. 1, eds D. F. Norton and M. J. Norton, Oxford: Clarendon Press; abbreviated as *Treatise*, and cited by book, part, section and paragraph number.
Izumiya, S. (1996), *Hyūmu* (Hume), Tokyo: Kenkyusha.
Josephson, P. (2002), *The Great Art of Government*, Lawrence: University Press of Kansas.
Klosko, G. (2012), 'The Moral Obligation to Obey the Law', in A. Marmor (ed.), *The Routledge Companion to Philosophy of Law*, 511–26, New York: Routledge.
Kojo, T. (2017), *Rokku Rinrigaku no Saisei* (Resurrecting Locke's Ethics), Kyoto: Koyo Shobo.
Kymlicka, W. (2002), *Contemporary Political Philosophy*, 2nd edn, Oxford: Oxford University Press.
Locke, J. (1988), *Two Treatises of Government*, ed. P. Laslett, Cambridge: Cambridge University Press; abbreviated as TT, and cited by treatise and section number.
Locke, J. (1997), *Political Essays*, ed. M. Goldie, Cambridge: Cambridge University Press.
Rawls, J. (1999), *A Theory of Justice*, revised edn, Cambridge, MA: Harvard University Press.
Rawls, J. (2007), *Lectures on the History of Political Philosophy*, ed. S. Freeman, Cambridge, MA: Belknap Press.
Russell, P. (1986), 'Locke on Express and Tacit Consent', *Political Theory*, 14 (2): 291–306.
Shimokawa, K. (2000), *Jon Rokku no Jiyūshugi Seijitetsugaku* (The Liberal Political Philosophy of John Locke), Nagoya: The University of Nagoya Press.

Simmons, A. J. (1979), *Moral Principles and Political Obligations*, Princeton: Princeton University Press.
Simmons, A. J. (1993), *On the Edge of Anarchy*, Princeton: Princeton University Press.
Steinberger, P. J. (2002), 'Political Obligation and Derivative Duties', *The Journal of Politics*, 64 (2): 449–65.
Waldman, T. (1957), 'A Note on John Locke's Concept of Consent', *Ethics*, 68 (1): 45–50.

5

Locke's political constitutionalism
A re-examination of his idea of the prerogative

Ryuichi Yamaoka

1 Locke's constitutionalism and his theory of the prerogative

It is quite dangerous to use the political language of today for describing the thought of a past thinker; many words of political ideology were invented after the nineteenth century, so that there is always a risk of anachronistic misrepresentation in calling a certain seventeenth-century thinker a 'liberal' or 'socialist'. Therefore, we must be careful when we embark on a study of Locke's constitutionalism. Although both the idea of constitutionalism and the thought of Locke are slippery, it seems an established opinion that Locke contributed in some way or other to the formation of the tradition of constitutionalism. For instance, one scholar writes: 'Everyone agrees, I think, that the American constitution – not just the document which is often given that name but the whole body of what might be called American constitutional practice – is pervaded by a Lockean spirit' (Armour 1988: 9). Likewise, Gordon Schochet, a respected scholar in the history of political thought, locates Locke without difficulty in the tradition of constitutionalism. Schochet justifies his interpretation by a quotation from Locke's text:[1]

> It is easie to conceive, that in the Infancy of Governments, when Commonwealths differed little from Families in number of People, they differ'd from them too but little in number of Laws: And the Governours, being as the Fathers of them, watching over them for their good, the Government was almost all *Prerogative*. A few establish'd Laws served the turn, and the discretion and care of the Ruler supply'd the rest. But when mistake, or flattery prevailed with weak Princes to make use of this Power, for private ends of their own, and not for the publick good, the People were fain by express Laws to get Prerogative determin'd, in those

points, wherein they found disadvantage from it: And thus declared *limitations of Prerogative* were by the People found necessary in Cases, which they and their Ancestors had left, in the utmost latitude, to the Wisdom of those Princes, who made no other but a right use of it, that is, for the good of their People. (TT II. 162)

Indeed, this quotation looks like a description that supports Schochet's understanding. This, however, is a passage from chapter 14 of Locke's 'Second Treatise' which deals with the prerogative, and if we examine Locke's definition of it, the interpretation of Locke as a liberal constitutionalist will prove to be seriously contestable. For Locke defines the prerogative as follows:

This Power to act according to discretion, for the publick good, without the prescription of the Law, and sometimes even against it, *is* that which is called *Prerogative*. (TT II. 160, underlining added)

The prerogative is here considered to belong to the executive power; it is nothing but the royal right. Locke approved of the royal prerogative, and admitted that it could be a power that goes against the law, as well as a power independent of the provisions of the law. If the ordinary doctrine of constitutionalism requires the legislative power to control or restrain the administrative power as found in kingship, Locke's theory of the royal prerogative is contradictory to the vindication of constitutionalism.

Why did Locke make an assertion which could yield such a contradiction? The four chapters that precede chapter 14 of the 'Second Treatise' deal with the typological theory of polities. Locke there actually says very little about the traditional Aristotelian consideration on the typology of government, only briefly dealing with monarchy, oligarchy, democracy and mixed forms of government. The main point in Locke's theory of government is to divide the power of the government into legislative, executive and federative powers, according to its functions, and to discuss their mutual relations. What is important from the viewpoint of constitutionalism is that Locke insists on the strict separation of legislative and executive powers (TT II. 143, 144), and claims that the legislative power is the supreme of the three (II. 149, 150), and this supreme authority is the fiduciary power exercised for a specific purpose, so that the community, which is the subject or author of the trust, always remains the real supreme authority (II. 149). Having presented this sort of constitutionalist argument, Locke goes on to begin his discussion of the status of the prerogative in chapter 14 by making the following statements:

Where the Legislative and Executive Power are in distinct hands, (as they are in all moderated Monarchies, and well-framed Governments) there the good of the Society requires, that several things should be left to the discretion of him, that has the Executive Power. For the Legislators not being able to foresee, and provide, by Laws, for all, that may be useful to the Community, the Executor of the Laws, having the power in his hands, has by the common Law of Nature, a right to make use of it, for the good of the Society, in many Cases, where the municipal Law has given no direction, till the Legislative can conveniently be Assembled to provide for it. Many things there are, which the Law can by no means provide for, and those must necessarily be left to the discretion of him, that has the Executive Power in his hands, to be ordered by him, as the publick good and advantage shall require: nay, 'tis fit that the Laws themselves should in some Cases give way to the Executive Power, or rather to this Fundamental Law of Nature and Government, *viz*. That as much as may be, *all* the Members of the Society are to be *preserved*. For since many accidents may happen, wherein a strict and rigid observation of the Laws may do harm; (as not to pull down an innocent Man's House to stop the Fire, when the next to it is burning) and a Man may come sometimes within the reach of the Law, which makes no distinction of Persons, by an action, that may deserve reward and pardon; 'tis fit, the Ruler should have a Power, in many Cases, to mitigate the severity of the Law, and pardon some Offenders: For *the end of Government* being the *preservation of all*, as much as may be, even the guilty are to be spared, where it can prove no prejudice to the innocent. (TT II. 159)

We may identify what is at issue here as a criticism of legalism as an ideology.[2] Locke is acutely conscious of the limit of the rule of law in real governance, and he exposes the imprudence of applying laws to governance in a strict or literal way. Locke as a natural law theorist holds that we have to make an appeal to natural law as the higher rule when civil laws appear to be seriously defective in dealing with some real political problems and thus override the positive provisions of established civil laws. This seemingly commonsensical (i.e. not so awkward) view poses two problems, however. First, there can be a discrepancy between the ideology supporting royal prerogative in the political context of seventeenth-century England, on the one hand, and, on the other, the political position to which Locke was actually committed. Second, theoretically, such a practice of discretionary power could neutralize the politics of constitutionalism, which gives rise to the question whether the royal prerogative is really compatible with constitutionalism. These are two serious problems for us, and I would like to analyse Locke's theory of the royal prerogative to clarify where he really stands.

Before proceeding to an analysis, I would like to state what I take to be the essence of Locke's political theory. This is a prerequisite for the argument of this chapter, and I would like to clarify Locke's constitutionalist standpoint in particular. It is widely believed that a large portion of the *Two Treatises of Government* was composed in the period of Exclusion Crisis (1679–81) in order to support the cause of the Whigs' leader and Locke's patron, the First Earl of Shaftesbury. Though the precise dating of the composition of the work has been debated, this might be regarded as an established point in modern Locke scholarship. And it is also commonly acknowledged that the publication of Robert Filmer's *Patriarcha* in 1680 provided an important occasion for Locke to formulate his theory. The theoretical task of the *Two Treatises*, which was written primarily as a criticism of Filmer, was to reaffirm what Filmer, the Tory's (rather extreme) ideologue, had denied. Filmer had rejected, first of all, the idea of natural freedom which stresses humankind's inborn equal freedom; second, the idea of a social contract which affirms that political authority is based on the people's consent; and third, the theory of tyrannicide which is concluded from the first and second ideas.[3] Instead, Filmer had contended that all human beings are naturally subordinate to their superiors; the royal power being a natural authority based on the creation of God, all monarchies are naturally absolute; and there is no such ruler as a tyrant.[4] It follows from this claim of the king's absolute authority that the private properties of the subjects are nothing but the king's grant, so that none can deny the king's arbitrary power of taxation. Locke deliberately and tactically reversed this line of Filmer's arguments.

Locke, therefore, argued that the idea of political society, based on the principle of natural freedom and conceived by social contract theory, could be justified from the viewpoint of Christian premises and rationality, that is, the authorities on which Filmer had also relied. In addition, Locke showed that the people's right of resistance, directed against a corrupt government, does not necessarily result in anarchy as Filmer had feared. And Locke concluded that a legitimate government is required to perform its function of preserving the properties (i.e. lives, liberties and possessions) of the people, and that absolute monarchy, being naturally contrary to this function, cannot be recognized as a form of political society because by its own nature it must lack political legitimacy.

Central to Locke's political theory thus summarized is, of course, the principle of natural freedom. Locke stipulates freedom negatively as 'Freedom from Absolute, Arbitrary Power' (II. 23), and positively as living only under the legitimate rules, i.e. the natural law which is God's rational will, and the laws of political society based on the consent of the people (II. 22). Given this understanding of freedom, alleged Lockean constitutionalism would appear most clearly as a government of the legitimate rules. And Locke actually expresses the idea of constitutionalism as follows:

> *Freedom of Men under Government*, is, to have a standing Rule to live by, common to every one of that Society, and made by the Legislative Power erected in it; A Liberty to follow my own Will in all things, where the Rule prescribes not; and not to be subject to the inconstant, uncertain, unknown, Arbitrary Will of another Man. As *Freedom of Nature* is to be under no other restraint but the Law of Nature. (TT II. 22)

This interpretation of Locke's constitutionalism, while being based on his conception of freedom, also reveals the problematic nature of his argument for the royal prerogative. Locke's idea of freedom, as it is shown in the remark that 'The Natural Liberty of Man is to be free from any Superior Power on Earth, and not to be under the Will or Legislative Authority of Man, but to have only the Law of Nature for his Rule' (II. 22), appears to be very close to what Quentin Skinner calls the republican or 'neo-Roman' conception of liberty in his study of the ideas of seventeenth-century English republican thinkers. According to Skinner, republican thinkers opposed freedom to servitude, and contended that those put under the arbitrary will of others lose their freedom, regardless of whether they are actually restrained or not. Republican freedom therefore means the freedom to live under the law that they themselves have set up.[5] Skinner emphasized that what republicans denounced as the source for the loss of freedom was 'the exercise of any discretionary or prerogative powers' which the government constitutionally allowed for the king.[6] Republicans insisted that tyrannical rule deprives the people of their civil liberties, and upheld the thesis that 'if you live under any form of government that allows for the exercise of prerogative or discretionary powers outside the law, you will already be living as a slave' (Skinner 1998: 69–70).

Locke appears to be free from the intense hatred that such republicans shared against the royal power. This point becomes clearer when we compare Locke with Algernon Sidney, who shared the same fate with Locke in many respects, but was, unlike Locke, executed in 1683 in connection with the Rye House Plot. As criticisms of Filmer, Locke's *Two Treatises* and Sidney's *Discourses Concerning Government* do share a great many arguments. Nevertheless, there is little overlap between the two regarding the theory of a king's prerogative power. For Sidney, the royal power of England is always under the laws of the country. '(O)ur kings are subject to law', Sidney says, 'because they can make no law, and have no power but what is given by the laws' (Sidney 1990: 364). When he discusses the issue of pardons which was usually a matter of the royal prerogative, he reemphasized that royal power should be under the limits of laws, and insisted that 'the power of altering, mitigating, explaining or correcting the laws of England, is only in the Parliament, because none but the Parliament can make them' (Sidney 1990: 451). Given the fact that the dissolution of the Parliament by the exercise of Charles II's prerogative power prevented the campaign for the Exclusion Bill, it is very unlikely that Locke justified the royal prerogative. So we begin to wonder what kind of logic there is that would make Locke's theory of royal prerogative compatible with his conception of liberty, or his constitutionalism?

2 The necessity of prerogative power

For many years Locke's theory of royal prerogative was not recognized as having any theoretical significance; at least, it did not become a full-scale subject of research. I should add, however, that there were some notable exceptions, such as the historical works by Dunn and Pasquino, and theoretical studies of Mansfield and Pangle.[7] One major turning point was the September 11 terrorist attacks in 2001. Since this unprecedented (at least for Americans) event, the nature of administrative authority in a liberal and constitutional regime has become a substantial subject for many political theorists, and a considerable number of researchers have turned to Locke's theory of prerogative power.[8]

Here we take up Fatovic's paper 'Constitutionalism and Contingency', which can be regarded as particularly important from the perspective of both historical and theoretical studies, and I would like to use its arguments in order to examine Locke's theory of prerogative power from the viewpoint of its necessity. It is the concept of contingency that Fatovic pays close attention to as the title indicates. Fatovic points out that the political theory of Locke does not easily fit into the idea of *liberal* constitutionalism, that is, what John Gray calls 'a legalistic or jurisprudential paradigm of political philosophy' (Gray 1995: 6). In other words, we can find in Locke's political theory a sort of sceptical epistemology which has a keen sense of the essential unpredictability of events or contingencies in this world. And this kind of sense, Fatovic insists, is absent from Kantian or legalistic liberalism.[9] This sense of unpredictability is already apparent in the quotation above from the *Two Treatises* II. 159, but Fatovic focuses on Locke's scepticism in his argument for the separation of the legislative and executive powers.

Things of this World are in so constant a Flux, that nothing remains long in the same State. Thus People, Riches, Trade, Power, change their Stations; flourishing mighty Cities come to ruine, and prove in time neglected desolate Corners, whilst other unfrequented places grow into populous Countries, fill'd with Wealth and Inhabitants. (TT II. 157)

This is the place where Locke explains the reason why representatives of the legislative assembly can become inequitably distributed, and he argues that it is the executive power, rather than the legislative, that should respond to such changes in the world. For Locke, the legislative was not suitable for responding to changes in the world: 'Constant *frequent meetings of the Legislative*, and long Continuations of their Assemblies' will be a heavy burden for the people and create more inconveniences. As a result, he comes to hold that in 'the Exigencies Of the Commonwealth', the role of watching the public good should be in the hand of the executive power, and the right to convene the assemblies should depend on the prudence of the man who holds the prerogative authority (II. 156).

It may be affirmed that the sense of human society's fluidity as expressed earlier is quite modern. From this Fatovic goes on to offer a rather controversial interpretation that '[Locke's] theory of prerogative is predicated on the assumption that the extraordinary is an ordinary part of politics' (Fatovic 2004: 282). And to buttress this interpretation, he emphasizes the influence of Machiavelli on Locke. Despite the absence of any explicit reference by Locke himself, this question of influence is a theme that has often attracted attention of Locke scholars.[10] A type of political theory which makes an appeal to political prudence (*virtù*) in the context of an unstable historical world (*fortuna*) might not appear to be a proper description for the political theory of Locke. Pocock, for one, regards Locke as an unhistorical thinker because of his indifference to the immediate and urgent historical and political issues in his time.[11] However, Fatovic reads the Pocockean theme of 'politics of time' (found in his *Machiavellian Moment*) into Locke's thought.[12] By using the texts of Machiavelli's *The Prince* and *The Discourses* and by critically examining Mansfield's account of Locke, Fatovic seeks to clarify, with a comparison with Aristotle's idea of equity,[13] Locke's theory of prerogative from a Pocockean perspective. According to Fatovic, 'Lockean constitutionalism is an attempt to respond to the necessities and exigencies of political life that the strictest legal formalism cannot accommodate.' Thus Locke emerges as a theorist who discloses 'an awareness of a political truth' by giving great latitude to the prerogative power (Fatovic

2004: 295). Fatovic presents an interpretation that 'Locke's innovation was to reconcile the seemingly antithetical doctrines of necessity and constitutionalism by showing that they both serve the same master: *salus populi*, as defined by the laws of nature' (Fatovic 2004: 284). On the strength of it, he claims that Locke's acute sense of politics accords with, and even makes a great contribution to, liberalism.

The validity of this interpretation will be discussed later. Here, I would rather like to relativize Fatovic's image of Locke as a thinker who developed himself to be a political theorist with a keen political sense by learning from Aristotle and Machiavelli – an image which is not so wrong in itself – and then try to put forward a certain hypothesis about the historical meaning of the Lockean theory of royal prerogative. The idea of responding to the fluidity of the historical situation and pointing out the limits of the legalistic approach in politics was, at least for Locke, a natural theme to uphold, without having to study Machiavelli or Aristotle. As already confirmed, one of the direct reasons why Locke began to write the *Two Treatises* was the publication of Filmer's *Patriarcha*. And Filmer was, contrary to his public image, a very learned and reasonable theorist.[14] The third chapter of *Patriarcha* discusses the relationship between regal authority and natural law, where Filmer says that natural law obliges a king to protect 'the safety of the kingdom'. In order to fulfil the duty, the king needs to exercise his prudence 'according to the infinite variety of times, places, persons'. And this vocation gives the king unlimited freedom and makes him accountable to God alone, because 'there were kings long before there any laws' (*Patriarcha* 35) – this was a typical historical view held by royalists, for they had the ideas of the superiority of the king's authority over the laws.

Filmer admits that there is a (republican) opinion that obedience to those who are not bound by law is slavish and dangerous. But he presents two objections against it. The first is taken from Bodin's theory of sovereignty, and it is the objection that living under a person with the absolute legislative power is inevitable no matter what regime one happens to live in. True, a straightforward Bodinian doctrine that the sovereign majesty with legislative power is not under any human law was a radical minority opinion among England's royalists, but it was a rational discourse for Filmer who was familiar with Roman law and other recourses that supported Bodin's argument.[15] The second is the argument that the ultimate purpose of the king's prerogative is the good of the subjects under the law, and that to protect their liberty might sometimes necessitate a discharge from the rigidity of the law. Filmer here emphasizes the need for policies like amnesty, advocating that *summum jus* is *summa injuria*.[16]

This proposition, '*summum jus* is *summa injuria*', was one which James I made frequent use of.[17] James insisted on the necessity of the flexible exercise of justice based on political prudence, and said that the application of rigid justice would create tyranny. He also insisted that such prudence should abide by the criterion that 'the health of the common-wealth is the highest law'. The proposition that '*summum jus* is *summa injuria*' was originally from Cicero's *De Officiis*, although there he criticized, rather than justified, the right of discretion as going beyond legal restraints.[18]

An appeal to the principle, 'public safety is the highest law' (*Salus populi suprema lex*), for the vindication of the necessity of political prudence was a staple justification of the reason of state by the royalists. For example, Francis Bacon used the principle in his essay 'Of Judicature' in the following way:

> Judges ought above all to remember the conclusion of the Roman Twelve Tables, *Salus populi suprema lex*; and to know that laws, except they be in order to that end, are but things captious, and oracles not well inspired. Therefore it is an happy thing in a state when kings and states do often consult with judges; and again, when judges do often consult with the king and state.... For many times the things deduced to judgement may be *meum* and *tuum*, when the reason and consequence thereof may trench to point of estate: I call matter of estate, not only the parts of sovereignty, but whatsoever introduceth any great alteration or dangerous precedent, or concerneth manifestly any great portion of people. And let no man weakly conceive that just laws and true policy have any antipathy: for they are like the spirits and sinews, that one moves with the other. (Bacon 1972: 165)

Speaking of the royal prerogative, Bacon stated that if it concerns the matter of state, the Parliament (the place to discuss *meum* and *tuum*, according to Bacon) must never challenge its authority.[19]

Let us return to Filmer. He points out the instability of customs on which Common Law relies, and stresses the importance of the judgement based on the authority of the king, asserting that '(d)iversity of the cases are infinite, and impossible to be regulated by any law' (*Patriarcha* 45-6). What Filmer is discussing here is the significance of equity, according to which the Lord Chancellor justified his judgement. Filmer reinforces this argument with quotations from Aristotle's works:

> Every law (saith he) is in the general, but of some things there can be no general law.... When therefore the law speaks in general, and something falls out after beside the general rule, then it is fit that what the lawmaker hath omitted, or

> where he hath erred by speaking generally, it should be corrected or supplied, as if the lawmaker himself were present to ordain it. (*Patriarcha* 46)[20]
>
> The governor, whether it be one man or more, ought to be lord over all those things whereof it was impossible the law should exactly speak, because it is not easy to comprehend all things under general rules. . . . Whatsoever the law cannot determine, it leaves to the governors to give judgement therein, and permits them to rectify whatsoever upon trial they find to be better than the written laws. (*Patriarcha* 46–7)[21]

This is Aristotle's idea of equity (*epikeia*), or the principle for the application of laws which was handed down to Thomas Aquinas and others in the Middle Ages.[22] The thought it expresses on the relationship between law and politics is closely related to Aristotle's idea of practical judgement (*phronesis*), and it can be regarded as quite rational.

It is clear from all this that Locke must have learned a great deal from the discussions on the prerogative by the royalists including Filmer. Since the theory of royal prerogative concerns justification for the power of the king, it was very natural for Locke to absorb royalists' arguments in this respect. This is a fact whose importance we may not find it necessary to stress now. Locke, however, needed to learn above all from Filmer in order to refute him. When developing the theory of resistance in the *Two Treatises*, Locke carefully tried to demonstrate that it would not evoke anarchy. This was because he seriously responded to Filmer's political argument that the claim of resistance based on natural freedom must inevitably fall into anarchy. Locke had an assured idea that the political theory which guarantees stability is a realistic one. Likewise, in the theory of prerogative, Locke was able to make a realistic response to Filmer, the critic of legalistic theory, by first absorbing into his own position Filmer's contentions for royal prerogative.

And learning is, of course, an act of selective acceptance rather than total acceptance. In this selection, the uniqueness of the philosopher Locke appears. While learning from Filmer's theory of royal prerogative, Locke seems to have utterly rejected the logic of justification which relies on the concept of sovereignty. Like Filmer, Locke certainly does not adopt the feudalist theory of kingship, which greatly restricts the king's powers. However, Locke does not explicitly use Bodin's theory of sovereignty. The royal prerogative, Locke insists, belongs to the executive power, not the legislative power. In other words, because its authority ultimately emanates from the legislative authority, the executive power cannot assert its intrinsic superiority over the legislative power. We can reconstruct the discussion of Locke so far as follows. In constitutional government, the legislative power is the supreme power while the executive power is subordinate to it. However, the executive power can execute policies that are against the rules established by legislative authority for justifiable reasons. Then, how should we understand the relationship between the king's prerogative and the constitutional government?

3 The nature of the prerogative: Natural or legal?

In order to consider this question, I would like to examine Locke's understanding of the nature of the royal prerogative power. If we briefly examine the controversies between royalists and parliamentarians (and their ideologues, i.e. theologians and common lawyers) in seventeenth-century England over this subject, it will become clear that the most fundamental issue was the question, whether the royal powers be natural or legal. As a royalist argument, divine rights theory is certainly well known, but this was not actually the mainstream doctrine. Rather, the arguments based on Aristotelian cosmology which justified the naturalness of the king's rulership were typical. Those arguments – Filmer's theory was also among them – insisted on the naturalness of the hierarchical relationship such as God and creatures, fathers and children, masters and slaves, and they justified the power of the kings by using the analogy of father's absolute right at household. Such Aristotelianism was decisively non-Aristotelian in denying the distinction between *oikos* and *polis* which Aristotle himself seriously relied on, but it was an influential royalist outlook shared by thinkers such as James I, Filmer and Roger Manwaring.[23] All laws were thought to originate from the king's right whose authority is natural, and therefore original. On the other hand, those thinkers who took the ancient constitution seriously, including common lawyers, among others, tried to situate the royal powers thoroughly within the framework of the laws. The scope of the royal power was claimed to be limited to that of the law. There were constitutionally accepted rights that approved the discretion of the king, but they were limited to those that would not infringe the freedom of the people. Regarding war, which is a typically extra-legal act, common lawyers insisted that it was not the king, but the law, that would define a war. According to common lawyers, the king may exceed statutory laws, but he cannot exceed the common law. The royal prerogative was therefore regarded as legal power.[24]

However, if the issue is simplified and understood as described above, the very meaning of the royal prerogative will become obscure. Indeed, if the king is not bound by any law, in the sense that the kingship is the source of all laws, the idea of royal prerogative is not necessary in the first place. On the other hand, if the kingship is completely under the restraint of the law, there cannot be a prerogative power in the sense of outright power. The fact that the two sides actually used the same term 'prerogative' means that both sides accepted its ambiguity, and held that kingship is legal *and* extra-legal at the same time. And in English constitutional history, controversy and struggle indeed had arisen over the matter of concrete rights of a king authorized as a prerogative, not over that of an abstract authority. In other words, in each particular case, the ambiguity of the meaning of the prerogative was appropriately interpreted in its discrete, historical contexts.[25] However, in the case of Locke, since his arguments are derived from the nature of government rather than historical examples, this ambiguity requires further theoretical consideration.

The same kind of ambiguity can be found in our contemporary studies of Locke's political theory. In a paper entitled 'The Extraconstitutionality of Lockean Prerogative', Corbett sorted recent researches on Locke's concept of prerogative into two types: one takes it as a legal (constitutional) concept, and the other a natural (extraconstitutional) concept. Corbett himself takes the second position.[26] Corbett's problem is as follows. Locke's executive power is a part of the government based on the people's consent, and of a constitutional scheme in which the legislative power holds the supreme authority. Is it, then, contradictory for the prerogative, which is a power of the executive, to be able to go against statutes as an extraconstitutional power? Corbett's answer is that executive power and prerogative power are completely two distinct powers, the former being legal while the latter being natural. Locke understood, Corbett's interpretation goes, that legal (constitutional) power had a decisive limit in dealing with the events of this world for the purpose of people's security; and therefore, Locke attributed the original, natural and extraconstitutional power (which is the very power men had in the state of nature) to the executive power in order to preserve the public good. From this reading Corbett derives an interesting conclusion: 'being extraconstitutional, prerogative can be authoritatively controlled only by another extraconstitutional power' (Corbett 2006: 447). Thus, it becomes clear that there is a close relationship between Locke's theory of the prerogative and his theory of resistance, and that Locke conceives the right of revolution as a guard against the misuse of the governmental powers, and the prerogative in particular.

Corbett's interpretation of sharply dividing the executive and prerogative powers is analytically clear, but it does not capture the ambiguity of the theory of prerogative, especially its political ambiguity. Here we should note that Locke shows his acute sense for ambiguity elsewhere, by recognizing that the same subject can be both legal and natural at the same time. We can find it in Locke's argument for the state of war. When Locke says, '*Want of a common Judge with Authority, puts all Men in a State of Nature: Force without Right, upon a Man's Person, makes a State of War*, both where there is, and is not, a common Judge' (TT II. 19), he understands that the state of war is something like a sudden assault by a robber, which can happen even when we live in civil society (political society). A state of war is a lawless state which ultimately could come into being by chance. When in such a state, citizens can exercise the right of executing natural law, especially of punishing others for their own self-preservation, which is supposed to have been given up when participating in political society. In other words, by accident, citizens suddenly become members of the state of war while they are still in a civil society.

This logic of the state of war is also important for Locke's theory of the right of resistance. When Locke says, '[f]or Rebellion being an Opposition, not to Persons, but Authority, which is founded only in Constitutions and Laws of the Government; those, whoever they be, who by force break through, and by force justifie their violation of them, are truly and properly *Rebels*' (TT II. 226), he indeed maintains that when the king abuses his power and thus creates a state of war, it is legitimate to exercise the natural right of the people against this tyrant and to restore the right authority. In other words, Locke holds that if an extraconstitutional evil was brought in in a way that threatens civil peace and order, that is, the constitutional good, extraconstitutional resistant power should be invoked, and the public good should be restored in an extraconstitutional way.

It follows that on this account, the prerogative power and tyranny are the two faces of the extraconstitutional exercise of power. Constitutional power (executive authority), which has the role of conserving the public good, in order to deal with the world of fluidity, sometimes has to exercise extraconstitutional power. It is impossible to know in advance whether this invocation of extraordinary power is good or bad. Even the intention of the actor is not a complete guarantee. The result will inevitably be judged afterwards. This uncertainty might be part of the inherent nature of political judgement because of the predicament of any political actor. And who is responsible for such a political judgement? This was a decisively important question for Locke, and his famous answer was that the people should judge.

4 Politics of trust

One of the characteristics of Locke's theory of royal prerogative was the positive absorption of royalists' arguments. There was a precedent in the way that an anti-monarchical theorist plundered the arguments of his enemy. A case in point is the political thought of Henry Parker, who is called the first advocate of parliamentary sovereignty in England.[27] Parker's thought was developed while the contentions of the parliamentarians fighting against the expansion of the royal powers became fierce. England's constitutional history from the beginning of the seventeenth century to the civil wars saw the tension and conflict between two main camps: the royalists who supported the successive expansion of royal power as a solution for the financial crisis, and the parliamentarians opposing it by making an appeal to the ancient constitution. There were constitutionally important disputes in which the anti-constitutional exercise of the royal powers was contested, including Bates's Case in 1606, the Five Knights Case in 1627 and the Ship money Case in 1637. Through these cases, parliamentarians made fierce contentions against a series of attempts by the king to exercise a high degree of governance, that is, financial power based on the reason of state, which was judged necessary by the king to deal with the national crisis, such as tariffs, mandatory public bonds and ship taxes. Parliamentarians asserted that there was no taxation without consent, and no arrest without legitimate procedures. Therefore, the king's attempts were judged to be rebellious as an infringement of the promises embodied in the ancient constitution. In these controversies, men on the royalist side used certain categories to justify their own causes. They used them in the following way:

> The King's power is double, ordinary and absolute, and they have several laws and ends. That of the ordinary is for the profit of particular subjects, for the execution of civil justice, the determining of *meum*; and this is exercised by equity and justice in ordinary Courts, and by the Civilians is nominated *jus privatum* and with us Common Law: and these laws cannot be changed without Parliament, and although that [sic] their form and course may be changed and interrupted, yet they can never be changed in substance. The absolute power of the King is not that which is converted or executed to private use, to the benefit of any particular person, but is only that which is applied to the general benefit of the people and is *salus populi*; as the people is the body and the King the head; and this power is [not] guided by the rules which direct only at the Common Law, and is most properly named policy and government; and as the constitution of this body varieth with the time, so varieth this absolute law according to the wisdom of the King for the common good. (Tanner 1930: 340–1)

These are the words of Chief Baron Fleming in the Bates Case, and the category of 'ordinary/absolute' used here, together with the category of 'ordinary/extraordinary', was one that was frequently used in the constitutional controversies of those days. The former category itself can be traced back to no less than theological controversies in the Middle Ages; the controversies about the character of God's authority were carried on between the voluntarists who emphasized God's omnipotence, and the intellectualists who emphasized the rationality of God. The voluntarists like Ockham and d'Ailly used the category of 'God's absolute power' (*potentia Dei absoluta*) and 'God's ordinary power' (*potentia Dei ordinata*) in order to defend their view against the criticism that if God's will (i.e. power) is absolutely unconstrained, God then must be regarded as a tyrant.[28] According to their apologies, God does obey his own volitions which are ordinarily revealed to us (which must be rational laws for us); but God can always actualize his potential powers which are absolutely unconstrained and can go beyond rationality, by way, for instance, of bringing a miracle in this world. What is important here is that the absolute power is considered a potential power that will be exercised in an abnormal way, whereas the ordinary power is an actual power corresponding to the historical world. The absolute nature of God exists as a possibility and will not be invoked arbitrarily. This category of ordinary/absolute was also adopted in the controversies over the authority of the pope and the king.

The reason why royalists used this category was to justify extraconstitutional powers without accusing kingship of being arbitrary.[29] While confronting this kind of royalist rhetoric, Henry Parker, unlike other parliamentary thinkers, approved the reason of state arguments which involved the concept of the public good or *salus populi*. And he developed the criticism that the actual king's power was utilized not for its real ends, that is, the necessities of the state, but abused privately by the king's flatterers: papists, prelates and court parasites (projectors).[30] In other words, he abstracted the theory of the reason of state from the argument of the royalists, and used it to defend the ideological cause of the parliamentarians. This was a politically effective method in that it could criticize the actual uses of royal prerogative, without denying the sacred nature of the kingdom itself. In the controversy over the militia ordinance in 1642, Parker, taking into consideration the historical situation of the time, totally usurped the royalist argument, and led himself to the assertion of the sovereignty of Parliament. The militia ordinance, he insisted, consequently should be supposed to correspond to the emergency situation of the state, and therefore legality in the normal sense was out of question in this context. In 'an extraordinary necessity of State', Parker argued, the Parliament can act as council and can exercise a power not bound by any law. And when king and Parliament confronted each other and came into conflict over which side should exercise such sovereign power, Parker said that the Parliament should, and his reason was that 'the sence of the whole Parliament, is the judgement of the whole Kingdom; and ... the judgement of the whole Kingdom, is more vigorous, and sacred, and unquestionable, and further beyond all appeal, then that which is the judgement of the King alone' (Parker 1642a: 9). Thus Parker stated the following:

> both Houses have an arbitrary power to abridge the freedom of the Subject, and to inlarge the Kings prerogative, beyond a measure.... To have then an arbitrary power placed in the Peers and Comm. is naturall and expedient at all times, but the very use of this arbitrary power, according to reason of State, and warlick policy in times of generall dangers and distresse is absolutely necessary and inevitable. (Parker 1643: 30)

Although this idea can be treated as an epoch-making declaration of parliamentary sovereignty from the viewpoint of constitutionalism, it is also true that it ends up being a mere replacement or transfer of the old theoretical problem. The real problem concerning the proper relationship between the prerogative and constitution still remains, even if the site of sovereignty released from the constitutional constraints is transferred from the king to the Parliament.[31] And as the civil wars in England show, the claim of sovereignty in Parliament was forced into a theoretical impasse when it directly confronted the sovereignty of the king. After all, the Parliament was forced to appeal to the violence of war.[32]

As for the question of the supremacy between the legislative and executive powers when they violently confront each other, Locke, unlike Parker, does not support any side. He plainly asserts 'there can be no Judge on Earth' in such case. No one but the people, the extraconstitutional agent, can make a judgement upon the question of earthly peace in this situation.

> And therefore, tho' the *People* cannot be *Judge*, so as to have by the Constitution of that Society any Superiour power, to determine and give effective Sentence in the case; yet they have, by a Law antecedent and paramount to all positive Laws of men, reserv'd that ultimate Determination to themselves, which belongs to all Mankind, where there lies no Appeal on Earth, *viz.* to judge whether they have just Cause to make their Appeal to Heaven. (TT II. 168)

The people in this way will be entitled to exercise their original and natural right of judgement over the peace or safety of their society. And Locke further insists that it is not only the natural right, but the natural duty, for the people to make an appeal of this.

> And this Judgment they cannot part with, it being out of a Man's power so to submit himself to another, as to give him a liberty to destroy him; God and Nature never allowing a Man so to abandon himself, as to neglect his own preservation: And since he cannot take away his own Life, neither can he give another power to take it. (TT II. 168)

Thus we have reached again Corbett's conclusion: 'being extraconstitutional, prerogative can be authoritatively controlled only by another extraconstitutional power'. However, is this not another way to cause instability of the constitutional regime? What guarantees political stability if the natural power of the people can be invoked?

In Locke's political theory, it is his conception of political trust that is considered to be the stabilizer of the political. Locke regards trust as the principle which can give the crucial reason for restricting (as well as warranting) the royal prerogative.

> The Power of *calling Parliaments* in *England*, as to precise time, place, and duration, is certainly a *Prerogative* of the King, but still with this trust, that it shall be made use of for the good of the Nation, as the Exigencies of the Times, and variety of Occasions shall require. For it being impossible to foresee, which should always be the fittest place for them to assemble in, and what the best Season; the choice of these was left with the Executive Power, as might be most subservient to the publick good, and best suit the ends of Parliaments. (TT II. 167)

Let me here return to Fatovic's interpretation that 'Locke's innovation was to reconcile the seemingly antithetical doctrines of necessity and constitutionalism by showing that they both serve the same master: *salus populi*, as defined by the laws of nature'. It can be said that this is an attempt to reconcile the reason of state argument and constitutionalism by not considering either one as another's means, but by considering both as the means to a higher end. In other words, Locke's theory of the royal prerogative is considered to have a teleological structure. The raison d'être of royal prerogative consists in its instrumental value for the purpose of the public good (*salus populi*). Certainly, Locke understands the prerogative as a purposive power. The people's attempts to restrain or transform the prince's prerogative power, he holds, does not constitute any infringement of the government, if it is apparent that his power will be misused.

> For the end of government being the good of the Community, whatsoever alterations are made in it, tending to that end, cannot be an *incroachment* upon any body: since no body in Government can have a right tending to any other

end. And those only are *incroachments* which prejudice or hinder the publick good. Those who say otherwise, speak as if the Prince had a distinct and separate Interest from the good of the Community, and was not made for it, the Root and Source, from which spring almost all those Evils, and Disorders, which happen in Kingly Governments. (TT II. 163)

Thus if the prerogative is misused against its primary purpose, it would become 'an Arbitrary Power to do things hurtful to the People' (II. 163), and if it is used according to its end, it would become 'Power to do good' (II. 164) or '*the Power of doing publick good without a Rule*' (II. 166). Because it is such a purposive power, the most important question is who is the agent that can accomplish its end. Therefore the distinction between 'a good Prince' (II. 164) or 'our wisest and best Princes' (II. 165) on the one hand and 'weak Princes' (II. 162) or 'a weak and ill Prince' (II. 164) on the other hand is critical. For Locke, a strong government is a good government, not a weak government.

However, this teleological interpretation raises two theoretical problems. The first is the cunning of history. The advent of a wise prince can be an opportunity to generate unlimited power. Consequentialism, that is, one of teleological arguments, sometimes justifies the extra-legal exercise of the executive power. Locke gives us a historical example as follows:

And . . . he, that will look into the *History of England*, will find, that Prerogative was always *largest* in the hands of our wisest and best Princes: because the People observing the whole tendency of their Actions to be the publick good, contested not what was done without Law to that end; or if any humane frailty or mistake (for Princes are but Men, made as others) appear'd in some small declinations from that end; yet 'twas visible, the main of their Conduct tended to nothing but the care of the publick. The People therefore finding reason to be satisfied with these Princes, whenever they acted without or contrary to the Letter of Law, acquiesced in what they did, and, without the least complaint, let them inlarge their *Prerogative* as they pleased, judging rightly, that they did nothing herein to the prejudice of their Laws, since they acted conformable to the Foundation and End of all Laws, the publick good. (TT II. 165)

Because the prerogative power can become an extraconstitutional power, in order to defend the freedom of the people, not only legal regulation but political regulation is also required at all times, because political judgement concerns the natural rights as well as the good of the people.[33]

The second problem is more fundamental. Filmer said, 'they that say the law governs the kingdom, may as well say that the carpenter's rule builds the house and not the carpenter' (*Patriarcha* 39). This remark shows that Filmer has a shrewd insight into the nature of governance. He holds that it is ultimately the will of man that determines the governance, no matter how much one may emphasize the point of the rule of law. Locke, who also recognizes the royal prerogative as an extraconstitutional power, actually shares this insight. And to deal with the contingency coming from the fluidity of the human world, we have to rely on another contingency, that is, the ability or virtue of a person who fortuitously occupies the office of power. The issue of Lockean politics depends on how to control in a rational way such contingencies.

There are further problems with the teleological understanding of the prerogative and trust if we look at it from the viewpoint of our contemporary political theory of liberal constitutionalism. In a paper that places Locke in a tradition of liberalism, Shirley Letwin criticizes Locke's teleology by insisting that 'Locke sees the law as a set of instructions for performing the right actions', because he embraces the moralistic conception of the higher law or natural law which presides over statutory laws and the government, and because he envisions the model of government directed to the purpose of public good. And she contends that '[i]f the rule of law is part of the liberal tradition, then Locke cannot be counted among its friends' (Letwin 1988: 22, 28).

Sheldon Wolin makes a severe criticism of Locke's theory of the prerogative. Wolin pays attention to the substantive connection of the prerogative power and the federative power. The federative power is what Locke himself clearly calls 'natural power' (TT II. 145), which includes the right of war. Wolin insists that the reason of state which resides in this power will naturally require the extension of its power as a matter of necessity. Locke's justification of the requirement of the reason of state for a more flexible and prompt power would amount to 'a criticism of the political system of his own creation, to a deconstruction of his own theory'. According to Wolin, this logic of extension will not stop as long as modern society pursues its own logic of modernity. As the reason of state proceeds to purge the irrational from modern society, 'statecraftiness has disappeared to be replaced by the well-being of society'. 'Briefly put, the modern state experienced a crisis expressed in its own increasing rigidification and a consequent deficit in variability.' 'The pivotal figure in the expansion of Reason of State', therefore, 'proved to be Locke rather than Hobbes' (Wolin 1989: 167–71).

If we want to protect constitutional freedom, it is dangerous to understand the principle of trust in a teleological way. Then, what should we do? We should recall that Locke stipulated 'an appeal to heaven' as a last resort to be taken against the breach of trust by the government. Just like the judgement of whether the government breaks the trust or not, the judgement of the validity for such a judgement becomes possible only *ex post facto*. Logically, this chain of post hoc analyses can be infinite, but at the end there must be, at least for Locke, the Last Judgement. Political judgement is inevitably the kind of wager which is made more or less in an open-ended, historical (providential[34]) situation. Lockean citizens have to question for themselves to what extent such a wager is reasonable.

5 Conclusion

Any attempt to unite constitutionalism and sovereignty tightly in a rational system of theory is bound to be unreasonable. No matter how detailed the plan of a constitutional system may be, it is in the nature of human beings and the political world that unexpected accidents always happen. It can be said that trying to suppress this uncertainty with an authoritarian power is foolish. Nonetheless, something can and should be done about extraconstitutional power. Extraconstitutional power after all emerges from the constitutional power, and the way that constitutional power – the ordinary power – is constructed will influence the potential extraconstitutional power. Indeed, it should influence the power and virtue of the agent who can exercise this unpredictable power.

The problem with the prerogative theory consists in the fact that it was often triggered in emergency situations. In such situations this power often reveals its brute absoluteness. Parker did not hesitate to declare Parliament's arbitrary superiority as England pushed to its civil war. He dared to say that 'there is an Arbitrary power in every State somewhere tis true, tis necessary, and no inconvenience follows upon it' (Parker 1642b: 34). And Filmer declared in a similar manner that '[t]here never was, nor ever can be any people governed without a power of making laws, and every power of making laws must be arbitrary'. 'For', he argued, 'to make a law according to law, is *contradictio in adjecto* [self-contradictory]' (Filmer 1991: 132).[35] Justification of the restraint on arbitrary power, only to be blown out in the state of emergency like a civil war, is clearly contradictory to Lockean constitutionalism which envisions freedom from arbitrary power. However, Locke dared to acknowledge the legitimacy of the absolute power of the king in an emergency while excluding it at ordinary times because of its arbitrary nature. He claimed that what should control this fundamental risk is the natural power of the people. Regarding the use of this 'natural power', Locke was extremely cautious, but it certainly was the ultimate appeal for him.

Finally, let us note that the people's power is a 'natural' power. The fact that the people's power appearing in such a moment of emergency is natural means that it is also extraconstitutional (or superconstitutional). It is, I dare say, a wild power. Once constitutionalized, its peculiar nature would disappear. We can affirm that Locke's political constitutionalism was an attempt to protect constitutional freedom by incorporating such an extraconstitutional power. We can take it as an attempt made by Locke the political realist to strive not to easily invoke this potential wild power while also acknowledging the possibility of this ultimate risk. For Locke closes the chapter on the royal prerogative with the following words:

> Nor let any one think, this [the appeal to heaven] lays a perpetual foundation for Disorder: for this operates not, till the Inconvenience is so great, that the Majority feel it, and are weary of it, and find a necessity to have it amended. But this the Executive Power, or wise Princes, never need come in the danger of: And 'tis the thing of all others, they have most need to avoid, as of all others the most perilous. (TT II. 168)

Locke was, after all, fundamentally a *political*, rather than legal or constitutional, theorist, in spite of the fact that he was undoubtedly a natural law theorist. Therefore, Lockean liberalism (if there is such a thing) should be also *political* liberalism, although what this means is different from our contemporary meaning which is heavily influenced by Rawlsian political theory. If we can attribute constitutionalism to Locke's thought, it must be *political* in the sense that it contains prudential and consequentialist elements as well as the sharp sense of time, history and providence.

Notes

1 Schochet (1979: 1).
2 Legalism is, according to Shklar, 'the ethical attitude that holds moral conduct to be a matter of rule following, and moral relationship to consist of duties and rights determined by rules'. This attitude can be an ideology if upheld as a categorical imperative. See Shklar (1964: 1 and *passim*).
3 See Sir Robert Filmer, *Patriarcha*, in Filmer (1991).
4 The last theme that 'there is no such ruler as tyrant' was, strictly speaking, not the opinion of Filmer in *Patriarcha*, but that of his later work. See Filmer, *Patriarcha* 29 and *passim*; idem., *The Anarchy of a Limited or Mixed Monarchy*, in Filmer (1991:147–8). For the historical survey of Filmer's thought, I heavily rely on Furuta (2016).

5 See Skinner (1998). Although Skinner does not count Locke as a theorist of republican freedom, Pettit who follows Skinner in many respects does count Locke as an advocate of it. See Pettit (1997: 40–1).
6 See Skinner (1998: 50–1 and 72–3).
7 Dunn (1969: ch. 11), Pasquino (1998), Mansfield (1989: ch. 8) and Pangle (1987).
8 On the impact of 9/11 on the studies of Locke's theory of the prerogative, see Feldman (2013: 75). On the relationship of security fetishism to Locke, see Neocleous (2008: 13–24). There are many recent works dealing Locke's theory of the prerogative. See Fatovic (2004), Ward (2005), Mattie (2005), Corbett (2006), Kleinerman (2007), Arnold (2007), Feldman (2008) and Casson (2008).
9 See Fatovic (2004: 278).
10 See Laslett, 'Introduction' to Locke (1988: 87), Harrison and Laslett (1971: 21–2).
11 Pocock and Ashcraft (1980: 1–11).
12 See Fatovic (2004: 282, n. 19). See also Pocock (1975: 117).
13 See Fatovic (2004: 287).
14 See Allen (1928: 27–46).
15 On the reception of Bodin in seventeenth-century England, see Salmon (1959, 1996) and Burgess (2013). According to Burgess, Bodin's theory of sovereignty could be utilized by the supporter of mixed constitution to criticize absolute monarchy.
16 See *Patriarcha* 44.
17 'Vse Iustice, but with such moderation, as it turne not in Tyrannie: otherwaies *summum Ius*, is *summa iniuria*'. '[A] good king will not only delight to rule his subjects by the lawe, but euen will conforme himselfe in his owne actions thervnto, alwayies keeping that ground, that the health of the common-wealth be his chiefe lawe: And where he sees the lawe doubtsome or rigorous, hee may interpret or mitigate the same, lest otherwise *Summum ius* bee *summa iniuria*' (James VI and I 1994: 43, 75). For James's political thought, I rely on Kobayashi (2014).
18 See Cicero (1913: I. x.33).
19 See Bacon (1868: 183). On Bacon's idea of political prudence, see Kimura (2003: especially, 124–8).
20 Aristotle, *Nicomachean Ethics*, 1137b.
21 Aristotle, *The Politics*, 1282b. Care must be taken here because Filmer modified the translation to support his political cause. Compare this with the modern translation in Aristotle 1984.
22 On Aristotle's idea of *epikeia*, see Takahashi (2016: especially, 90–2).
23 See Wormuth (1939: ch. VI). See also Greenleaf (1964: especially, ch. 2).
24 See Sommerville (2014: 96–100).
25 See Kelley (1970: 199).
26 See Corbett (2006: 429–30).

27 On Parker's political thought, see Mandel (1995), Judson (1988) and Sakai (1997: ch. 4).
28 See Oakley (1961: 66–70; 1964). On my understanding of this category, see Yamaoka (1997: 79–83). On the importance of this category for modern constitutional thought, see McIlwain (1947: ch. 6).
29 An important fact about the usage of a political concept is that there were attempts in England in the seventeenth century to separate the concept of absolute monarchy and that of arbitrary rule. In this respect, Locke's tendency to equate despotic, absolute and arbitrary power appears to be ideological, that is, non-philosophical (TT II. 172). Locke indeed argues the separateness of these ideas elsewhere (see II. 139). See Daly (1978: 227–50) and Burgess (2012).
30 See Sakai (1997: 281–6).
31 This kind of criticism was already available in the seventeenth century. See Hunton (1643: 70). Indeed, we can find ambiguity in the arguments of Parker, an occasionally sensitive propagandist. In a theoretical treatise published in 1644, Parker took the principle of *salus populi* to be the interests of the governed, and he understood the power of Parliament, that is, the representative of the people, as a legal power. See Cromartie (2016: especially, 155–9).
32 Therefore, both parties of royalists and parliamentarians were in general very cautious to make a direct appeal to the idea of sovereignty; they rather tended to make constitutionally grounded arguments. See Smith (1994) and Cromartie (2006).
33 The relationship between the natural rights and the (public) good in Locke's political theory is a complex and interesting issue which I regret I cannot examine here.
34 Locke's conception of history is theological as well as teleological. More precisely, the dispute between Filmer and Locke was carried out in theological terms, where the idea of providence played an important role. See Dunn (1969).
35 In Filmer's *The Anarchy of a Limited or Mixed Monarchy*.

References

Allen, J. W. (1928), 'Sir Robert Filmer', in F. J. C. Hearnshaw (ed.), *The Social and Political Ideas of Some English Thinkers of the Augustan Age: A.D. 1650–1750*, 27–46, London: Dawsons of Pall Mall.

Aristotle (1984), *The Complete Works of Aristotle*, 2 vols, ed. J. Barnes, Princeton: Princeton University Press.

Armour, L. (1988), 'John Locke and American Constitutionalism', in A. S. Rosenbaum (ed.), *Constitutionalism: The Philosophical Dimension*, 9–30, New York: Greenwood Press.

Arnold, K. (2007), 'Domestic War: Locke's Concept of Prerogative and Implications for U.S. "Wars" Today', *Polity*, 39 (1): 1–28.
Bacon, F. (1868), *The Works of Francis Bacon*, vol. 11, eds J. Spedding, R. L. Ellis, D. D. Heath, London: Longmans.
Bacon, F. (1972), *Essays*, ed. M. J. Hawkins, London: Everyman's Library.
Burgess, G. (2012), 'Tyrants, Absolute Kings, Arbitrary Rulers and the Commonwealth of England: Some Reflections on Seventeenth-Century English Political Vocabulary', in C. Cuttica and G. Burgess (eds), *Monarchism and Absolutism in Early Modern Europe*, 147–58, London: Pickering and Chatto.
Burgess, G. (2013), 'Bodin in the English Revolution', in H. A. Lloyd (ed.), *The Reception of Bodin*, 387–407, Leiden: Brill.
Casson, D. (2008), 'Emergency Judgement: Carl Schmitt, John Locke, and the Paradox of Prerogative', *Politics & Policy*, 25: 944–71.
Cicero, M. T. (1913), *De Officiis*, trans. W. Miller, Cambridge, MA: Harvard University Press.
Corbett, R. J. (2006), 'The Extraconstitutionality of Lockean Prerogative', *The Review of Politics*, 68: 428–48.
Cromartie, A. (2006), *The Constitutionalist Revolution: An Essay on the History of England, 1450–1642*, Cambridge: Cambridge University Press.
Cromartie, A. (2016), 'Parliamentary Sovereignty, Popular Sovereignty, and Henry Parker's Adjudicative Standpoint', in R. Bourke and Q. Skinner (eds), *Popular Sovereignty in Historical Perspective*, 142–63, Cambridge: Cambridge University Press.
Daly, J. (1978), 'The Idea of Absolute Monarchy in Seventeenth-Century England', *The Historical Journal*, 21: 227–50.
Dunn, J. (1969), *The Political Thought of John Locke: An Historical Account of the Argument of the 'Two Treatises of Government'*, Cambridge: Cambridge University Press.
Fatovic, C. (2004), 'Constitutionalism and Contingency: Locke's Theory of Prerogative', *History of Political Thought*, 25 (2): 276–97.
Feldman, L. C. (2008), 'Judging Necessity: Democracy and Extra-Legalism', *Political Theory*, 36 (4): 550–7.
Feldman, L. C. (2013), 'Lockean Prerogative: Productive Tensions', in C. Fatovic and B. A. Kleinerman (eds), *Extra-Legal Power and Legitimacy: Perspectives on Prerogative*, 75–93, Oxford: Oxford University Press.
Filmer, Sir R. (1991), *Patriarcha and Other Writings*, ed. J. P. Sommerville, Cambridge: Cambridge University Press; abbreviated as *Patriarcha*.
Furuta, T. (2016), 'Robāto Firumā no Shisō Sekai: 1588–1945' (The Thought World of Robert Filmer: 1588–1945), PhD thesis submitted to Keio University.
Gray, J. (1995), *Enlightenment's Wake: Politics and Culture at the Close of the Modern Age*, London: Routledge.
Greenleaf, W. H. (1964), *Order, Empiricism and Politics: Two Traditions of English Political Thought 1500–1700*, Oxford: Oxford University Press.

Harrison J. and P. Laslett (1971), *The Library of John Locke*, 2nd edn, Oxford: Clarendon Press.
Hunton, P. (1643), *A Treatise of Monarchie*, London: John Bellamy and Ralph Smith.
James VI and I, King (1994), *Political Writings*, ed. J. P. Sommerville, Cambridge: Cambridge University Press.
Judson, M. A. (1988), *The Crisis of the Constitution: An Essay in Constitutional and Political Thought in England, 1603–1645*, London: Rutgers University Press, 1st edn, 1949.
Kelley, D. R. (1970), *Foundations of Modern Historical Scholarship: Language, Law, and History in the French Renaissance*, New York: Columbia University Press.
Kimura, T. (2003), *Komonkan no Seijigaku: Furanshisu Beikon to Runessansuki Ingurando* (Politics of the Counsellor: Francis Bacon and Renaissance England), Tokyo: Bokutakusha.
Kleinerman, B. A. (2007), 'Can the Prince Really Be Tamed? Executive Prerogative, Popular Apathy, and the Constitutional Frame in Locke's "Second Treatise"', *The American Political Science Review*, 101 (2): 209–22.
Kobayashi, M. (2014), *Kinsei Sukottorando no Ōken* (Kingship in Early Modern Scotland), Kyoto: Minerva Shobo.
Letwin, S. R. (1988), 'John Locke: Liberalism and Natural Law', in K. Haakonssen (ed.), *Traditions of Liberalism: Essays on John Locke, Adam Smith and John Stuart Mill*, 3–29, St Leonards, NSW: The Centre for Independent Studies Limited.
Locke, J. (1988), *Two Treatises of Government*, ed. P. Laslett, Cambridge: Cambridge University Press; abbreviated as TT, and cited by treatise and section number.
Mandel, M. (1995), *Henry Parker and The English Civil War: The Political Thought of the Public's "Privado"*, Cambridge: Cambridge University Press.
Mansfield, Jr. H. C. (1989), *Taming the Prince: The Ambivalence of Modern Executive Power*, Baltimore: Johns Hopkins University Press.
Mattie, S. (2005), 'Prerogative and the Rule of Law in John Locke and the Lincoln Presidency', *The Review of Politics*, 67: 77–112.
McIlwain, C. H. (1947), *Constitutionalism Ancient and Modern*, Ithaca, NY: Cornell University Press, 1st edn, 1940.
Neocleous, M. (2008), *Critique of Security*, Edinburgh: Edinburgh University Press.
Oakley, F. (1961), 'Medieval Theory of Natural Law: William Ockham and the Significance of Voluntarist Tradition', *Natural Law Forum*, 6: 65–83.
Oakley, F. (1964), *The Political Thought of Pierre d'Ailly: The Voluntarist Tradition*, New Haven: Yale University Press.
Pangle, T. L. (1987), 'Executive Energy and Popular Spirit in Lockean Constitutionalism', *Presidential Studies Quarterly*, 17 (2): 253–65.
Parker, H. (1642a), *Some Few Observations upon his Majesties late answer to the Declaration, or remonstance of the Lords and Commons of the 19. of May, 1642*, London, [s.n.].
Parker, H. (1642b), *Observations upon some of His Majesties Late Answers and Expresses*, London, [s.n.].

Parker, H. (1643), *The contra-replicant, his complaint to his majestie*, London, [s.n.].
Pasquino, P. (1998), 'Locke on King's Prerogative', *Political Theory*, 26 (2): 198–208.
Pettit, P. (1997), *Republicanism: A Theory of Freedom and Government*, Oxford: Oxford University Press.
Pocock, J. G. A. (1975), *The Machiavellian Moment: Florentine Political Thought and the Atlantic Republican Tradition*, Princeton: Princeton University Press.
Pocock, J. G. A. and R. Ashcraft (1980), *John Locke: Papers Read at a Clark Library Seminar 10 December 1977*, Los Angeles: William Andrew Clark Memorial Library.
Sakai, S. (1997), *Kongō Ōsei to Sozei Kokka: Kindai Igirisu Zaiseishi Kenkyū* (Mixed Monarchy and the Tax State: Studies on the Financial History of Modern England), Tokyo: Koubundo.
Salmon, J. H. M. (1959), *The French Religious Wars in English Political Thought*, Oxford: Clarendon Press.
Salmon, J. H. M. (1996), 'The Legacy of Jean Bodin: Absolutism, Populism or Constitutionalism?', *History of Political Thought*, 17: 500–22.
Schochet, G. J. (1979), 'Introduction: Constitutionalism, Liberalism, and the Study of Politics', in J. R. Pennock and J. W. Chapman (eds), *Constitutionalism*, NOMOS XX, 1–15, New York: New York University Press.
Shklar, J. N. (1964), *Legalism: Law, Morals, and Political Trials*, Cambridge, MA: Harvard University Press.
Sidney, A. (1990), *Discourses Concerning Government*, ed. T. G. West, Indianapolis: Liberty Fund.
Skinner, Q. (1998), *Liberty Before Liberalism*, Cambridge: Cambridge University Press.
Smith, D. L. (1994), *Constitutional Royalism and the Search for Settlement, c.1640–1649*, Cambridge: Cambridge University Press.
Sommerville, J. P. (2014), *Royalists and Patriots: Politics and Ideology in England 1603–1640*, 2nd edn, London: Routledge.
Takahashi, H. (2016), *Arisutoteres no Hōshisō: Sono Kontei ni arumono* (The Legal Thought of Aristotle: Its Foundations), Tokyo: Seibundo.
Tanner, J. R. (1930), *Constitutional Documents of the Reign of James I A.D. 1603–1625 with an Historical Commentary*, Cambridge: Cambridge University Press.
Yamaoka, R. (1997), 'Morality and Politics of a Modern Self: A Critical Reconstruction of Lockean Liberalism', PhD thesis submitted to the University of London, available at EThOS.
Ward, L. (2005), 'Locke on Executive Power and Liberal Constitutionalism', *Canadian Journal of Political Science*, 38 (3): 719–44.
Wolin, S. S. (1989), *The Presence of the Past: Essays on the State and the Constitution*, Baltimore: Johns Hopkins University Press.
Wormuth, F. D. (1939), *The Royal Prerogative 1603–1649*, Ithaca, NY: Cornell University Press.

6

The death penalty and a Lockean impossibilism

Masaki Ichinose

1 Attitudes towards the death penalty

Of late, two-thirds of all the countries in the world, institutionally or virtually, have already abolished the death penalty. Nevertheless, the death penalty still deserves scrutiny. There are two reasons for this. First, there are countries that retain the death penalty, such as the United States, Japan and China, and their retention of it regularly causes controversies, domestically as well as internationally. Moreover, even in those countries where the death penalty has already been abolished, some people still hope to revive it because of the fact that horrible crimes are sometimes committed that cause terrible fear and anger. This circumstance seems to require us to take seriously any controversy related to the death penalty and examine the meaning of the death penalty. Second, since the death penalty is actually taken to be the ultimate punishment, we can expect to clarify the significance of the system of punishment in general through examining the death penalty. An acquittal sentence and a death sentence represent the two, extreme ends of sentencing and punishment (0 and 1, as it were) so that we could delineate one extreme of the system of punishment by analysing the death penalty. The point may be understood in an analogous way to the concept of probability. The concept of probability is usually defined in terms of Kolmogorov's axioms, in which there is an axiom concerning probability 1. In this axiom, probability 1 is defined as the probability of the whole sample space.[1] In other words, we need to clearly comprehend what probability 1 is, that is, what the ultimate value of probability is, in order to understand the concept of probability in general. Analogously, it seems clear that we need to figure out how the death penalty should be dealt with in order to make sense of what the system of punishment in general should be like.

In fact, Japanese public opinion in recent years strongly supports the death penalty, as is shown, for instance, in an opinion poll conducted by the Japanese government in 2019. Surprisingly, 80.8 per cent of the people support the retention of the death penalty. If democracy is understood as the social system that attaches importance to what the majority supports, it is politically and morally justified for Japan to retain the death penalty, although the United Nations urges Japan to abolish it. However, this surprising result seems to be based only upon their reluctant agreement to the retention of the death penalty, because, as a matter of fact, most of those surveyed only answered 'yes' to the question which asks whether it is unavoidable to impose the death penalty in some extreme cases. This is not positive support. As evidence of this we could give the result of another questionnaire. In Japan the citizen judge system began in 2009, in which ordinary people take part in judicial decisions including death sentences. A newspaper company carried out an opinion poll with regard to this new system of citizen judge. This poll included the question, 'Can you announce the death sentence by yourself as a citizen judge?' The outcome showed that only 48.8 per cent of the people answered 'Yes'. One suspects that had the poll included a question about whether the citizen judges themselves should execute criminals on death row, the percentage of the positive answer would radically decrease.

What does this result suggest? People who support the death penalty, positively or reluctantly, seem to regard it as conforming to justice. Nevertheless, the more directly they come to take part in it by themselves, the more reluctant they are to endorse it. Why do they have mixed feelings of that kind? One of the most plausible and likely answers to this question is that they perceive killing persons (no matter what the reason) not to be perfectly compatible with justice. Of course, this is just a conjecture. However, as far as the result of the opinion poll is concerned, there is no doubt that people's honest response to the death penalty is indeterminate. On the one hand, the death penalty somehow seems morally just; on the other, it looks as if it ought to be avoided. I am sure that this ambivalence surrounding the death penalty could be generalized, for it agrees with our naïve intuitions. Nevertheless, this ambivalence is still to be investigated from a philosophical point of view. So in this chapter I will aim to analyse this peculiar kind of ambivalence. Such an analysis might provide a clue to the general issue of punishment, first because the death penalty, as I said, constitutes the ultimate punishment, which is the outer extreme of punishment in general, and second, because this ambivalence could be applied to other punishments as well. To impose punishment, particularly to do it by means of physical confinement, tends to cause an ambivalence in the observer. It seems to conform to the rule of justice, while simultaneously raising doubts as to its desirability. Thus, it seems clear that one of our philosophical tasks about the issue of punishment is to clarify the nature of this ambivalence.

2 Turning to Locke

In discussing the ambivalence over the death penalty in the following, I will presuppose two points. First, I take it for granted that any present judicial system that includes the death penalty, or present system of punishment in general, is based upon a modern theory of human or natural rights or a modern concept of persons, or at least is consistent with them. Indeed, this is true of the Japanese legal system as well as any Western systems, since the respect for fundamental human rights and the principle of *nulla poena sine lege* (no punishment without law) are clearly stated in the Constitution of Japan (Articles 11 and 31, respectively). Thus, it logically implies that the system of punishment, including the death penalty, ought to be based upon the theory of fundamental human rights. As far as we presuppose this first point, we should set aside some premodern or medieval views that appear inconsistent with the modern theory of rights, like *Bushido* or *samurai-spirit* in Japan or the frontier spirit found among early Americans. We might admit that such kinds of premodern ideas inform people's emotional reactions to the system of punishment. However, those who live in constitutional states should regard the modern theory of rights or the modern concept of persons as the basis of their legal system.

Second, I also take it for granted that one primary source of the modern theory of rights and the modern concept of persons is the philosophy of John Locke, that is, the most influential political philosopher of the seventeenth century. It is quite true that Grotius, Hobbes and Pufendorf developed arguments for modern society prior to Locke and that their philosophies are indispensable to understand the notions of rights and persons. But it is not a great mistake, historically speaking, to suppose that the ideas of rights and persons which Locke proposed, the right of resistance among others, provided the philosophical basis of our modern society, as clearly shown in such later documents as the Declaration of Independence in 1776 and the Declaration of the Rights of Man and of the Citizen in 1789.

Granted those two presuppositions, I intend to discuss the issue of the death penalty and the system of punishment in general by coming back to Locke. Of course, I do not think that all the aspects and phases of the contemporary theory of human rights perfectly conform to Locke's original arguments. One ought to admit that the theory of human rights has been modified and changed since Locke's era. In addition, it is hard to say that Locke's views are fully digested or accepted in non-Western countries, including Japan, despite their official declaration of the respect for fundamental human rights. Thus, I should say, what I am going to do here is to seek one possible approach towards the death penalty by experimentally coming back to one origin of the theory of rights, i.e. Locke's theory of rights, and then try to find some clues in order to clarify the nature of the ambivalence previously mentioned. As this plan suggests, I mainly aim to present a reasonable account of the problem of the death penalty itself by applying and expanding Locke's philosophy in a creative way.

3 The labour theory of property

Let us begin by briefly confirming the main points of Locke's classical argument for property rights and persons, which underpins punishment. This is not the place to delve deeply into scholarly controversies over the interpretation of Locke's philosophy. The aim here is to pick up some hints as to how to understand the general issue of the death penalty and punishment by taking a look at particular aspects of his philosophy. Thus, I will skip controversial issues and will simply present arguments herein on the basis of my own understanding of Locke. First of all, let us confirm the main scheme of Locke's argument developed in the 'Second Treatise'. In order to understand his argument for property rights, we must consider the notion of the state of nature as it forms its background. He describes it as follows:

> that is, a *State of perfect Freedom* to order their Actions, and dispose of their Possessions, and Persons as they think fit, within the bounds of the Law of nature. (TT II. 4)

On the basis of this notion of the state of nature, Locke offers an account of the origin of property rights in this historically famous passage:

> Though the Earth, and all inferior Creatures be common to all Men, yet every Man has a *Property* in his own *Person*. This no Body has any Right to but himself. The *Labour* of his Body, and the *Work* of his Hands, we may say, are properly his. Whatsoever then he removes out of the State that Nature hath provided, and left it in, he hath mixed his *Labour* with, and joyned to it something that is his own, and thereby makes it his *Property*. (TT II. 27)

These words form the core of Locke's argument for property rights and the concept of persons. The argument is based upon his notions of the state of nature and the law of nature. It is usually called 'the labour theory of property' (LTP hereafter). In short, Locke claims that property rights should be established by our labour and effort. This idea conforms well with the contemporary notion of intellectual property in our present society, for intellectual property rights are undoubtedly a kind of rights attributed to creators because of their labour or effort to create something. (Set aside the issue of inheritance.)

In any case, what we can certainly draw from Locke's LTP is that property rights are not what is naturally given but what we should acquire or obtain by our own effort (perhaps, that might seem to conform to the popular phrase, 'no pain, no gain'). Namely, LTP is defined like this:

> [LTP] If we need to have a property in something, we must labour to get it.

The gist of LTP is taken up, albeit in an attenuated form, by the Constitution of Japan whose Article 12 declares, 'The freedoms and rights guaranteed to the people by this Constitution shall be maintained by the constant endeavour of the people.' The Constitution also declares, 'The fundamental human rights by this Constitution guaranteed to the people of Japan are fruits of the age-old struggle of man to be free' (Article 97). Those statements are sympathetic with LTP, at least in the sense that they capture its core idea emphasizing the aspect of labour in terms of 'endeavour' and 'struggle'. However, those points in the labour theory contrapositionally imply that what cannot be obtained by our labour by definition, either because of its being given from the outset inseparably from us or because of its status being completely beyond the range of our labour, is excluded from the category of property rights. This contraposition of LTP (CP-LTP hereafter) could be expressed as follows:

> [CP-LTP] If something is outside what we can labour to get, we cannot have a property in it at all.

I will come back to this point later.

4 Life, liberty and estate

I want to make three points about the labour theory to prepare for the further arguments which are to follow. The first point concerns the context of Locke's philosophy. As Locke's LTP, built on the basis of the law of nature, is developed with reference to the state of nature, we may be inclined to think that if our society shifts to a political state by our consent, the law of nature will no longer be binding and LTP will become invalidated. However, this is not the case. Locke claims that the obligations of the law of nature 'cease not in Society, but only in many Cases are drawn closer . . . to inforce their observation' (TT II. 135). Therefore, we should accept the labour theory as generally applicable to any possible situation of property, even though the introduction of money might make the situation highly complicated.

Second, the concept of property that Locke discusses covers so wide a range that many of the rights enjoyed by human beings are included in Lockean property, though at first glance Locke's concept of property looks applicable only to rights to material objects. This is confirmed by Locke's famous phrase, 'Life, Liberty and Estate' (TT II. 87 et al.). Locke defines the concept of property with this phrase, which suggests that other rights such as the right to life and the right to liberty are covered by Lockean property. In other words, in the context of Locke, those rights are all described in the form of having, possessing or owning something exactly in the same way as property rights are. Actually, this approach to rights is applicable even in our contemporary context of rights. For example, H. L. A. Hart once argued that legal rights are nothing but legal powers to require others to meet correlative obligations, and then pointed out that 'we also speak of the person who has the correlative right as *possessing* it or even *owning* it' (Hart 1982: 185). If this is the case, we could understand that property rights encompass all rights.

Third, although at first sight it looks strange to apply the labour theory literally to all cases of rights, particularly in the contemporary context where there are many immaterial forms of property without the medium of physical labour, nevertheless, we could say that the labour theory remains intuitively convincing. Actually, the labour theory could be seen as more widely applicable than we expect if we take the notion of labour in a broad way. For instance, we could suppose ourselves to be labouring when we collect information about stock market via the internet to earn profits. Historically speaking, the standard interpretation holds that the labour theory is contrasted to the convention theory of property which was developed, for example, by Hume. However, the convention theory could be subsumed under the labour theory, because we need a certain kind of labour to observe and keep a convention, particularly when someone tries to violate it. A similar point is true of contemporary theories of rights. Roughly speaking, there are two types of theories of rights in our contemporary discussions, that is to say, 'the choice theory' and 'the interest theory'. The choice theory 'regards rights as protecting the exercise of choice'

(Harel 2006: 194). This protection is conducive to the autonomy and self-realization of right-holders. To put it another way, the right-holders in this case make some choice autonomously and try to protect it. This mode of rights has a great affinity with the one described by Locke's labour theory in that their rights are established by the holders' decision and their effort to keep them, probably by a powerful protest.

We turn next to the interest theory. Generally speaking, 'the interest theory of rights holds that the point of rights is to protect and promote (some of) the right-holders' interests' (Harel 2006: 195). This concept of rights 'emphasizes the status of right-holders as the passive beneficiaries of protective and supportive duties imposed on others . . . it can also ascribe rights to entities which are not agents, as long as these entities have interests, that is, as long as they can be made better or worse off' (Harel 2006). This interest theory is helpful to justify a universal application of rights not only to healthy adult humans but also to young infants, those who suffer from senile dementia, or animals, as we treat them at present. However, at first glance, the rights based on this interest theory seem to conflict with Locke's labour theory, as interests in this case can be ascribed to the subjects who are incapable of labour or effort (e.g. infants). Nevertheless, in reality, the protection of such kinds of interests could not be provided without the assistance (i.e. a kind of labour) of other (healthy adult) people's claims, as our history obviously shows. In this sense, the interest theory of property could be theoretically subsumed under Locke's labour theory. Thus, our rights are what we should obtain by our labour or effort. Actually, this is generally true of our ordinary usage of the concept of rights as well as Lockean rights. Probably, the right or the qualification to be seeded in sports tournaments as in tennis or football would be an appropriate example, which typically represents the signification of the concept of rights. For the right to be seeded must be gained by making efforts to achieve good results in advance of the particular tournaments. Our rights are intrinsically different from those of the natural objects which exist in the world (e.g. oxygen) in that they are not passively provided but actively gained.

5 The concept of persons

However, there is one crucial point developed in Locke's argument for rights, about which we should raise a fundamental question. He says, 'dispose of persons' and 'has a property in his own person'. But how on earth can we dispose of our persons, and how can we have a property in our persons? How are these claims to be understood? These questions might lead us to chaotic controversies concerning how to interpret Locke, but if we take Locke's argument at face value, the situation is simple. Here we need to confirm the two basic points that are deduced from Locke's argument. First, according to his remarks that I have already quoted, it is grammatically obvious that our persons are regarded as objects of property rights. If this is the case, the labour theory must apply to our persons, and our persons must share common characteristics of property rights with other objects of property rights. This is not so strange at the level of our ordinary life. We could say, for example, 'cultivate an attractive personality', when we take the concept of person or personality to be capable of being improved by our effort. This must fit in well with the labour theory. We could gain a new personality through our labour. In addition, our persons can be treated in the same way as other possessions, particularly when actors and actresses or music players earn their living through, as it were, selling their personas or personalities. In these cases, our persons are treated as exchangeable objects which are even convertible into money. Of course, those personas or personalities could be achieved or cultivated by their everyday efforts. In fact, even Locke himself accepts those points, which I will discuss later.

The second basic point to be confirmed about Locke's claim about persons is that he sharply distinguishes our persons from our lives themselves. Property rights or rights of ownership are sometimes described as a bundle of rights because it is a package that contains within itself many kinds of rights, for example, the rights of consumability, tradability and alienability.[2] But we could summarize the meaning of those rights by saying that when we have property rights in something, we have a kind of power to control or treat those things as we like, so long as such treatment would not harm others.[3] This is exactly what we mean by having property. Without the power, we are simply in the same position as not having that property. Locke also uses the concept of power when he discusses various aspects of property rights. Among those, we should pay attention to the following remark:

> For a Man, not having the Power of his own Life, *cannot*, by Compact, or his own Consent, *enslave himself* to any one, nor put himself under the Absolute, Arbitrary Power of another, to take away his Life, when he pleases. (TT II. 23)

Locke also says this:

> no Man can, by agreement, pass over to another that which he hath not in himself, a Power over his own Life. (TT II. 24)

On the one hand, as I have confirmed a couple of times, Locke founds his LTP rights on our property in our own persons. However, on the other hand, according to his remarks here, he claims that we do not have a property in our own lives. What should we deduce from this? The answer is simple: Locke supposes that we have no property rights in our own lives or bodies themselves, or, more exactly, no property rights in controlling and destroying our own lives as a whole. It is for this reason that Locke claims that we cannot alienate them. In other words, he regards our own lives or bodies themselves as totally different from our own persons. In the background of this argument, there seems to be a Christian idea that we are God's creatures; thus, we ourselves are not ours but God's property. Actually, we cannot create our own lives as a whole through our labours. Who claims that our DNA is what we intentionally create? These points exactly correspond to CP-LTP that I previously formulated. Thus, if we adopt the labour theory, our lives or our bodies themselves as a whole cannot be our property at all. Of course, not everything in our lives or bodies is excluded from the category of property rights. If we acquire muscular strength by our tough training or gain bodily health by our abstinence, we are qualified to have those results. Probably, we might earn money by means of those results. However, to make our own lives as a whole or to create our own bodies as a whole is fundamentally beyond human control apart from our parents' subsidiary role on occasions to make the process smooth. Therefore, suicide has been prohibited as a crime particularly in the Christian tradition since St Augustine and St Thomas Aquinas, for in the tradition suicide is nothing but destroying God's property.

On the contrary, those arguments of Locke suggest that characteristics of property rights should be applied to our own persons in contrast to our lives or bodies. In other words, it seems to follow that we could consume, trade or alienate our own persons. This point was previously examined along with the first basic point about Locke's theory of persons from a general point of view, and I pointed out that it is not so strange. What did Locke himself think about it? How did he ever come to regard a person as an object of property? Locke supposed that there was an objection to his claim of the impossibility of our transferring our own lives to others to be slaves. The objection concerns the case of Jews who did sell themselves. To this Locke replies:

> but, 'tis plain, this was only to *Drudgery, not to Slavery*. For, it is evident, the Person sold was not under an Absolute, Arbitrary, Despotical Power. (TT II. 24)

Locke obviously accepts that our persons can be sold in the same manner as other objects of property rights, while he also claims that there is a distinction between selling them to drudgery and selling them to slavery.

However, we still need to ask how we are to understand Locke's phrase, 'Life, Liberty and Estate'. Does he mention 'life' as a representative of our property rights? Yes, he does. So we should understand 'life' in this context not as our life as a whole, but as a bundle of bodily functions or abilities, which we could gain by our efforts and use or alienate in a way that in principle was convertible into money.

6 Punishment as forfeiture

In fact, Locke's argument is so surprisingly consistent that the labour theory even conforms to the argument developed in the second edition of his masterpiece *An Essay concerning Human Understanding*. Locke discusses the problem of personal identity in his *Essay* with his unique strategy. First, he introduces the following theoretical distinction:

> to conceive, and judge of it aright [i.e. *identity*], we must consider what *Idea* the Word it is applied to stands for: It being one thing to be the same *Substance*, another the same *Man*, and a third the same *Person*, if *Person*, *Man*, and *Substance*, are three Names standing for three different *Ideas*. (*Essay* II. xxvii. 7)

'Man' in this case means our biological existence as a set of organizations or lives. Thus, his distinction suggests that there must be a clear-cut, theoretical difference between a biological life and a person, to say nothing of the difference between substance and person. Additionally, we must not miss the next famous point Locke makes in his theory of personal identity. He says:

> we must consider what *Person* stands for; which, I think, is a thinking intelligent Being, that has reason and reflection, and can consider it self as it self, the same thinking thing in different times and places; which it does only by that consciousness. (*Essay* II. xxvii. 9)

'Consciousness' is the key to establishing personal identity. Roughly speaking, in the scheme of Locke's philosophy, 'consciousness' is supposed to be connected with an active aspect of our experience to intentionally understand something, as his criticism of innate notions shows. In criticizing innatism, Locke develops the view that our knowledge is not naturally given but gained by our experience or experiments; in particular, he sees it as applicable to complex ideas (particularly ones of mixed modes) and the kind of propositional knowledge which is made up of combinations of ideas. Certainly, and amazingly, those main claims on knowledge in Locke's *Essay* perfectly correspond to his LTP, as the notion of consciousness here implies a certain motivation to experimentally understand something, and that motivation has affinity with activities of our labour. In addition, Locke's distinction between person and life in the *Essay* has a corresponding distinction in his crucial argument in his LTP that I have scrutinized. There Locke distinguishes between our person capable of being an object of property rights and our life as a whole incapable of being an object of property rights.[4]

How, then, is punishment understood in Locke's scheme? In fact, Locke introduced another concept of right into his account of the state of nature, while introducing property rights. He says this:

> all Men may be restrained from invading others Rights, and from doing hurt to one another, and the Law of Nature be observed, which willeth the Peace and *Preservation of all Mankind*, the *Execution* of the Law of Nature is in that State, put into every Mans hands, whereby every one has a right to punish the transgressors of the Law to such a Degree, as may hinder its Violation. (TT II. 7)

The reason Locke introduces the right to punish others here is that if nobody has a power or right to execute the law of nature, the law would be 'in vain'. This right in the state of nature also justifies punishing foreigners who violate the law. In this case, by violations of the law, Locke obviously means violations of other's property, including their property in their persons. For the contents of the law of nature amount to nothing but the preservation of each other's rights or the preservation of mankind, which can be evidently reduced to the preservation of property. But how could anyone be justified in executing the right to punish others? Locke stipulates the following:

> in the State of Nature, *one Man comes by a Power over another*, but yet no Absolute or Arbitrary Power, to use a Criminal when he has got him in his hands ... but only to retribute to him, so far as calm reason and conscience dictates, what is proportionate to his Transgression, which is so much as may serve for *Reparation* and *Restraint*. For these two are the only reasons, why one Man may lawfully do harm to another, which is that we call *punishment*. (TT II. 8)

And he adds:

> From these *two distinct Rights*, the one of *Punishing* the Crime *for restraint*, and preventing the like Offence, which right of punishing is in every body; the other of taking *reparation*, which belongs only to the injured party. (TT II. 11)

As to the reparation, Locke gives an explanation in the context of his discussion of an unjust war, which is a kind of crime:

> Let the *Conqueror* have as much Justice on his side, as could be supposed, he *has* no *right* to seize more than the vanquished could forfeit; his Life is at the Victors Mercy, and his Service and Goods he may appropriate to make himself reparation; but he cannot take the Goods of his Wife and Children. (TT II. 183)

Here we should pay special attention to Locke's introduction of the concept of forfeiture because it seems clear that he offers here the logic of punishment in terms of forfeiture. His argument seems to rely upon the idea that 'by performing acts contrary to natural law one forfeits that portion of one's own rights against others that will make an interference in one's own life, proportionate to one's interference with others, morally permissible' (Simmons 1992: 149).[5]

One element of punishment, namely, reparation, can be easily understood in this way. If we deprived others of some property or possessions, we ought to make reparation for those. This reparation is explained by our forfeiting or losing our property or possessions, proportionate to what we deprived others of. In this case, reparation as one element of punishment is explained as arising from a forfeiture of offenders' property rights. This is an idea of retributive equilibrium. However, what about the other element of punishment, namely, restraint? Could we understand it as a kind of forfeiture of offenders' property rights, following the logic of forfeiture? There might be two interpretations. First, we could understand restraint as only an emergency treatment of offensive behaviours when those behaviours are really dangerous. If the danger continues, we can justify detention. If we take this view, the core of the Lockean idea of punishment lies in the idea of reparation, where the restraint works not as the main function of punishment but rather as playing an essentially temporary role. Second, we could even understand restraint as a kind of forfeiture of offenders' property rights. That is to say, the offenders deprived our society of our rights to safety or free actions so that they ought to forfeit or lose their rights to safety or free actions proportionally. In this context, what was harmed is supposedly our society as a whole rather than a specific individual, so it is conceptually distinguishable from reparation. If we take this second view, we consistently hold the logic of forfeiture to understand the Lockean idea of punishment in an integrated way. In any case, Locke's use of the category of restraint can be interpreted without violating his logic of the forfeiture of rights which Locke seems to adopt in explaining punishment.

7 Impossibilism

This view of punishment corresponds to retributivism in the philosophy of punishment in general. However, the view is not necessarily opposed to the utilitarian idea of punishment, although, generally speaking, retributivism tends to be considered incompatible with the utilitarian theory in the context of the philosophy of punishment. As I said, any offences are regarded as violations of people's rights to safety and free actions in our human societies, so we could punish or detain the offenders to recover the others' rights to safety and freedom according to the Lockean logic of forfeiture. As a matter of fact, this virtually plays the same role as deterrence. We can make another related point. Whatever theory of punishment we may adopt, it is undoubtedly true that we can still keep the traditional system of punishing offenders. Why is this the case? It is because we rely upon the basic idea of retribution in sustaining the system of punishment. Actually, if we purely follow the utilitarian idea, we might more effectively deter future offences and achieve the greatest happiness of the greatest number by inflicting punishment on family members of offenders. For this could cause more serious pain in the minds of would-be offenders and make them more scared. Nevertheless, we do not adopt such a system because we virtually accept the basic point of retributivism at the fundamental level. In this respect, the Lockean view of punishment, while being classical, still deserves consideration. Moreover, his LTP rights, which constitutes the basis of his view of punishment, is more convincing than we usually expect, as I have shown. Therefore, it might turn out to be one of the promising approaches to the issues about punishment if we applied Locke's view to some of our contemporary problems. At least, it is worth attempting an application.

Our task here is to apply Locke's view to the issue of the death penalty, and investigate what significant perspectives we might draw from that. In what follows, I will argue by presupposing that crimes to which the death penalty is applicable are murders. This is only to make my argument as simple as possible, and I am perfectly aware that the death penalty has been actually applied in some countries to other kinds of crimes like rebellion, drug dealing and adultery, rather than murders alone. I believe that the simplified strategy is not highly misleading in light of the fact that the death penalty has been actually imposed on many cases of homicide in many countries. Anyway, it is quite well known that the conflict between retentionists and abolitionists constitutes the very core of the debate on the death penalty. Moreover, some of the main points in the debate are also widely acknowledged. For example, the retentionists claim that our human society must cope with the suffering of the bereaved families of murder victims by executing the murderers; that the death penalty is necessary to deter future crimes; that public opinion strongly supports it (in Japan and many other countries) and so on. On the other hand, the abolitionists maintain that the death penalty is cruel; that it fails to respect the dignity of each human being; that there is a possibility of the court making misjudgements while it is irrevocable; that there is vagueness and arbitrariness in deciding between a death sentence and a life sentence, and so on. Those points are so persuasive in their own right that the debate appears to have reached a deadlock.

Surprising as it may seem, however, this debate as a whole can be severely criticized as misguided or as resting on a fundamental mistake if we consider it from the viewpoint that Locke originally took. All we need to do here is to reapply Locke's view of rights and punishment to the debate on the death penalty. This is not a complicated matter at all, but rather a logical consequence of his own view. I propose the consequence in the form of an indicative conditional sentence: if we accept the theory of rights and the concept of persons in their original form, we must regard the death penalty as conceptually impossible. That is, as long as we accept the theory of rights as Locke proposed it, the death penalty must be taken to be a contradiction like 'a round triangle' or 'a married bachelor'. I call this position 'the impossibilist view of the death penalty', or simply 'impossibilism' about the death penalty, as distinct from either retentionism or abolitionism.[6]

There are three justifications to deduce impossibilism from the arguments that I have presented thus far. First, and most importantly, in the theory of rights, a person is sharply distinguished from life itself as a whole in that we have property rights in our own persons while we do not have them in our own lives as a whole (our lives are created not by ourselves through our labour but by God; thus, our lives themselves are beyond the category of property rights), so that it is *impossible* to make someone forfeit his or her life as a whole in punishment, that is, the act which is defined as reparation that is equated with the forfeiture of rights. Of course, this point is bolstered by CP-LTP discussed earlier. It is logically true that we cannot forfeit or lose anything that we do not have. The situation is the same as the plain fact that we cannot lose gills because we do not have gills. Then, how should we understand the actual practice of death penalty or actual executions in countries like Japan, where the respect for fundamental human rights is clearly stated in their constitutions? The answer is quite simple. That practice cannot be seen as the death penalty according to impossibilism, but the practice is purely violence or a murder committed by the power of a state. That is a strange contradiction in our societies.

Second, as far as we accept the definition of punishment as reparation that is equated with forfeiture of rights, the death penalty remains logically opposed to the definition of punishment because it eliminates the possibility for an offender to make reparation for harmed victims. The death penalty must then be judged to be impossible. Instead, the death penalty should come to be regarded as a counter-punishment, as it prevents punishment from being imposed. What should be noted here is that what I mean by harmed victims are basically bereaved families of the murdered persons, as there is a metaphysical question about whether the murdered persons themselves could be named victims or not. I understand that not all bereaved families suffer the same kinds of harm, but I believe that it is not a big mistake to treat bereaved families as (indirect) victims, at least in an institutional sense. Furthermore, I maintain that families of death-row convicts are harmed victims as well. Obviously, they are deprived of rights to live peacefully with family members without suffering prejudices from other members of the society. Death-row convicts must also make reparation for their own families. Nevertheless, the death penalty makes such reparation altogether impossible. Thus, the death penalty is not what is properly regarded as the punishment.

Third, the concept of persons, which founds the modern system of punishment upon property rights, is established by 'consciousness', but death (as distinct from the process of dying) is by definition what we cannot be conscious of, so that death has nothing to do with persons and any property rights at all. For this reason, imposing death in the form of a punishment is impossible. According to the modern concept of persons, punishment is supposed to make sense only when a punished person can be conscious of being punished. Actually, even in the present world, offenders who are insane or suffer from mental disorder are treated as being less responsible for offences in most countries. This fact evidently corresponds to the original sense of punishment such that punishment should be what the punished can be conscious of, in other words, what the punished can reasonably understand as results of their own behaviours while being punished, whereas offenders who are insane or suffer from mental disorders might not, supposedly, reach such clear understanding. However, death is definitely beyond consciousness, for if we can be conscious of our death, we have not died yet. Thus, the concept of the death penalty is a confused, or rather a contradictory, idea. What I have said earlier about consciousness supports impossibilism.[7]

How, then, does Locke himself deal with the death penalty? Locke describes how to treat a murderer:

> every Man in the State of Nature, has a Power to kill a Murderer . . . a Criminal, who having renounced Reason, the common Rule and Measure, God hath given to Mankind, hath by the unjust Violence and Slaughter he hath committed upon one, declared War against all Mankind, and therefore may be destroyed as a *Lyon* or a *Tyger*, one of those wild Savage Beasts, with whom Men can have no Society nor Security. (TT II. 11)

Do these remarks suggest that Locke approves of the death penalty? There has been a debate concerning how to understand Locke's view of the death penalty, one which is constituted at least in part by the remarks I have just quoted. Some interpret Locke as positively supporting the death penalty, while others claim that Locke takes a view of restricting applications of the death penalty as much as possible.[8] However, if my interpretation of Locke is correct, he cannot support the death penalty. How can we interpret Locke that way, given his aforementioned remarks where he says that a murderer may be destroyed? I want to pay attention to the fact that Locke asserts that a murderer may be destroyed as a lion or tiger. Could killing dangerous lions or tigers be classified as punishment? I do not think so. That is not any kind of punishment, but simply an extermination of harmful beasts. Thus, we could say that Locke's argument is developed in a quite consistent way.[9]

8 Implications of impossibilism

My proposal thus far of the impossibility of the death penalty is, as I noted, the consequence of an experiment to apply Locke's original theory of persons and property rights to the issue of the death penalty. So if Locke's theory does not deserve consideration at present despite its historical significance, my argument will cease to be persuasive and remain just an anachronism that is not worth discussing. However, objectively speaking, the situation is quite different. The Christian tradition, which constitutes the background of his concept of persons, is still a viable option for many people, particularly in Western countries, where they have the religious belief that our lives are created by God, as clearly shown in the debate between evolutionary theory and creationism, for instance. That is, our lives are not supposed to be just our own property, so that committing suicide has been prohibited in the Christian context since medieval era as destroying

God's property. Additionally, Locke's LTP still remains influential and looks like a realistic option, as revealed in the current trend of thought about intellectual property. The ground of intellectual property seems to lie in inventors' labour and efforts. I believe that this Lockean tradition of thought has exerted some influence over Western countries, with the result that most of them have come to abolish the system of death penalty.

I will conclude my argument by briefly pointing out three implications of the impossibilism I have presented. First, I want to emphasize that impossibilism is offered in the form of a conditional sentence. Namely, the impossibilist simply claims: If the Lockean theory of rights is accepted, then the death penalty is impossible. Probably, a natural reaction to this is to ask how different this view is from the abolitionist one. For, actually, the modern theory of rights, like that of Locke, has been universally accepted so that, at least theoretically (rather than practically), it is a common default for us. Therefore, even though the impossibilism is presented as a conditional, the conditional may be said to be virtually the same as the categorical denial of the possibility of the death penalty. So it may be claimed that the assertion of the impossibility is not distinguishable from the abolitionist view. To this reaction, I will first answer that the impossibilist claims that the death penalty is conceptually impossible, whereas the abolitionist asserts that the death penalty is so morally problematic that it ought to be abolished. Unlike the impossibilist, the abolitionist assumes that the death penalty is a form of punishment and then claims that it is undesirable. Thus, we can see that impossibilism is structurally different from abolitionism. Additionally, that reaction rests on a misunderstanding of the universality of the concept of rights. As some scholars have pointed out, and as I have briefly discussed in my own account, the notion of rights is basically a Western and Christian one, so that objectively speaking, it has not permeated all nations on the globe even though they officially declared the respect for rights.[10] In this sense, exactly speaking, the antecedent in the impossibilist's conditional is not the default. To put it another way, we could suppose or consider the different situation where the antecedent does not hold true. For example, as I said at the beginning, Japanese public opinion strongly supports the retention of the death penalty in spite of the fact that the Constitution of Japan clearly states that fundamental human rights ought to be respected. I suspect that there is a different system of morality like *Bushido* or the spirit of *samurai* influencing, secretly and unconsciously, the minds of Japanese people. That culturally determined view is quite different from the theory of rights in that people living with the view pay special attention to dying in a brave manner, though in some other respects of human affairs, it is similar to the theory of rights. We may conjecture that if we adopt or revive that (possibly premodern) kind of culturally determined view instead of the notion of universal rights, the antecedent of the impossibilist's conditional will be rejected. Of course, the conditional is still true according to the standard logical rule, but it will lose its practical impact. In that case, impossibilism might virtually lead to the retentionist position. This is one important implication of impossibilism. This partially explains why the death penalty and punishment in general are surrounded by the peculiar kind of ambivalence which I touched on earlier.

Second, as long as impossibilism depends upon the original theory of rights where the system of punishment is, as I argued, ultimately based upon the notion of reparation (i.e. forfeiture), impossibilism implies the existence of a legal system according to which reparation for the harm caused by offences matters more than the retributive imposition of physical punishment including restraint or detention. In my view, although it is deduced from the classical standpoint, the impossibilist position tends to support what is nowadays called 'restorative justice', or a new theory of criminal responsibility that underpins it. This is a quite surprising implication, but on reflection we can easily find the implication very natural. Impossibilism eventually removes what is known as the ultimate punishment because it is not really a punishment at all. To put it differently, impossibilism is that position that considers how seriously each victim is harmed without trying to solve the problem at one stroke by executing offenders. If this is the case, impossibilism has an affinity with the system of restorative justice in considering degrees of harm in each case carefully.

Third, impossibilism conversely allows us to analyse and explain our psychological tendency to accept a conceptual possibility of the death penalty in terms of retributive schemes, despite its theoretical impossibility. By the retributive scheme I mean the idea that when someone deprived others of some property, that person must offer an equivalent of the property taken. This is the idea of retributive equilibrium, which is basically the same as the Lockean scheme of reparation or forfeiture. People tend to apply this scheme to the death penalty to justify it. They apparently do so because they really perceive an equivalent offered to us when someone dies. They have no hesitation in applying the retributive scheme in this case. But what is offered? We could not think that the life of the executed person is offered, since it is a completely nonsensical idea. Who receives the life offered? Does the recipient have the two lives then? Offering a life is simply a violation of grammar. Then, what is offered? How about supposing that 'a death' is offered rather than 'a life'? Certainly, the notion of offering a death seems more realistic (even though not perfectly realistic) at least in comparison to that of offering a life. For a dead body is actually given, or some emotions like sorrow and guilt are given, when someone dies. Those are quite realistic in a sense. However, if we suppose that a dead person offers 'a death' when he or she dies, we should also suppose, logically speaking, that he or she owns 'a death' before they die, i.e. when they are living. Otherwise they cannot offer 'deaths'. How can we make sense of such a strange way of thinking? I suggest that what we might call the notion of 'the ownership of a death' comes up here to clarify this issue. In fact, it is possible, for example, to think that we own 'deaths' while we are living as long as we can die freely whenever we like.[11] This idea might be compared to the idea of 'owning a marriage', namely, that of single people holding a qualification to marry someone unlike married people, in a society of monogamy.

In any case, if we accept the notion of 'the ownership of a death' in one way or another, we are likely to keep the retributive justification of the death penalty. A person deprives others of the 'deaths they have owned' by killing them irrespective of their own wills. Then the offender must offer 'the death which he or she has owned' by being executed. It may be that this way of thinking is secretly working in us, affecting many aspects of human cultures. However, 'offering a death' is an irregular idea, just as much as 'offering a life', though the former looks more plausible than the latter. Actually, if we are offered a death, what should we do? Must we die? So we should note that the notion of 'the ownership of a death' is also a purely fictitious idea. But if people believe that they can justify the death penalty within a retributive scheme, it is plausible that they unconsciously use the notion of 'the ownership of a death'. This seems to be another origin of the ambivalence which surfaces in the debate on the death penalty.

Notes

1 See Jaynes and Bretthorst (2003: 651–2).
2 See Honoré (1961: 107–47) and Becker (1977: 18–22).
3 As to the relation between 'rights', 'power' and 'control', the following interpretation of Shimokawa could be helpful. 'Everyone is free with respect to the control of his person or his possessions. In other words, everyone has a power to control those objects, while he is also allowed to exercise his power within the bounds of the laws. To have the right of disposal over specific objects means both that one has his power and that one may exercise it' (Shimokawa 2006: 191).

4 Some scholars seem to, as if traditionally, refuse to connect Locke's notion of person in his 'Second Treatise' with the same notion in his *Essay*, probably because the former notion is discussed in the context of political philosophy, whereas the latter appears in the context of metaphysical or ethical argument. However, I do not agree with this standpoint, because, obviously, there is a strong connection between those two texts. That is to say, the issue of punishment is discussed in both texts as one of main subjects. In the *Essay*, Locke defines the concept of person as 'a Forensic Term appropriating Actions and their Merit; and so belongs only to intelligent Agents capable of a Law, and Happiness and Misery' (*Essay* II. xxvii. 26). Actually, Locke discusses the issue of drunken man's answerability for his mischief, and justifies punishing him (*Essay* II. xxvii. 22). In reality, punishment essentially matters in Locke's argument over the notion of person in his *Essay*. And, it is needless to say that punishment constitutes one of the main issues in his 'Second Treatise', as I have argued. In this respect, we must interpret Locke's concept of person, taking a connection of both texts seriously.

5 In the contemporary context concerning the philosophy of punishment, the concept of forfeiture actually works well. For example, Wellman criticizes the dominant debates on punishment by pointing out that those debates have not tried to show the moral permissibility of punishment. Instead, Wellman proposes the importance of the rights-based analysis, according to which rights forfeiture as a result of violating others' rights is a necessary and sufficient condition for the system of punishment to be morally permissible. See Wellman (2017).

6 Peter Anstey pointed out that my proposal of 'impossibilism' sounds trivial, as the proposal simply depends on how to define the notion of the death penalty. I answer this criticism by offering two points. First, if my impossibilism were accepted together with the Lockean view of human rights, then the system of the death penalty still sustained in many countries must be stopped as long as those countries adopt the theory of human rights as their basic legal principle. For that would be judged not as a system of punishment, but merely as that of unjustifiable violence. In this sense, impossibilism is not a trivially verbal view at all. Rather, it could exert some practical impact. Second, if we focus on the fact that my impossibilist view is made of a conditional sentence whose antecedent is, 'if the Lockean theory of rights is accepted', then we could come to find that there would be room for rejecting the consequent, 'the death penalty is impossible'. That is to say, if we could adopt a view of morality which is different from the Lockean view of human rights, then the death penalty might be consented to as a kind of punishment. In this way, the impossibilist view could open up a possibility of taking into account other views of morality than the theory of human rights. That could be of philosophical significance. See Panikkar (1982).

7 In addition to my arguments for impossibilism, there might be another argument for it. That is to say, the Epicurean view of regarding death as neither beneficial

nor harmful could support some standpoint similar to my idea of impossibilism, because, according to the Epicurean view, being killed is harmless so that homicide is nothing harmful, thus not qualified to be an offence! Of course, the Epicurean view must suppose that being executed cannot be punishment either, as killing causes nothing harmful. See Ichinose (2017), where I discuss the issue of the death penalty from a general point of view while mentioning the idea of impossibilism and the Epicurean view. I also touch upon the Lockean view in the 2017 article, but this chapter exclusively focuses upon Locke's arguments. In addition, I would like to acknowledge that my arguments after Section 5 of this chapter partially depend upon my arguments in chapter 1 of my Japanese book, Ichinose (2011). I have, however, revised my past arguments and added some new points.

8 For example, Simmons (1994) claims that Locke positively supports the system of the death penalty, whereas Calvert (1993) focuses upon an aspect of Locke's argument which shows that he carefully restricts execution, by highlighting a utilitarian flavour found in Locke's argument. As these exemplify, what has been commonly presupposed in the previous debates on Locke's commitment to the death penalty is that Locke basically accepts the system of the death penalty as a kind of punishment. My argument is a challenge to this presupposition.

9 It is true that Locke mentions 'Penalties of Death' at the end of the opening chapter of the 'Second Treatise' (TT II. 3), but I interpret this reference as standing for the case of killing dangerous beasts as Locke develops in TT II. 11. We could interpret the terminology 'penalty' in Locke's text in a broad sense, and in a sense distinct from 'punishment'. That could be a consistent reading of Locke's argument.

10 See, for example, Panikkar (1982).

11 Note that the ownership of a death should not be understood to be the same as the right to die. The notion of the ownership of a death is a kind of strange fiction by definition (although we unconsciously tend to introduce the notion), so that the notion is not expected at all from the outset to function in a realistic way like the right to die.

References

Becker, L. C. (1977), *Property Rights: Philosophic Foundations*, London: Routledge and Kegan Paul.

Calvert, B. (1993), 'Locke on Punishment and the Death Penalty', *Philosophy*, 68 (264): 211–29.

Harel, A. (2006), 'Theories of Rights', in M. P. Golding and W. A. Edmundson (eds), *The Blackwell Guide to the Philosophy of Law and Legal Theory*, 191–206, Oxford: Blackwell.

Hart, H. L. A. (1982), *Essays on Bentham: Jurisprudence and Political Theory*, Oxford: Oxford University Press.

Honoré, A. M. (1961), 'Ownership', in A. G. Guest (ed.), *Oxford Essays in Jurisprudence*, 107–47, Oxford: Oxford University Press.

Ichinose, M. (2011), *Shi no Shoyū: Shikei, Satsujin, Dobutsu Riyō ni mukiau Tetsugaku* (The Ownership of Death: A Philosophy towards the Death Penalty, Homicide and the Use of Animals), Tokyo: Tokyo University Press.

Ichinose, M. (2017), 'The Death Penalty Debates: Four Problems and New Philosophical Perspectives', *Journal of Practical Ethics*, 5 (1): 53–80.

Jaynes, E. T. and G. L. Bretthorst, eds (2003), *Probability Theory: The Logic of Science*, Cambridge: Cambridge University Press.

Locke, J. (1975), *An Essay concerning Human Understanding*, ed. P. H. Nidditch, Oxford: Clarendon Press.

Locke, J. (1988), *Two Treatises of Government*, ed. P. Laslett, Cambridge: Cambridge University Press.; abbreviated as TT, and cited by treatise and section number.

Panikkar, R. (1982), 'Is the Notion of Human Rights a Western Concept?', *Diogenes*, 120: 75–102.

Shimokawa, K. (2006), 'Locke's Concept of Property', in P. R. Anstey (ed.), *John Locke: Critical Assessments of Leading Philosophers*, Series II, vol. 1, 177–216, London: Routledge.

Simmons, A. J. (1992), *The Lockean Theory of Rights*, Princeton: Princeton University Press.

Simmons, A. J. (1994), 'Locke on the Death Penalty', *Philosophy*, 69 (270): 471–7.

Wellman, C. H. (2017), *Rights Forfeiture and Punishment*, Oxford: Oxford University Press.

Part III

Religion and toleration

7

Locke's harm argument and the largeness of toleration[1]

Kiyoshi Shimokawa

1 Introduction

In this chapter, I try to show that Locke is more tolerant than is usually thought by many commentators. To put it specifically, I want to show that Locke defended a rather extensive scope of toleration, which allowed for a peaceful coexistence of Jews, Muslims and pagans as well as all Christians, including Roman Catholics. He defended what he called the 'largeness' of toleration.[2] How did Locke do it? He defended it mainly by deploying a secular argument, which may be called 'the argument from the absence of harm' or 'the harm argument' for short. It is the argument which says that religious beliefs and practices ought to be tolerated within or beyond a political society *if they do not harm others*. Though the argument is largely neglected by Locke scholars, it deserves special notice, for it significantly expands what would otherwise be a much narrower scope of toleration.

This extensive scope of toleration alarmed Locke's opponent Jonas Proast. Proast acutely remarked that while the author of the *Letter* initially discussed the mutual toleration of Christians, he ended up defending the broader toleration. He said that the design of the author was to show that 'all the Religions and Sects in the World, that are but consistent with Civil Society, and ready to tolerate each other, ought everywhere to be equally tolerated and protected' (Proast 1984: 2). Proast was perceptive and accurate in saying this. But neither he nor any later commentator seems able to understand Locke's deployment of the harm argument. In what follows, I try to clarify how Locke developed it in *A Letter Concerning Toleration*.

By highlighting the way he developed it, I intend to achieve one primary objective. I aim to show how he expanded the scope of toleration which would have remained much narrower if he had relied solely on the other arguments available to him. Locke was able to go beyond Christianity to include non-Christian religions because he made use of the harm argument.[3] My intention is to propose an alternative to the dominant view, propounded by John Dunn among others, that Locke developed 'arguments for tolerating varieties of *Christian* belief and practice within a *Christian* state and society' (Dunn 1990: 19, emphasis added).[4] Locke's defence of toleration is clearly not restricted in this way, as we have already seen in Proast's reaction to the *Letter*. Dunn neglects some of what Locke actually said, and establishes too strong a connection between Christianity and his theory of toleration. Consequently, he makes Locke's theory irrelevant to our contemporary problem of religious liberty and freedom of expression, and pronounces it to be 'dead'. My argument proceeds in a contrary direction. In order to recover the continuing relevance of Locke's theory, I shall look at how extensive his scope of toleration actually was, and show that he defended that extensive scope by a secular argument which I have called the harm argument.

This chapter also has two subsidiary aims. First, I shall show that contrary to the common supposition that Locke wanted to exclude Roman Catholics, he took the harm argument seriously and maintained that they ought to be *included* like any other religious group *if they do not harm others*. Second, I shall reconsider why Locke placed one significant limit on toleration, that is, the belief in a deity. The real reason for the exclusion of atheists, as I shall show, is that Locke thought that their denial of a deity would necessarily cause *harm to others*. This makes the scope of toleration too narrow for us, but he delimited it by making use of the harm argument. This shows, at least, that he took the harm argument seriously.

2 Locke's four considerations

Let me begin with what is *not* the harm argument, namely, with Locke's other better-known arguments. By discussing those familiar arguments, I intend to show that they rather narrowly restrict the scope of toleration, in just the way Dunn supposed his theory did. In the *Letter*, Locke offers three 'Considerations' to explain why the magistrate ought not to use force to punish his subjects for their religion.[5] This means that Locke offers the considerations to explain why the magistrate has a duty of toleration towards his subjects.

Here I should point out that there is a significant connection between the use of force and toleration. To see this connection, we need to understand that toleration, as Locke sees it, essentially consists in the negation of force, or removing the force that is applied to what we disapprove of. As he puts it, 'Toleration is but the removing that force' (*Second Letter* 62).⁶ He never defined the term 'toleration' since his readers clearly understood it as an opposite of persecution, but the remark just quoted comes close to his own definition, or at least, what we regard as the negative or minimal definition of it. On this definition, to tolerate X is to remove force from X, or to refrain from applying force to X. Toleration, on this view, is the negation of intolerance or persecution, just as justice can be understood as the negation of injustice or the violation of rights. Since intolerance involves the use of force, it is possible to define 'toleration' minimally as the removal of force. This negative definition may appear strange to those recent commentators who are inclined to use the term 'toleration' in a more positive, extended sense.⁷ Careless readers of the opening paragraph of the *Letter*, where Locke discusses the mutual toleration of Christians, might also identify 'toleration' with 'charity'. It is clear, however, that Locke actually operates with the negative definition or something close to it.⁸ And it is also clear that he keeps a sharp conceptual distinction between 'force' (hence, intolerance) and 'love' (hence, charity). For he states that nobody can be a Christian 'without Charity', or 'without *that Faith which works, not by Force, but by Love*' (*Letter* 8). Locke keeps this conceptual distinction intact, while he also seems aware of the causal influence of charity over toleration. He notes that clergymen, in particular, should appeal to charity and meekness and not just to toleration or the mere removal of force.⁹

Now Locke is most concerned with a particular type of toleration, called 'civil' toleration. It is the removal of 'civil force', that is, the force of the magistrate (*Second Letter* 67). The 'purpose' of the *Letter*, he says, is 'plainly to defend toleration, exempt from all force; especially civil force, or the force of the magistrate' (*Second Letter* 67). The violence from our neighbours is bad enough, but the force from the head of the state is far worse. It can undermine the legal order of the whole society, and can systematically destroy the lives, liberties or possessions of a large number of subjects. Having understood these conceptual connections, we are in a position to affirm that Locke's three considerations are offered to explain why the magistrate has the duty of toleration over religious matters, that is, the duty to refrain from applying force to them.

What are those considerations? This is a matter of recent debate among scholars.¹⁰ As I interpret them, they are: (1) The magistrate is not 'committed',¹¹ either by God or 'by men',¹² to the care of their souls (*Letter* 13). (2) Given the nature and function of the understanding, neither the magistrate nor anyone else can effectively or appropriately change our belief by force (13–14). Such a change can be, and ought to be, brought about by 'light'¹³ rather than by compulsion. (3) Even if the magistrate's force could change our belief, it would bring about an absurd (hence, impossible) consequence of local, rather than universal, salvation (14–15).

These appear to be presented as three separate considerations, but a careful reading reveals that they are linked to Locke's concern about the ultimate purpose of religion, that is, the salvation of human souls. In stating the first consideration on the absence of commission, Locke claims that even if one may want to commit the care of his soul to any other agent, 'no man can so far abandon the care of his own *Salvation*, as blindly to leave it to the choice of any other [such as a magistrate]' (*Letter* 13; emphasis added). In stating the second consideration, Locke also links the inefficacy of force in changing our belief with that of achieving *salvation* and states that 'true and *saving Religion* consists in the inward Perswasion of the Mind' (13; emphasis added). And obviously, the third consideration directly relates to a feature of salvation. What is most important of all, Locke comes to state a fourth consideration on salvation, as '[t]he *Principal Consideration*' which 'absolutely determines this Controversie' (31) about the liberty of conscience. Here is what he says:

> Although the Magistrates Opinion in Religion be sound, and the way that he appoints be truly Evangelical, yet if I be not thoroughly perswaded thereof in my own mind, there will be no safety for me in following it. . . . I may grow rich by an Art that I take not delight in; I may be cured of some Disease by Remedies that I have not Faith in; but I cannot be saved by a Religion that I distrust, and by a Worship that I abhor. . . . Faith only, and inward Sincerity, are the things that procure acceptance with God. . . . Men cannot be forced to be saved whether they will or no. And therefore, when all is done, they [i.e. the subjects] must be left to their Consciences. (*Letter* 31–2)

This principal consideration may be called 'the salvation argument'. It says that the magistrate's use of force destroys the necessary conditions of salvation, that is, the full persuasion and inward sincerity of the mind. Locke seems to subjectivize the conditions at one point.¹⁴ But the real point of the argument is that the magistrate's use of outward force destroys the conditions of salvation because it is logically incompatible with the liberty of judgement which is presupposed by those conditions. A 'liberty' of judgement, which must accompany the conditions, is 'essentially necessary' for 'the End of all Religion' (33), that is, to please God and make salvation possible, but since the force is incompatible with the liberty, it makes that end unachievable. This ingenious argument is of the type which George Fletcher calls 'the logical argument against intervention'.¹⁵

So far we have seen Locke's four considerations. They can be treated as distinct arguments, and each can be developed further in different directions. But Locke himself treats the salvation argument as the principal argument that underpins the other arguments or provides the point of their convergence. If we focus on its centrality, it is plausible to treat Locke's theory as defending the toleration of Protestants. For it is closely linked to the Protestant doctrine of salvation which stresses the function of internal faith (*sola fide*) rather than external deeds or works. Locke's own doctrine of salvation is not presented in full in the *Letter*, but the general tone of his argument clearly stresses faith, persuasion and sincerity, rather than works.[16]

But if this is the case, it is also clear that Locke's salvation argument does not work well for the toleration of Roman Catholics, insofar as they hold that one is saved by one's works rather than faith. Nor does it work for Judaism, insofar as it requires the Jewish people to externally observe their laws for their salvation.[17] And it is not at all clear how the salvation argument is linked to pagan beliefs. Thus, as long as Locke relies on the salvation argument, the scope of toleration is confined to Protestants and remains very narrow.

In order to expand the scope, we might try to separate the first, second and third considerations from the salvation argument, and try to develop new independent arguments for the defence of a broader toleration. For instance, we might try to separate the second consideration from it, and argue that given the function of the understanding, its relation to truth and its independence from will, it is inappropriate for the magistrate to use force to change our belief about the truth of a doctrine.[18] But if this argument is carried to its logical conclusion, it would make possible a defence of the toleration of any belief or any expression of it, including an irreligious belief. This is not the strategy Locke takes in the *Letter*. He has no intention to defend the toleration of an irreligious belief. He is neither a Mill nor a Spinoza. What he does instead is to retain the salvation argument along with the other arguments and simply *add a fifth consideration* that is independent of any of those arguments.[19] This new consideration is what I called the harm argument, to which we now return.

3 The harm argument

3.1 The harm principle

The harm argument makes use of the harm principle which Locke adopts. He holds that the magistrate can legitimately use force to punish people only if they harm others. This is Locke's harm principle. Unlike Mill's, it only concerns 'physical force in the form of legal penalties', but not 'the moral coercion of public opinion' (Mill 1989: 13).

Locke's statement of the harm principle is found in his discussion of the inappropriateness of punishing sins. Granted that idolatry is a sin, he says that it does not follow that it ought to be punished. Here is what he says:

> If they said, it [i.e. a sin] were therefore to be avoided, the Inference were good. But it does not follow, that because it is a Sin, it ought therefore to be punished by the Magistrate. For it does not belong unto the Magistrate to make use of his Sword in Punishing every thing, indifferently, that he takes to be a Sin against God. Covetousness, Uncharitableness, Idleness, and many other things are sins, by the consent of all men, which yet no man ever said were to be punished by the Magistrate. (*Letter* 41)

Why is it that those sins are not punishable? The reason, Locke states, is 'because they are not prejudicial to other mens Rights, nor do they break the publick Peace of Societies' (*Letter* 41). Those sins do not harm or injure any particular neighbour, nor do they disturb the public peace of societies. Locke goes on to say that 'even the Sins of Lying, and Perjury, are no where punishable by Laws', except in the cases where we consider 'the Injury done unto Mens Neighbours, and to the Commonwealth' (41).[20]

Locke uses here two terms interchangeably, 'harm' (*damnum*, which originally meant a damage to someone's goods) and 'injury' (*injuria*). He means by them the violation of any right, regardless of its object. In this, he seems to follow in the footsteps of Pufendorf.[21] But in the *Letter*, Locke clearly thinks that the paradigm case of harm or injury is found in the violation of another's perfect, rather than imperfect, rights. By the 'perfect' rights I mean those rights which can be enforced at court or by arms, while the 'imperfect' ones are those moral claims which should be realized without recourse to force. The distinction goes back to Grotius at least. To use Locke's own terminology, one man can be said, paradigmatically, to harm or injure another man, when he violates another's *property*. 'Property' here means another's exclusive right of disposal over his person and his goods (i.e. his life, liberty and possessions).[22] This is Locke's terminology in the *Two Treatises*, and it is equivalent in meaning to what he calls 'civil interests' (*bona civilia*) in the *Letter*. So when Locke claims that the sins of lying and perjury do not injure our neighbours, he means that they do not violate their exclusive rights. When he talks about the injury to the commonwealth, he has in mind an attempt to do serious damage to the legal order, which protects the lives, liberties and possessions, or a consequent breakdown of that order.

3.2 Applications of the harm principle

Locke's harm argument is a result of applying the harm principle to three items, that is, speculative opinions, outward worship and practical opinions. In the case of 'Speculative Opinions', that is, those 'Articles of Faith' which 'terminate simply in the Understanding' (*Letter* 44), the harm argument takes the following form: the magistrate has no right to punish his subjects for their speculative opinions since they cannot by nature harm others. He says: 'The Magistrate ought not to forbid the Preaching or Professing of any Speculative Opinions in any Church; because they have no manner of relation to the Civil Rights of the Subjects' (44). In the case of outward worship, and 'Practical' opinions, that is, those which 'influence the Will and Manners' (44), he argues that the magistrate has no right to interfere with them because, and insofar as, they do not harm others. This argument is different from the first in that it not only offers the reason for toleration, but qualifies it by stating the limit of toleration.

Locke takes up the Roman Catholic doctrine of transubstantiation, together with a Jewish and a pagan speculative opinion:

> If a *Roman Catholick* (pontificius, EPIS 120) believe that to be really the Body of Christ, which another man calls Bread, he does no injury thereby to his Neighbour. If a *Jew* do not believe the New Testament to be the Word of God, he does not thereby alter any thing in mens Civil Rights. If a Heathen doubt of both Testaments, he is not therefore to be punished as a pernicious Citizen. (*Letter* 44)

The point is that the civil rights or 'properties' of the people are perfectly secure, even if those speculative opinions are expressed. 'I readily grant', says Locke, 'that these Opinions are false and absurd' (44). But the truth or falsity of the opinions does not matter. What counts is whether an opinion can do harm or injury to any neighbour or to the commonwealth. For 'the business of Laws' is 'not to provide for the Truth of Opinions, but for the Safety and Security of the Commonwealth, and of every particular mans Goods and Person' (44–5). We should note that Locke's claim about the toleration of speculative opinions is applicable to all religious groups, including Roman Catholics, Jews and pagans, and it is independent of their truth.

What does Locke say about the relationship of harm to various forms of outward worship? Ordinary forms of worship, which do not take away or diminish the lives, liberties or possessions of the subjects, are to be tolerated. But those peculiar forms of worship in which some congregations '*sacrifice Infants*' or '*lustfully pollute themselves in promiscuous Uncleanness*'[23] (*Letter* 37) ought not to be tolerated by the magistrate. The reason is because they clearly harm others in that they involve violations of the subjects' rights over their lives, bodies, health or liberty.[24] Locke puts the point in the following way: 'These things are not lawful in the ordinary course of life, nor in any private house' (37), so they are not lawful in religious worship either; therefore, they are punishable. But if someone lawfully kills his own calf at his home, he can do the same for a religious worship. In this case, the magistrate has no right to prohibit it by a law since there is 'no Injury done to any man, either in Life or Estate' (37). Thus any form of worship should be tolerated as long as it does no injury to anyone.

Locke extends the liberty of worship to those pagans who live in the new world, that is, native Americans. They practise what modern Europeans regard as idolatry. Locke claims that Christians in Europe have no right to punish them or wage wars against them for the purpose of rooting out what they take to be a sin.[25] Their form of religious worship is not punishable because it harms none of their neighbours or Christians.

Locke's defence of the liberty of worship rests not only on the harm principle but also on its impartial application. This becomes increasingly clear towards the end of the *Letter*. In its concluding part, he states that if the Roman way of worshipping God is permitted, the Genevan way should also be permitted. He says:

> The *Sum of all* we drive at is, *That every Man may enjoy the same Rights that are granted to others*. Is it permitted to worship God in the *Roman* manner? Let it be permitted to do it in the *Geneva* Form also. (*Letter* 57)

What Locke is claiming here is that the harm principle should be applied impartially to all religious groups. He initially applies the harm principle to all Christian sects and claims that they should have equal rights to religious worship, just as they have equal rights to their dwelling and trade. Then he goes on to extend this principle to other non-Christians:

> Nay if we may openly speak the Truth and as becomes one Man to another; neither *Pagan*, nor *Mahumetan*, nor *Jew*, ought to be excluded from the Civil Rights of the Commonwealth, because of his Religion. (*Letter* 58–9)

Here Locke affirms that pagans, Muslims and Jews should enjoy their civil rights in their lives, liberties and possessions. The magistrate has no right to punish them on account of their religion. The reason for including them, he says, is partly because '[t]he Gospel commands no such thing' as exclusion, and partly because 'the Commonwealth, which embraces indifferently all men that are honest, peaceable, and industrious, requires it not' (*Letter* 59). The latter contains the secular argument we have been seeking to recover. The key words here are 'indifferently' and 'peaceable', which mean 'impartially' and 'harmless'. So what Locke is claiming here is that we can include pagans, Muslims and Jews and indeed all religions in the world by impartially applying the harm principle to all, regardless of their religion.

It is clear from all this that Locke defends the equal toleration of all religions, rather than the toleration of any particular religion or sect. In the Preface added to the English translation of the *Letter*, Popple speaks of the 'equal and impartial liberty' for all. Though commentators often stress that Popple and Locke differ in their opinions on toleration, this particular statement of Popple's is a faithful representation of Locke's own position. In defending the impartial liberty, Locke is putting into use his own conception of justice, according to which all human beings ought to be governed by one and the same law, and judged by impartial judges.[26] We should also note that Locke's reference to Muslims is not incidental but is supported by a degree of knowledge and concern which he cherished about them.[27]

Locke applies the harm principle to practical opinions in a similar way. He considers the absence or presence of harm to others as the criterion for judging whether a particular practical opinion should be tolerated. In the next section, we will examine what Locke says about the limits of toleration, and see that he regards as punishable those practical opinions which are pernicious to civil society and are bound to harm the lives, liberties or possessions of its members. Before we do so, however, it is important to remind ourselves that religion, as Locke understands it, consists of a set of speculative opinions which cannot by nature harm others, and those forms of outward worship and practical opinions which are harmless to others. People are 'of the same Religion', he says, when they have 'one and the same Rule of Faith and Worship' (*Letter* 63). In saying this, Locke supposes that the religion in question consists of those opinions and practices which are peaceful. It does not contain, within itself, any of the dangerous practical opinions which cause harm to others. Punishment, and any form of violence to the person or goods of another, involves the use of force which is incompatible with religion. As we are about to consider Locke's view of the possible connections between religion and dangerous practical opinions, it is worth stressing that he holds the view that *religion as such is a peaceful activity* and *has nothing to do with the use of force*. This view is found in his remarks on how Christians should behave. Locke states that 'True Religion' is instituted for 'the regulating of Mens Lives according to the Rules of Vertue and Piety' (*Letter* 8), and not for the establishing of an empire over others. He adds that a true Christian should 'make War upon his own Lusts and Vices', and seek 'Holiness of Life, Purity of Manners, and Benignity and Meekness of Spirit' (8). And the clergymen who preach 'the Gospel of Peace' (25) should 'admonish' their hearers of 'the Duties of Peace and Good-will towards all men', the erroneous as well as the orthodox, and 'exhort all men' (24) to charity and meekness as well as to toleration. Locke famously states that a church is 'a free and voluntary Society' for 'the public worshipping of God' (15). Such a church is 'a thing absolutely separate and distinct from the Commonwealth' (24) in that the latter, unlike the former, involves the use of force as its characteristic method of obtaining outward conformity.

4 The limits Locke places on toleration: Further applications of the harm principle

We now consider what sorts of practical opinions, churches and individuals Locke takes to be harmful to civil society and its members. He considers two types of practical opinions, one type of church, and one type of individual, to be harmful or dangerous to civil society and its members. For that reason, he excludes them from toleration. They are subject to the magistrate's punishment.

The first type of dangerous practical opinions is a set of 'Opinions contrary to human Society, or to those moral Rules which are necessary to the preservation of Civil Society' (*Letter* 49–50). Locke gives the following examples: 'Men are not obliged to keep their Promise'; 'Princes may be dethroned by those that differ from them in Religion'; and 'the Dominion of all things belongs only to themselves' (50). Locke observes, however, that no sect would be so insane as to teach these opinions openly since they plainly show that they undermine the foundations of society.

The second set of dangerous practical opinions is of a more subtle kind, and those who profess them 'arrogate to themselves' certain special privileges over others. For example, they claim that '*Faith is not to be kept with Hereticks*'; that '*Kings excommunicated forfeit their Crowns and Kingdoms*' (*Letter* 50); or that '*Dominion is founded in Grace*' (51). By professing these opinions, a particular group of people try to monopolize the right to break promises or to depose kings, or they lay claim to the possession of all things. They have 'no right to be tolerated by the Magistrate'. For they are 'ready upon any occasion to seise the Government, and possess themselves of the Estates and Fortunes of their Fellow-Subjects' (51),[28] that is, to injure the government and its subjects. Besides, they are partial to themselves and neglect the mutual duty of toleration.

Of the three concrete examples offered here, the first two, on heretics and excommunication, were widely believed, at least by Protestants, to be the views held by Catholics. The third view on dominion and grace is attributed by some scholars to Puritans alone, but others suggest that it could also be attributed to Catholics.[29] Thus, these examples seem to show that Locke intended to exclude Catholics. In fact, as Adam Wolfson has pointed out, the exclusion of Catholics has been a constant theme in the Locke scholarship for more than forty years, from Gough and Cranston, to Dunn and Ashcraft, and to Vernon and Wootton.[30] Scholars committed to this view stress Locke's practical aim of defending Protestantism in England against the threat of Catholicism. Richard Ashcraft, who studied anti-popery sentiments in seventeenth-century England, made a strong indictment against Locke. He says that the *Letter* 'represents an attempt both to occupy the higher ground of principles and at the same time to rake up the most basic antipopery prejudices and fears' (Ashcraft 1986: 498). He goes on to claim that Locke defended 'the application of force to Catholics as a means by which they might be "converted" to the truth of Protestantism', and that the *Letter* 'actually contributed to the efforts to foster and justify the anti-Catholic fear shared by his countrymen', which had 'manifested itself as a national hysteria during the "popish plot" crisis a few years earlier' (Ashcraft 1996: 207).

Here I think we need more light than heat. We should carefully consider what status Roman Catholics enjoy within Locke's theory of toleration. In my view, it is not safe to infer from the *Letter* that Locke simply intended to exclude Roman Catholics from toleration.[31] As we have seen, he suggested that the magistrate should tolerate the Catholic doctrine of transubstantiation and their form of outward worship. What is more important, he consistently defends the thesis that the magistrate ought *not* to punish anyone *on account of religion*. As Locke sums up his own position, 'in *punishing others for religion*, the magistrate misapplies the force he has in his hands, and so goes beyond right, beyond the limits of his power' (*Second Letter* 135; emphasis added). It follows that if anyone is punishable at all, it is not because he has a particular religious belief or engages in a particular religious worship, but because he has or professes non-religious, dangerous practical opinions which are bound to harm others. Instead of claiming that Locke intended to exclude Roman Catholics, we should treat him as excluding *all* groups that hold and profess those dangerous opinions. The condition for inclusion is the same for all religions: *that they do not harm others*.

Of course, those dangerous, practical opinions which Locke specified can *get combined*, under some circumstances, with a particular religious group such as Roman Catholics. If that happens, they are tolerated only if the dangerous opinions are renounced by that group,[32] or their religion is securely separated from the influence of those opinions. This is a case for conditional toleration, one which is conditioned by the harm principle. Again, it applies not only to Catholics but to all religious groups. Some scholars may be inclined to connect Locke with the 'anti-popery fear' that Ashcraft stressed. But it is more reasonable to treat Locke's position in the *Letter* as one calling for a renunciation of those dangerous practical opinions on the part of Catholics or for a separation of their religion from the influence of those opinions. In fact, Locke began to think about the separation of one from the other as early as 1667, more than two decades before the publication of the *Letter*.

With regard to the separation issue, there is an important passage of *An Essay Concerning Toleration* where Locke observes that as evident among Roman Catholics, men often mix 'their religious worship, & speculative opinions' with 'other doctrines [which are] absolutely destructive to the society wherein they live' (Locke 2006: 284; Locke 1997: 146). He claims that those who blend them 'ought not to be tolerated by the magistrate in the exercise of their religion', unless he can be 'secur' [*sic*], that he can allow one part [i.e. their religion], without the spreading of the other [i.e. those destructive doctrines]', and that 'the propagation of these dangerous opinions may be separated from their religious worship' (Locke 2006: 284–5; 1997: 146). In 1667 Locke thought that it would be 'very hard' (Locke 2006: 284–5; 1997: 146) to secure this separation. It is not entirely clear whether he thinks the separation relatively easy at the time of writing the *Letter*.[33] But there is reason to believe that he continues to hold that *if their religion can be securely separated* from the influence of those dangerous opinions, they have a right to be tolerated by the magistrate. For in the *Letter*, Locke is deeply committed to the view that people should be punished for the harm they cause, and not for their religion.

The same commitment is found in a recently discovered manuscript of Locke's, entitled 'Reasons for Tolerating Papists Equally with Others'.[34] In this manuscript, which Walmsley and Waldmann take to date from 1667–8 and provide clues to the compositional history of *An Essay Concerning Toleration*, Locke states that there are reasons for tolerating Roman Catholics, while also holding that there are reasons for excluding them from toleration. The most important reason for exclusion is stated at the end of the manuscript:

> it is not the difference of their opinion in religion, or of their ceremonys in worship; but their dangerous and factious tenents in reference to the state. *which are blended with & make a part of their religion* that excludes them from the benefit of toleration who would thinke it fit to tolerate either presbiterian or

Independant, if they made it a part of their religion to pay an implicit subjection to a forraigne infallible power? (Walmsley and Waldmann 2019: 1115; emphasis in the original)

Here Locke repeats the claim that harm to others as well as to the state, which is caused by the *blending* of their religion and their dangerous practical opinions, is the real reason for excluding Roman Catholics.

Let us now return to the argument of the *Letter*. Locke's concern about the impossibility of separating religion from the influence of dangerous practical opinions manifests itself in the *Letter* when he places the third limit on toleration. A church has no right to be tolerated by the magistrate, he says, if 'all those who enter into it, do thereby, *ipso facto*, deliver themselves up to the Protection[35] and Service of another Prince' (*Letter* 52). It is useless for anyone 'to profess himself to be a *Mahumetan* only in his Religion, but in every thing else a faithful Subject to a Christian Magistrate', if he acknowledges himself 'bound to yield blind obedience to the *Mufti* of *Constantinople*', who in turn obeys the Ottoman Emperor (52). Some scholars have wondered whether this limit really relates to Muslims or Catholics,[36] but the exclusion of any particular religion is not Locke's concern. He should be seen as stating the general principle that if a church in one commonwealth is absolutely subordinate to the power of another commonwealth, hence, *inseparable* from its influence, then the church has no right to toleration because it is bound to cause harm to that commonwealth and its members.

It is clear from all this that toleration is not extended to those who hold or express the two sorts of dangerous practical opinions, or to the type of church that is absolutely subordinate to a foreign power. It is also clear that Roman Catholics, insofar as they are treated as a peaceful, religious group, can be included within the scope of toleration, while no religious group is to be tolerated if they inseparably connect their religion with any of the dangerous opinions.

The last limit Locke places on toleration pertains to the particular kind of practical opinion known as atheism or to the particular group of individuals called 'atheists'. Atheists are excluded from toleration, as Locke explicitly states that '[t]hose are not at all to be tolerated who *deny the Being of a God*' (*Letter* 52). We should keep in mind that he included pagans in general and native Americans in particular. So if he is to be consistent, 'a God' (*numen*) should be taken in the broad sense of any deity which we may find in monotheism or polytheism. But it is doubtful whether Locke is perfectly consistent here. The chief reason he offers for the exclusion of atheists is that 'Promises, Covenants, and Oaths, which are the Bonds of Humane Society, can have no hold' upon atheists (52–3). This suggests that he presupposes that there is one omnipotent God (*Deus*), who makes the law of nature and has a right to punish any transgression of it. Leaving aside the apparent lack of clarity, Locke is claiming here that those atheists can break their promises, and so forth, at any moment, whenever it suits their own interest. They do so because they have no faith in God, his power of punishment or eternal life.[37] Locke also stresses that the taking away of God (*Deus*), 'even in thought', 'dissolves all' (53). For our purpose, it is important to see the real reason which underlies Locke's exclusion of atheists. The underlying reason is to be found in the *harm* which is caused by the dissolution of the bonds of human society. The dissolution necessarily takes place according to Locke, because those untrustworthy atheists who do not fear God's punishment break their promises, and so forth, at any moment, whenever it suits their interests.

Today we are ready to point out that there are quite a few atheists who are harmless, peace-loving and trustworthy, or who respect the rights of others. Locke failed to see it, but for our purposes it is important to note that he did apply the harm principle consistently. For if we grant the premise that atheists can break the bonds of human society at any moment, or another one about the disastrous consequence of taking away God 'even in thought', it follows that either their actions or their atheistic belief always causes harm to others.

However, if we remove those unwarranted premises, we can use the harm principle for a contrary purpose, that is, to expand the scope of toleration to include atheists. This is actually what Thomas Jefferson did. He closely studied the text of Locke's *Letter*, and took over the harm argument to make the following provocative statement: 'But it does me no injury for my neighbor to say there are twenty gods or *no god*. It neither picks my pocket nor breaks my leg' (emphasis added).[38] By this simple move, Jefferson used the harm principle to include atheists. This is a radical use of Locke's harm principle. It brought about the further expansion of the scope of toleration, which Locke had never intended.

5 Conclusion

It goes beyond the scope of this chapter to evaluate Locke's harm argument. No doubt, it requires critical scrutiny. The argument appears to ignore, to a certain extent, some of the distinctions which are important for the evaluation of various forms of liberty of conscience or freedom of expression – those between holding and expressing opinions, between opinions and actions, between the probability of harm and the necessity of it, or between a remote, unspecific danger and a 'clear and present danger'.[39] So it is plausible to suggest that the argument needs further refinement as well as critical scrutiny.

But I hope to have shown that Locke not only presented four 'Considerations' but developed the harm argument with the aid of the impartial application of the harm principle, in order to defend the toleration of all peaceful, religious groups, that is, Christians (Catholics as well as Protestants) and non-Christians (polytheists like native Americans, as well as monotheists like Muslims and Jews). The scope of toleration is clearly not restricted to Christians or Protestants. After all, Locke is more tolerant than has been generally allowed. He only excluded those who harm others. The harmful people may or may not be Catholics; they can be Protestants or non-Christians. The exclusion of atheists, or of those whom Locke thinks necessarily harm others, rests on what we regard as unwarranted premises. But like the exclusion of other individuals, this exclusion is a logical consequence of applying the harm principle to the problem of toleration.

Notes

1 Earlier versions of this chapter were read at Gakushuin University in December 2016 and June 2018, and at the John Locke Conference held at Mansfield College in July 2018. I am grateful for the comments received from Peter Anstey, James Harris, Luisa Simonutti and J. C. Walmsley. I would also like to acknowledge that this chapter is an updated English version of the Japanese article 'Locke Kan'yōron ni okeru Kigai no Fuzai to Kan'yō no Shatei' (The Absence of Harm and the Scope of Toleration in Locke's Theory of Toleration), which appeared in *Jinbun*, 17 (2018): 7–28, published by the Research Institute for Humanities at Gakushuin University.
2 The 'largeness' of toleration is the expression Locke used in his reply to Proast: 'The first thing you seem startled at, in the author's letter, is the largeness of the toleration he proposes' (*Second Letter* 62).
3 Marshall notes that in *A Philosophical Commentary*, Pierre Bayle also included Jews, Muslims and pagans within the scope of toleration. See Marshall (2006: 593).
4 See Dunn (1990: chap. 2), entitled 'What Is Living and What Is Dead in the Political Theory of John Locke?'.
5 The 'subjects' (subditi) are those who are subject to, or governed by, the laws of a political society. The term, as Locke uses it, does not imply the existence of a monarch. The 'magistrate' (magistratus) is the supreme legislative agent, called the

'Legislative' in the *Two Treatises* (TT II. 132, 134–6, 138, 149–51), who exercises power over his subjects, independently of any particular form of government. See Locke's definition of 'magistrate' in *Two Tracts on Government* (Locke 1967: 125).

6. Locke offers what we may regard as an approximation to the minimal definition of toleration when he makes the following statement: 'Force, you allow, is improper to convert men to any religion. Toleration is but the removing that force' (*Second Letter* 62).

7. An example of this extended sense is found, for instance, in Peter Nicholson's discussion. See Nicholson (1985).

8. I say 'something close to it' here because Locke could easily add the idea of peaceful coexistence to his minimal definition, and arrive at a slightly expanded definition.

9. See my comment, in the last paragraph of section 3.2, on the role of the clergymen who preach 'the Gospel of Peace'.

10. Vernon (1997), Wolfson (2010) and Tate (2016).

11. The Latin word is 'demandatur' in EPIS 66, and the sense involved here is that of 'entrusted'. Locke seems to have in mind the idea of trust, which figures prominently in the *Two Treatises*.

12. The Latin is 'ab hominibus' (by men) in EPIS 66. In Popple's translation it is rendered as 'by the *Consent of the People*' (*Letter* 13).

13. 'Lux' in EPIS 68; 'Light and Evidence' in *Letter* 14.

14. He says that if we 'cram a Medicine down a sick Mans Throat', 'his particular Constitution will be sure to turn [it] into Poison' (*Letter* 32).

15. On Fletcher's account, no coercive agents can intervene to bring about the desired behaviour in question, because 'in the nature of things, individuals must do it on their own, and coercive threats – from the state or anybody – prevent (or tend to prevent) individuals from acting with internal motivation'. See Fletcher (1996: 162).

16. When Locke does present his own doctrine of salvation in *The Reasonableness of Christianity*, he offers what seems to be a significantly modified version of the *sola fide* doctrine. There Locke stresses that one is justified by faith, or by believing the proposition 'Jesus is the Messiah' to be true (*Reasonableness* 19–22, 32–3), yet he adds that another condition of 'repentance' needs to be fulfilled if one is to be saved (*Reasonableness* 110–64, 131–2). Whether or not this amounts to the abandonment of the *sola fide* doctrine, or how it relates to the salvation argument in the *Letter*, is an interesting issue that I cannot pursue here. For a discussion of the roles of faith and repentance in the *Reasonableness*, see Keisuke Takei's account in Chapter 8, Section 4.3 of this volume.

17. See Fletcher (1996: 161), though he goes on to qualify his view about Judaism.

18. An argument of this kind could be reconstructed out of some passages in the *Essay* and *Of the Conduct of the Understanding* in Locke (1823, 3: 203–89). For this, see Shimokawa (2000: 28–32 and 48–51).

19 On the account provided in this chapter, Locke's *Letter* provides *five* considerations or arguments for the magistrate's duty of toleration. Those are primary arguments, but there are other subsidiary arguments offered in it. One of them concerns the fallibility of our judgement and our responsibility to take risks, while the other makes use of the analogy between the care of souls and that of possessions. For these subsidiary arguments, see Shimokawa (2000: 33–4, 51–2). We may also find other arguments outside of *A Letter Concerning Toleration*, but those are not the concern of this chapter, either. The present chapter is concerned only with the main arguments for toleration which Locke presents in the *Letter*.

20 Popple's translation does not fully capture the sense of directedness, attempt or threat. The original Latin is 'intentata vel rei publicae vel vicino iniuria' (EPIS 114). This is translated by Gough as 'the threat of injury to the commonwealth or to a man's neighbour' (EPIS 115), and by Silverthorne as 'an attempt to do harm to the commonwealth or a neighbour' (Locke 2010b: 28).

21 Pufendorf (1995, 3.1.3).

22 For a detailed analysis of Locke's concept of property, see Shimokawa (2006).

23 Popple seems to exaggerate here. The Latin text says 'in promiscua stupra ruere', which Gough translates as 'plunge into promiscuous unchastity' (EPIS 108/109).

24 We should note, however, that it is not entirely clear from the text of the *Letter* on what grounds Locke really thought of the promiscuous sexual relations as punishable. The context seems to make it fairly clear that it has something to do with the harm or injury of one kind or another. In *Letter* 37, n. 86, Goldie states that 'Locke takes for granted forbidding sexual immorality is a proper role for civil governments'. See also his explanatory note in Locke (2016: 187). The issue, however, deserves a more careful examination. For a detailed examination of Locke's view of the so-called 'sexual immoralities' and the role of the state, see Numao's discussion in Chapter 9 of this volume.

25 *Letter* 40.

26 For Locke's concept of justice, see Shimokawa (2003).

27 Behind his personal acquaintance with Islam lies the historical fact that England maintained a friendly relationship with the Ottoman Empire from the Elizabethan era onwards, because it fought a war with Spain. Quite a few Englishmen knew from travel literature that the religion of Islam was tolerant towards other religions. Edward Bagshaw referred to the status of Muslims in England to argue for the toleration of Protestant dissenters in the post-Restoration era. Henry Stubbe wrote an epoch-making work on Islam, *The Originall and Progress of Mahometanism*, which shows that Islamic theology contains at its foundation religious pluralism. Stubbe and Locke also had a common Orientalist teacher in Oxford named Edward Pococke. For these and other interesting pieces of information, see Matar (1999, 2015).

28 Popple's translation slightly diverges from the Latin original. In EPIS 132/133, 'data occasione reipublicae jura et civium libertatem ac bona invasuros'; 'given the opportunity, they will attack the laws of the commonwealth and the liberty and property of the citizens'.
29 See Gough's attribution of it to the Fifth Monarchy Men in note 27 in EPIS 157. For Goldie's attribution of it to Catholics as well as Puritans, see *Letter* 23, n. 50.
30 Wolfson (2010: 11).
31 Unlike other scholars, Jeremy Waldron propounds the view that there is no textual basis in the *Letter* for the exclusion of Catholics as such. See also Waldron (2002: 218–23). I agree with Waldron, but his position needs strengthening. So I try to explain Locke's position in the following paragraphs, in terms of his consistent application of the harm principle.
32 With respect to the renunciation of the dangerous opinions, we should note that there is a draft of an oath (*c.* 1674, not in Locke's hand, but endorsed 'Papists Test') containing the doctrines which Catholic priests must renounce. See 'The Particular Test for Priests' in Locke (1997: 222–4).
33 Waldron holds that Locke 'evidently' comes to think the separation easier, but he does not provide any evidence for this. See Waldron (2002: 223).
34 Walmsley and Waldmann (2019: 1093–115).
35 In EPIS 134/5: 'allegiance', rather than 'protection', is used for 'obedientiam'.
36 Ashcraft (1986: 504) and Marshall (2006: 597).
37 See Locke's comment on 'a Christian' and 'a Hobbist' in *Essay* I. iii. 5: 'If a Christian, who has the view of Happiness and Misery in another Life, be asked why a Man must keep his Word, he will *give* this as a *Reason*: Because God, who has the Power of eternal Life and Death, requires it of us.' But 'if a *Hobbist* be asked why; he will answer; Because the Publick requires it, and the *Leviathan* will punish you, if you do not'. The prudential reasoning involved in the Hobbist's answer suggests that the atheist breaks his promise if it suits his own interest.
38 See Jefferson (1977: 210) (Query XVII Religion).
39 This well-known phrase is derived from Oliver Wendell Holmes Jr. See Holmes (2010: 221–3).

References

Ashcraft, R. (1986), *Revolutionary Politics and Locke's Two Treatises of Government*, Princeton: Princeton University Press.
Ashcraft, R. (1996), 'Religion and Lockean Natural Rights', in I. Bloom, J. P. Martin and W. L. Proudfoot (eds), *Religious Diversity and Human Rights*, 195–212, New York: Columbia University Press.

Bayle, P. (2005), *A Philosophical Commentary on These Words of the Gospel, Luke 14: 23, "Compel Them to Come In, that My House May Be Full,"* eds J. Kilcullen and C. Kukathas, Indianapolis: Liberty Fund. First published 1708.
Dunn, J. (1990), *Interpreting Political Responsibility*, Cambridge: Polity Press.
Fletcher, G. (1996), 'The Instability of Toleration', in D. Heyd (ed.), *Toleration: An Elusive Virtue*, 158–72, Princeton: Princeton University Press.
Holmes, O. W. (2010), *The Fundamental Holmes*, ed. R. K. L. Collins, Cambridge: Cambridge University Press.
Jefferson, T. (1977), *Notes on the State of Virginia*, in M. D. Peterson (ed.), *The Portable Thomas Jefferson*, 23–232, London: Penguin Books.
Locke, J. (1823), *The Works of John Locke*, 10 vols, London: T. Tegg.
Locke, J. (1823a), *A Second Letter Concerning Toleration*, in *The Works of John Locke*, vol. 6, 61–137, London: T. Tegg; abbreviated as *Second Letter*.
Locke, J. (1967), *Two Tracts on Government*, ed. and trans. P. Abrams, Cambridge: Cambridge University Press.
Locke, J. (1968), *Epistola de Tolerantia, A Letter on Toleration*, ed. R. Klibansky, trans. J. W. Gough, Oxford: Clarendon Press; abbreviated as EPIS.
Locke, J. (1975), *An Essay concerning Human Understanding*, ed. P. H. Nidditch, Oxford: Clarendon Press; abbreviated as *Essay*.
Locke, J. (1988), *Two Treatises of Government*, ed. P. Laslett, Cambridge: Cambridge University Press; abbreviated as TT, and cited by treatise and section number.
Locke, J. (1997), *Political Essays*, ed. M. Goldie, Cambridge: Cambridge University Press.
Locke, J. (1999), *The Reasonableness of Christianity*, ed. J. C. Higgins-Biddle, Oxford: Clarendon Press; abbreviated as *Reasonableness*.
Locke, J. (2006), *An Essay Concerning Toleration and Other Writings on Law and Politics, 1667–1683*, ed. J. R. Milton and P. Milton, Oxford: Clarendon Press.
Locke, J. (2010a), *A Letter Concerning Toleration and Other Writings*, ed. M. Goldie, Indianapolis: Liberty Fund; abbreviated as *Letter*.
Locke, J. (2010b), *Locke on Toleration*, ed. R. Vernon, trans. M. Silverthorne, Cambridge: Cambridge University Press.
Locke, J. (2016), *The Second Treatise of Government and a Letter Concerning Toleration*, ed. M. Goldie, Oxford: Oxford University Press.
Marshall, J. (2006), *John Locke, Toleration and Early Enlightenment Culture*, Cambridge: Cambridge University Press.
Matar, N. (1999), 'The Toleration of Muslims in Renaissance England: Practice and Theory', in J. C. Laursen (ed.), *Religious Toleration: 'The Variety of Rites' from Cyrus to Defoe*, 127–46, New York: St. Martin's Press.
Matar, N. (2015), 'England and Religious Plurality: Henry Stubbe, John Locke and Islam', in C. Methuen, A. Spicer and J. Wolffe (eds), *Christianity and Religious Plurality*, 181–203, Rochester, NY: The Boydell Press.
Mill, J. S. (1989), *On Liberty and Other Writings*, ed. S. Collini, Cambridge: Cambridge University Press.

Nicholson, P. (1985), 'Toleration as a Moral Ideal', in J. Horton and S. Mendus (eds), *Aspects of Toleration*, 158–73, London: Methuen.

Proast, J. (1984), *The Argument of the Letter Concerning Toleration, Briefly Consider'd and Answer'd* (1690), reprinted with Proast's *A Third Letter Concerning Toleration* (1691) and *A Second Letter to the Author of the Three Letters for Toleration* (1704), New York: Garland.

Pufendorf, S. (1995), *De Jure Naturae et Gentium*, 2 vols, vol. 1: Reproduction of the edition of 1688, and vol., 2: English translation by C. H. Oldfather and W. A. Oldfather; repr. of the 1934 edn; Buffalo, NY: William S. Hein.

Shimokawa, K. (2000), *Jon Rokku no Jiyūshugi Seijitetsugaku* (The Liberal Political Philosophy of John Locke), Nagoya: The University of Nagoya Press.

Shimokawa, K (2003), 'Locke's Concept of Justice', in P. R. Anstey (ed.), *The Philosophy of John Locke: New Perspectives*, 61–85, London: Routledge.

Shimokawa, K. (2006), 'Locke's Concept of Property', in P. R. Anstey (ed.), *John Locke: Critical Assessments of Leading Philosophers*, Series II, vol. 1, 177–216, London: Routledge.

Tate, J. W. (2016), *Liberty, Toleration and Equality*, New York: Routledge.

Vernon, R. (1997), *The Career of Toleration*, Montreal and Kingston: McGill-Queens University Press.

Waldron, J. (2002), *God, Locke, and Equality*, Cambridge: Cambridge University Press.

Walmsley, J. C. and F. Waldmann (2019), 'John Locke and the Toleration of Catholics: A New Manuscript', *The Historical Journal*, 62 (4): 1093–115. doi:10.1017/S0018246X19000207

Wolfson, A. (2010), *Persecution or Toleration*, Lanham, MD: Lexington Books.

Salvation and reasonableness in Locke's *Reasonableness of Christianity*[1]

Keisuke Takei

1 Introduction

John Locke began addressing political and religious problems when he wrote *Two Tracts on Government* (*c.* 1660–2). His aim in this work was to establish a peaceful and stable social order in England after the civil wars had created so much turmoil. One of the prominent features of the work is the way he made use of the contrast which he drew between what is inward and what is outward. In particular, Locke was able to justify the obedience of subjects to their governor, on the one hand, and their liberty of conscience, on the other, by relying on the distinction he made between their outward behaviour and their inward belief.[2]

Following that work, Locke took a more liberal position on toleration and, as we know from his *An Essay Concerning Toleration* (1667), he discussed the scope of toleration at length. In *An Essay Concerning Toleration*, he classified 'the opinions & actions of men' into the following three categories: (1) 'all puerly speculative opinions & Divine worship', (2) 'all practicall opinions & actions in matters of indifferency' and (3) 'morall virtues & vices' (Locke 2006: 271). The first sort of opinions and worship have 'an absolute & universall right to toleration' because they do not concern 'government or society at all' (Locke 2006: 271). The second sort of practical opinions and actions 'have a title also to toleration' unless they 'doe not tend to the disturbance of the state' or 'doe not cause greater inconveniences, then advantages to the community' (Locke 2006: 276). As for the third sort, moral virtues and vices, if they could 'be seperated from the relation they have to the weale of the publike, and cease to be a meanes to setle or disturbe mens peace & proprietys', 'they would then become only the private & super-politicall concernment between god & a mans soule'. In that case, the magistrate's authority 'is not to interpose' (Locke 2006: 281).

To sum up, all inner beliefs (together with peaceful forms of divine worship) become the object of toleration because they belong to the inner world. In contrast, all outward actions, including the acts of expressing opinions, can be tolerated unless they do harm to society. In his *Essay Concerning Toleration* of 1667, Locke extended the range of toleration further than he had done in his *Two Tracts on Government*. Locke continued to discuss the problem of toleration, and he argued that we should extend toleration to people of all persuasions provided that they do not disturb the peace and order of civil society. This is one of the central claims he made in *A Letter Concerning Toleration* (1689).

It appears, however, that Locke developed his argument in the direction of connecting inward belief and outward behaviour in *The Reasonableness of Christianity* (1695), which is one of the most important works from Locke's later years. As I show herein, here he described Jesus as an exemplar who expressed the deity which was inside him through his outward behaviour, that is, his miracles and perfect obedience to the Law of God, without disturbing the social order. How should we understand this example of Jesus? There are at least two possible ways of interpreting the meaning of Jesus's life in *The Reasonableness of Christianity*.

The first possible interpretation is that Locke used it to defend toleration. According to Loconte, '[t]he example of Jesus – the supreme embodiment of divine love in Christian theology – was a recurring motif among the reformers' (Loconte 2014: 20). He explains that 'Locke was thinking seriously about the Biblical basis for toleration' while writing *The Reasonableness of Christianity*. Then he claims that Locke tried to justify toleration by showing 'Jesus Christ as the exemplar of toleration' (Loconte 2014: 183).[3] The second interpretation is that Locke used the example of Jesus to show what true Christianity is like, or what it is like to accept a religion that was closely connected with morality and love. Loconte also points out that Locke looked to 'the example of Jesus' and contrasted 'Christ's teaching about true worship', that is, what people were required by God to worship, 'with ritualistic religion' (Loconte 2014: 189).[4]

Although I cannot examine in detail the plausibility of each of the two interpretations, I should state that the first loses its plausibility once we understand that Locke minimally defines toleration as a matter of removing the use of force, in contrast to an act of charity or love,[5] and that his theory of toleration, as we have seen above with reference to his *Essay Concerning Toleration* of 1667, rests upon whether the opinions and actions of men are harmful to society. The second interpretation, by contrast, looks like a more promising candidate because Locke does stress, as we will see, that Christ accepts all the duties of morality embodied in the Old Testament, while he also inculcates teachings of love in the simplest possible manner. So I would like to take up the second position and consider the argument of *The Reasonableness of Christianity* in detail from that perspective, with a view to clarifying the sense of reasonableness Locke tried to convey to his readers.

I begin by explaining the historical contexts of *The Reasonableness of Christianity*, and then summarize some of the previous studies of this book and locate my own approach in Lockean studies. After that, I analyse Locke's theory of salvation in *The Reasonableness of Christianity* in detail from four viewpoints. First, I look at Locke's account of Adam's fall because this provides the foundation of his theory of salvation. Second, I examine the relationship between 'the Law of Works' and 'the Law of Faith', and clarify the meanings of 'repentance' and 'faith'. Both of them form the core of Locke's theory of salvation. Third, I confirm that believing that Jesus is the Messiah (Christ) is the only article of faith that is necessary for salvation and show that Locke developed his argument to link his inward belief with his outward behaviour. Fourth, I examine how Locke described Jesus's mission and show that the practical example of Jesus is important in Locke's theory of salvation. The reason is that it brings ordinary people to believe in Jesus as the Messiah and teaches them to obey his commands, both of which lead them to salvation. To come right to the point, I claim that Locke tried to show that people as rational creatures could understand true Christianity by reading the story of Jesus's life.[6] After analysing Locke's theory of salvation, I consider how his contemporaries criticized *The Reasonableness of Christianity*, and discuss his intentions with a view to clarifying the sense of reasonableness he tried to convey to readers.

2 Historical contexts of the *Reasonableness*

In general, two theological controversies are often mentioned as historical contexts for *The Reasonableness of Christianity*.[7] The first is the so-called Trinitarian Controversy, which is a debate within the Anglican Church that resulted from the Unitarian theologian Stephen Nye's *A Brief History of the Unitarians, Called Also Socinians* (1687). In this book, Nye overviewed the history of anti-Trinitarian doctrine and claimed that Trinitarians corrupted authentic Christianity.[8] However, William Sherlock, who became dean of St Paul's in 1691, tried to refute this work by publishing *A Vindication of the Doctrine of the Holy and Ever Blessed Trinity, and the Incarnation of the Son of*

God (1690).⁹ These two men mainly continued pursuing the debate over the doctrine of the Trinity. The second is the controversy over justification between strict and moderate Calvinists in 1690, which arose due to the republication of *Christ Alone Exalted* by the Antinomian Tobias Crisp (Tobias himself had died, and his son, Samuel Crisp, republished this work). They argued over justification by faith.¹⁰ According to Timothy Cooper, Richard Baxter, who is known as a moderate Puritan, was astonished by the republication of this book because he had spent a lifetime trying to remove Crisp's influence. He was alarmed at a renewed Antinomian threat, so he published three works to refute Crispianism.¹¹

Locke wrote, in his *A Second Vindication of the Reasonableness of Christianity, &c.*, about this controversy as follows:

> The Beginning of the Year in which it was Published, the Controversie that made so much noise and heat amongst some of the Dissenters, coming one Day accidentally into my Mind, drew me by degrees into a stricter and more through Enquiry into the Question about Justification. (Locke 2012: 34)

Although Locke did not refer directly to the Trinitarian Controversy, he owned some of the main books published in the same period and left plenty of notes.¹² Therefore, it is very likely that these debates motivated him to write *The Reasonableness of Christianity*.

Locke, however, may not have meant to engage actively in these debates. In a letter to Philipp van Limborch in 1695, he wrote that

> From an intent and careful reading of the New Testament the conditions of the New Covenant and the teaching of the Gospel became clearer to me, as it seemed to me, than the noontide light, and I am fully convinced that a sincere reader of the Gospel cannot be in doubt as to what the Christian faith is. I therefore set down my thoughts on paper, thereby the better to survey, tranquilly and at leisure, the agreement of the parts with one another, their harmony, and the foundations on which they rested. (Locke 2002: 210)¹³

As Locke stated in this letter, he had been engaged in reading the New Testament. K. I. Parker points out that Locke took an intense interest in hermeneutics while he stayed in France from 1675 to 1679. He met some French biblical scholars, Richard Simon and Nicolas Toinard, among others. When Locke fled to Holland in 1683, he also became acquainted with van Limborch and Jean Le Clerc, both of whom were theologians and biblical scholars.¹⁴ Locke continued to study the Bible, while being influenced by them. He spent a lot of time reading not only the Bible but also commentaries written by John Lightfoot, Joseph Mede, John

Spencer, John Selden and others and made many notes on the Bible.[15] Thus, *The Reasonableness of Christianity* can be seen as the first fruit of his biblical studies. In fact, Locke stated the following in the preface to this book:

> The little Satisfaction and Consistency is to be found in most of the Systems of Divinity I have met with, made me betake my self to the sole Reading of the Scripture... for the understanding the Christian Religion. What from thence by an attentive and unbiassed search I have received, Reader, I here deliver to thee. (*Reasonableness* 3)

Moreover, the book focuses entirely on interpreting the Bible and does not explicitly present arguments related to the issues discussed in such controversies, for example, the doctrine of the Trinity. Therefore, we can assume that Locke did not intend to actively take part in these debates and tried to relativize doctrinal conflicts by showing 'the sole Reading of the Scripture'.[16]

3 The place of the *Reasonableness* in Locke studies

Previous work on *The Reasonableness of Christianity* can be classified roughly into two groups, according to whether they stress such a historical context as the controversy over the Trinity.[17] The first group is concerned with its theoretical aspects and their relationship to Locke's intellectual development. A number of scholars have discussed the basis of moral obligation in relation to the distinction between reason and revelation, one which is found in *An Essay concerning Human Understanding*, Book 4, Chapter 17.[18] For example, John Dunn argues that Locke could not 'present morality as a system of universally intelligible obligatory truths' in his *Essay*, so he depended on 'his own interpretation of the Christian revelation' as the 'coercive instrument which he employed to bring home these obligations to his own society' in *The Reasonableness of Christianity* (Dunn 1969: 192).[19]

The second group is concerned with Locke's doctrinal views.[20] Scholars in this group have tried to clarify his religious position by locating the *Reasonableness* in one of the historical contexts that I discussed earlier. For example, John Marshall points out that, on the one hand, it is highly possible that Locke espoused Socinian or Unitarian views because he took notes on many books written by Unitarians and remained silent on the denial of original sin and the Trinity, which were important topics in the controversies.[21] On the other hand, Marshall emphasizes Locke's eclecticism. He says that the *Reasonableness* is also 'paralleled to a considerable degree by significant numbers of the writings of irenic trinitarians among the English latitudinarians and Arminians who were accused of "Socinianism'" (Marshall 2000: 164).[22]

I agree with the arguments of these two groups of scholars for the most part, but I hold that neither group pays enough attention to an important part of the *Reasonableness*, that is, an account of how Jesus's mission was carried out. This discussion occupies the middle part of the book, and constitutes about 40 per cent of the entire work. Very few researchers have focused on this part of the *Reasonableness*, yet Victor Nuovo significantly points out that the 'greater part of *The Reasonableness of Christianity* . . . gives an account of Jesus' propagation of the gospel, which was the main purpose of his ministry' and the 'importance that Locke attached to this part of the *Reasonableness* cannot be overstated' (Nuovo 2011: 69).[23] He also explains that this part 'is a narrative of Jesus' ministry from his baptism until his resurrection and ascension, which is to say, it is a narrative of the founding of Christianity' (Nuovo 2011: 69). According to him, Locke claimed that he 'discovered conclusive evidence of the authenticity of the Christian revelation and of the authority of the biblical account of it' 'in the pattern of Jesus' self-manifestation, his choice of disciples . . . and his overall management of events pertaining to his ministry'. As a result, he thinks that this part is 'the heart of the *Reasonableness*' (Nuovo 2011: 69). I also want to focus on Jesus's mission, but I intend to view it from a different perspective, one which allows us to grasp the meaning of Jesus's exemplary actions.

4 Locke's theory of salvation

4.1 Adam's fall

According to Locke, it is obvious to anyone 'who reads the New Testament, that the Doctrine of Redemption, and consequently of the Gospel, is founded upon the Supposition of *Adam*'s Fall', and the problem is 'what we are restored to by Jesus Christ' (*Reasonableness* 5). First, Locke examines the meaning of 'Adam's Fall'. He explains that 'by this Fall he [Adam] lost Paradise, wherein was Tranquility and the Tree of Life' (6), that is to say, 'Bliss and Immortality', so 'all Men are Mortal, and come to die' (7) based on Gen. 2.17, Rom. 5.12 and 1 Cor. 15.22. Here, Locke points out that people interpret 'the signification of the word *Death*' differently (*Reasonableness* 7, italics in the original). Some people think it 'to be a state of Guilt' and others think it 'a state of necessary sinning, and provoking God' (7, 8). Locke, however, rejects these interpretations as 'strange' and argues that '*all die in Adam*, yet none are truly *punished* but for their own deeds' by referring to Rom. 2.6, 9 and 2 Cor. 5.10 (*Reasonableness*: 10, 11).[24]

After confirming the meaning of 'Adam's Fall', Locke offers the following answer to the question of what Jesus Christ restored to us: 'the Life, which Jesus Christ restores to all men, is that Life, which they receive again at the Resurrection' (*Reasonableness* 12). This is based on 1 Cor. 15.21-2.[25] He concludes that 'men are by the Second *Adam* [Jesus Christ] restored to Life again' and that none of them lose 'Eternal Life' which they might have a title to 'by their own Righteousness', that is, by 'an exact obedience to the Law'. This conclusion is based on Rom. 4.4 and Mt. 25.46 (*Reasonableness* 12).[26] Locke summarizes his argument as follows:

> Immortality and Bliss belong to the Righteous; Those who have lived in an exact Conformity to the Law of God, are out of the reach of Death: But an Exclusion from Paradise, and loss of Immortality, is the Portion of Sinners, of all those who have any way broke that Law, and failed of a Compleat Obedience to it by the guilt of any one Transgression. And thus Mankind by the Law are put upon the issues of Life or Death; As they are *Righteous*, or *Unrighteous*; *Just* or *Unjust*; i.e. Exact Performers, or Transgressors of the Law. (13)

Immediately after this passage, however, Locke cites Rom. 3.9, 20, 23 and states that *all having sinned, both Jews and Gentiles, come short of the glory of God*, or 'the Kingdom of God in Heaven'. Therefore, 'it follows, that no one could . . . have Eternal Life and Bliss' because *by the deeds of the Law no one could be justified* (*Reasonableness* 13).[27] Here, one question arises: 'Why did God give so hard a Law to Mankind, that to the Apostles time no one of *Adam*'s Issue had kept it?' (*Reasonableness* 13). When Locke answers this question, he makes a claim about 'the Law of Faith', one which says that sinners are justified by having faith in Jesus Christ. Locke refers to Gal. 3.22 and contrasts the Law with the law of reason, that is, the law of nature, which is an equivalent of 'the Law of Works' in this context.[28] Next, I will examine Locke's account of the relationship between 'the Law of Works' and 'the Law of Faith'.

4.2 The Law of Works and the Law of Faith

First, Locke explains that 'the Law of Works' is the law 'which requires perfect Obedience, without any remission or abatement', and that 'by that Law a man cannot be Just, or justified without an exact performance of every tittle' (*Reasonableness* 17). This account is based on Lev. 18.5, Ezek. 20.11, Rom. 10.5 and Gal. 3.12.[29] Locke further says that we can find 'the Law of Works' in the 'Moral part' of the law given by Moses.[30] He also connects that part of Moses's law with 'the Eternal Law', and states that the 'Moral part' 'conformable to the Eternal Law of Right, is of Eternal Obligation, and therefore remains in force still under the Gospel; nor is abrogated by the *Law of Faith*' (*Reasonableness* 19). This is based on Rom. 3.31.[31] Thus, 'the Law of Works' is equal to the moral part of Moses's law, while the latter being equal to 'the Eternal Law of Right', so 'the Law of Works' is identical with 'the Eternal Law', that is, the law of nature. As for 'the Law of Faith', Locke explains that it is the law 'to supply the defect of full Obedience'. Thanks to this law, the believers who cannot perfectly obey the Law of Works 'are admitted to Life and Immortality as if they were Righteous' (19).

Here, by way of summary, I quote Locke's own words and show what 'the Law of Works' and 'the Law of Faith' are. Let me begin with what he says about 'the Law of Works':

> The Civil and Ritual part of the Law delivered by *Moses* obliges not Christians, though to the Jews it were a part of the Law of Works; it being a part of the Law of Nature, that man ought to obey every Positive Law of God, whenever he shall please to make any such addition to the Law of his Nature. But the Moral part of *Moses*'s Law, or the Moral Law, (which is every where the same, the Eternal Rule of Right) obliges Christians and all men every where, and is to all men the standing Law of Works. (*Reasonableness* 20)

Next, Locke says the following about 'the Law of Faith':

> Christian Believers have the Privilege to be under the *Law of Faith* too; which is that Law whereby God Justifies a man for Believing, though by his Works he be not Just or Righteous, *i.e.* though he came short of Perfect Obedience to the Law of Works. God alone does, or can, Justifie or make Just those who by their Works are not so: Which he doth by counting their Faith for Righteousness, *i.e.* for a compleat performance of the Law. (20–1)[32]

Locke thinks that people are required to obey 'the Law of Works' as strictly as the law of Moses. Practically, however, it is impossible for human creatures to obey his law strictly, so they cannot avoid committing sin. Then, Jesus Christ appears and shows the way of salvation by 'the Law of Faith'. As the case of Abraham indicates, 'the Law of Faith' means that everyone believes 'what God requires him to believe, as a condition of the Covenant he makes with him; and not to doubt of the performance of his Promises' (22). Here, another question arises: what does God require 'us to believe now under the Revelation of the Gospel'? (22). This question is about the content of faith. To answer the question and clarify the content is the purpose of Locke's *Reasonableness of Christianity*. So I will examine Locke's answer to it below.

4.3 Faith and repentance

A question arises as to whether people can really achieve salvation by 'the Law of Faith' alone, that is, simply by believing that Jesus is the Messiah. This is a question about justification by faith. Generally, the Roman Catholic Church regards not only faith but also good deeds as essential for justification. However, Martin Luther (or Lutherans) argues that faith is the only condition for salvation. As I have already mentioned in the introduction to this chapter, in the controversy over justification, the view of strict Calvinists was considered problematic because they argued that works 'played no role in preserving his "justification", which is to say, the salvation of his soul' (Foster 2005: 132). Although their position did 'not entail Antinomianism', it was also 'widely associated with lawlessness and immorality because it seemed too close to Antinomianism, the belief that saved Christians need not even try to obey God's law' (Foster 2005: 132).

Against this, Locke says that 'there is something more required to Salvation, besides believing' (*Reasonableness* 31).[33] He emphasizes that 'the Law of Faith' does not completely replace 'the Law of Works' and connects one's faith with one's outward behaviour. This connection is embodied in the concept of 'Repentance'.[34] According to Locke, 'God dealt so favourably with the Posterity of Adam' that 'God would Justifie them' if they would not only 'believe *Jesus* to be the *Messiah*' but also 'perform what other Conditions were required of them by the Covenant of Grace' (110). In other words, 'Repentance is as absolute a Condition of the Covenant of Grace, as Faith' (110). Locke argues, on the basis of Mk 1.14-15, 6.12, that 'Believing Jesus to be the Messiah, and Repenting, were so Necessary and Fundamental parts of the Covenant of Grace, that one of them alone is often put for both' (111).[35] Thus he concludes that 'believing *Jesus* to be the *Messiah*, and Repenting, was what the Apostles preached' (111). This conclusion is based on Lk. 8.3, 5, 16.30-1, 24.27.[36]

In addition, Locke says, on the basis of Acts 3.19, that repentance is 'not only a sorrow for sins past, but . . . a turning from them, into a new and contrary Life' (*Reasonableness* 111), and expresses this point as follows:

> Repentance is an hearty sorrow for our past misdeeds, and a sincere Resolution and Endeavour, to the utmost of our power, to conform all our Actions to the Law of God. So that Repentance does not consist in one single Act of sorrow. .

..But in *doing works meet for Repentance*, in a sincere Obedience to the Law of Christ, the remainder of our Lives. (112)

Concerning the relation between faith and repentance, Locke does not make just one of them essential for salvation. Rather, he regards the connection between one's inward faith and one's outward behaviour (good deeds) as important. This argument is similar to another one we have seen earlier about the relationship between 'the Law of Works' and 'the Law of Faith'. It is very hard to obey 'the Law of Works', so 'the Law of Faith' is needed to compensate for the gap and, hence, for salvation. Salvation can never be achieved by faith alone because repentance is an absolute condition in the new covenant of grace. '[I]t is not enough to believe him [Jesus] to be the *Messiah*, unless we also obey his Laws, and take him to be our King, to Reign over us' (128). Repentance contains both faith and works. In other words, we can find the unity of one's inward belief and one's outward behaviour in the matter of salvation. In contrast, the inconsistency between them, which takes the form of '*Faith* without *Works*, i.e. the Works of sincere Obedience to the Law and Will of Christ', is 'not sufficient for our Justification' (118).[37]

Now we ask how Christians should behave, and what works they are required to do. According to Locke, we know the answer to this is 'by the Laws he [Christ] gives them, and requires them to obey', and 'by the Sentence which he himself will give, when, sitting on his Throne, they shall all appear at his Tribunal, to receive every one his Doom from the mouth of this Righteous Judge of all Men' (*Reasonableness* 121). Concretely, the laws which Christians are required to obey are 'all the Moral Precepts in the Old Testament', and Locke states that 'not only Murder, but causeless Anger, and so much as words of Contempt' are forbidden. Furthermore, referring to Luke 6 and Matthew 5–7, the Sermon on the Mount, Locke says that 'actual Uncleanness', 'all irregular desires', 'Causeless Divorces', 'Swearing in Conversation', 'Forswearing in Judgment', 'Revenge', 'Retaliation', 'Ostentation of Charity, of Devotion, and of Fasting; Repetitions in Prayer, Covetousness; Worldly Care, Censoriousness' are all forbidden (*Reasonableness* 123). However, 'Loving our Enemies; Doing good to those that Hate us; Blessing those that Curse us; Praying for those that despightfully use us; Patience and Meekness under Injuries; Forgiveness; Liberality; [and] Compassion' are commanded (123). These moral duties are 'inculcated over and over again to his Followers in express terms' by Jesus and his Apostles (129), and 'All the Duties of Morality' stated in the Bible are 'clear, and plain, and easy to be understood', so reading the Bible is 'the surest, the safest, and most effectual way of teaching' them to those who have 'the lowest Capacities of Reasonable Creatures' (158–9).

We have considered Locke's account of the meanings of faith and works by focusing on the role of repentance. We have found that Locke regards the performance of works based on one's faith as necessary for salvation, which clearly shows that he respects the harmony between one's inward faith and one's outward behaviour. Moreover, Locke holds that this doctrine of salvation in the Bible is so clear that even those who have only the lowest capacities can understand it because they are reasonable creatures.[38] Locke makes the same point in different ways, so I now turn to his account of the way in which Jesus's mission was carried out.

4.4 Jesus's way of self-disclosure

According to Locke, Jesus revealed that he was the Messiah in three ways. First, by 'Miracles'. Second, 'by Phrases and Circumlocution, that did signifie or intimate his Coming; though not in direct words pointing out the Person'. 'The most usual' of the phrases and circumlocutions used are '*The Kingdom of God, and of Heaven*'. Third, by 'plain and direct words, declaring the Doctrine of the *Messiah*'. These, however, are the words used by the Apostles 'when they went about Preaching the Gospel, after our Saviour's Resurrection' (*Reasonableness* 38–9). Locke argues that Jesus 'made no other discovery of himself . . . at the beginning of his Ministry, but in the two former ways, which were more obscure'. In other words, Jesus did not declare 'himself to be the *Messiah*, any otherwise than as it might be gathered from the Miracles he did, and the conformity of his Life and Actions with the Prophesies of the Old Testament concerning him; and from some general Discourses of the Kingdom of the *Messiah* being come, under the name of the *Kingdom of God*, and *of Heaven*' (39). Why did Jesus not reveal that he was the Messiah from the beginning?

There are two reasons for 'this concealment'. One is that Jesus could not have fulfilled his mission 'if as soon as he appeared in Publick, and began to Preach, he had presently professed himself to have been the *Messiah*', that is, 'the King that owned that Kingdom he published to be at hand. For the *Sanhedrim* would then have laid hold on it, to have got him into their Power, and thereby have taken away his Life; at least, they would have disturbed his Ministry, and hindred the Work he was about' (*Reasonableness* 41). The other reason is that 'the whole Nation of the Jews expecting at this time their *Messiah*, and deliverance by him from the Subjection they were in to a Foreign Yoke, the body of the People would certainly, upon his declaring himself to be the *Messiah* their King, have rose up in Rebellion, and set him at the Head of them' (47).[39] That is to say, Jesus chose the first two ways to show that he was the Messiah because if he had declared himself to be the Messiah, the order of civil society would have been disturbed and he could not have fulfilled his mission.

Locke claims that we shall conclude 'this proceeding' is 'according to Divine Wisdom, and suited to a fuller Manifestation and Evidence of his being the *Messiah*' when 'we consider, that he was to fill out the time foretold of his Ministry; And, after a Life illustrious in Miracles and Good Works ... should be led as a sheep to the slaughter, and ... be brought to the Cross, though there were no guilt nor fault found in him' (*Reasonableness* 40–1).[40] He summarizes Jesus's way of carrying out his mission as follows:

> *Jesus*, by the admirable wariness of his Carriage, and an extraordinary Wisdom visible in his whole Conduct, weathers all these Difficulties, does the Work he comes for, uninterruptedly goes about Preaching his full appointed time, sufficiently manifests himself to be the *Messiah* in all the Particulars the Scriptures had foretold of him. (92)

As we saw earlier, Nuovo claims that Locke demonstrated the authority of the Bible, 'grounded in the rational assurance of the excellence of the Christian religion', by showing the wisdom and the reasonableness of Jesus's practice in his 'self-disclosure over the whole course of his ministry' (Nuovo 2011: 73, 70).[41]

I find his interpretation acceptable, but I think that it is more important to stress that Jesus had to reveal his Messiahship by his outward conduct. As for the choice of the Apostles, for example, Locke explains, on the basis of Mt. 11.25 and Lk. 10.21, that they are such 'A company of Poor, Ignorant, Illiterate Men' that they 'might be disposed to believe him to be the *Messiah*', 'convinced by the Miracles they saw him daily do, and the unblameable Life he led', that is, Jesus's outward conduct (*Reasonableness* 89). Locke also refers to Jn 14.10: 'Believest thou not that I am in the Father, and the Father in me? the words that I speak unto you I speak not of myself: but the Father that dwelleth in me, he doeth the works', and interprets it as 'he [Jesus] signifies such an Union with God, that God operates in and by him'. Finally, Locke emphasizes that Jesus revealed his Messiahship through his outward behaviour by interpreting Jn 14.11 as showing that 'the Works that I [Jesus] have done convince you that I am sent by the Father' (*Reasonableness* 99). Locke also refers to Jn 14.20 and interprets it as follows: 'By the works I shall enable you to do, through a Power I have received from the Father', and '[W]hoever sees me do [the works], must acknowledge the Father to be in me; And *whoever sees you do* [the works], *must acknowledge me to be in you*' (98, emphasis added).[42]

Here I consider the connection between Jesus's way of self-disclosure and salvation. As such, I quote a relevant part again: 'These two, Faith and Repentance; *i.e.* believing Jesus to be the Messiah, and a good Life; are the indispensable Conditions of the New Covenant to be performed by all those, who would obtain Eternal Life' (*Reasonableness* 112). Locke also argues, on the basis of Mt. 7.22-3, that 'Faith in the Penitent and Sincerely Obedient, supplies the defect of their Performances; and so by Grace they are made Just' (*Reasonableness* 133). As I have already discussed in Section 4.3 and quoted earlier, 'Faith and Repentance' are the absolute conditions of salvation. First, those who seek salvation are required to believe in Jesus as the Messiah. Then they should endeavour to obey his laws. According to Locke, '[w]hat those were to do, who believed him [Jesus] to be the *Messiah* . . . we shall best know by the Laws he gives them, and requires them to obey' (121).

Generally, whatever should 'be universally useful, as a standard to which Men should conform their Manners, must have its Authority either from Reason or Revelation'. Therefore, a lawgiver must show that 'he builds his Doctrine upon Principles of Reason, self-evident in themselves', or must show 'his Commission from Heaven; That he comes with Authority from God, to deliver his Will and Commands to the World' (*Reasonableness* 152). Locke argues that '[i]n the former way, no body that I [Locke] know before our Saviour's time, ever did; or went about to give us a *Morality*' (152–3). If nobody did it, it is plain that 'there was need of one to give us such a *Morality*; Such a Law, which might be the sure guide of those who had a desire to go right', and 'Such a *Law of Morality*, Jesus Christ hath given us in the New Testament' 'by the latter of these ways', that is, 'by Revelation' (153). Locke concludes as follows:

> We have from him a full and sufficient Rule for our direction; And conformable to that of reason. But the truth and obligation of its Precepts have their force, and are put past doubt to us, by the evidence of his Mission. . . . And the Authority of God in his Precepts cannot be questioned. Here *Morality* has a sure Standard, that Revelation vouches, and Reason cannot gainsay, nor question; but both together witness to come from God the great Law-maker. (153)

To sum up the above, 'the evidence of his Mission' is shown through his miracles and unblameable life, which is described as 'the Purity of his Life' in another place (*Reasonableness* 88). Ordinary people, for example, can understand that such miracles as '[t]he healing of the Sick, the restoring sight to the Blind by a word, the raising, and being raised from the Dead' are 'matters of Fact' if they 'can distinguish between sick and well, Lame and sound, dead and alive'. Furthermore, they can also conceive that 'he who does such things, must do them by the assistance of a Divine Power' (158). As a result, they are persuaded that 'Jesus Christ was sent by God to be a King, and a Saviour of those who do believe in him' and that his precepts were based on 'the Authority of God'. Now 'All his Commands become Principles: There needs no other Proof for the truth of what he says, but that he said it' (158). If they sincerely repent their bad behaviour and try to obey the Laws which he gives them, the door of salvation will be opened. As a means of instruction to the people, Locke concludes that 'there needs no more but to read the inspired Books, to be instructed' because 'All the Duties of Morality lye there clear, and plain, and easy to be understood' (158–9). He also adds that this is 'the surest, the safest, and most effectual way of teaching' if we take it into consideration that 'as it suits the lowest Capacities of Reasonable Creatures, so it reaches and satisfies, Nay, enlighten the highest' (159).[43]

5 Contemporary criticism of the *Reasonableness*

I have pointed out that the consistency between inward belief and outward behaviour is one of the most significant features in Locke's account of salvation. I have confirmed this with respect to the relationship between 'the Law of Works' and 'the Law of Faith', and then between faith and repentance. I have also shown this in Jesus's way of self-disclosure. Jesus fulfilled his mission by revealing his Messiahship (inwardness) through his outward behaviour (miracles and good works) without disturbing the existing order in civil society. Those who believe in Jesus as the Messiah should sincerely endeavour to obey his commands for salvation.

What implications did Locke's description of Jesus's ministry have for readers? There are several possibilities. For example, it implies a criticism against strict Calvinists who claim antinomianism in the controversy over justification or against strict Anglicans (members of the High Church) who force people to obey their outward rules and invade people's liberty of conscience. Or it differentiates itself from Thomas Hobbes, who justifies absolute obedience to the sovereign by separating belief from outward behaviour. In the following discussion I will clarify its implications from the perspective of a dispute Locke had with his contemporaries. Specifically, I will examine Richard Willis's criticism of *The Reasonableness of Christianity* and Locke's response to it.[44]

Richard Willis (1664–1734), who became bishop of Winchester in 1723, published *The Occasional Paper* anonymously in 1697. This journal continued to be published up to volume 10 until 1698. In 'A Letter to a Friend' in volume 1, Willis states the following:

> I Think you have very good reason to complain of the present Liberty of the Press, and to wish it were under some better Regulation; for I cannot imagine it a fit thing that a Way shou'd lie open for *ill Men* to vent what they please, and to disperse abroad in the World Discourses which tend to the perverting of our Faith, or the corrupting of our Manners. (Willis 1697a: 1, italics in original)

Willis does not deny that better men also have the same liberty to publish refutations of those discourses, and he acknowledges that the present liberty of the press is very useful. However, he is worried that 'A Man may be heated beyond measure by a Zeal even for the *Truth* it self, and may be pusht beyond the limits of *good Manners*, in his Fury against such as would corrupt them' (Willis 1697a: 2). He adds that especially in the case of religion, people 'are acted by a Principle of *Resentment* rather than of *Christian Zeal*', so that 'it wou'd be of great Service both to *Religion* and *good Manners*, to have *ill Books* as they are publish'd, consider'd calmly by some Men of *Temper* and *Moderation*, who are Friends to Morality, to the Church and Government' (Willis 1697a: 4). It is *The Occasional Paper* that played this role.

Willis criticizes 'our *Plays*' for having 'the greatest Share in the Corruption of our Age' (Willis 1697a: 5). The reason is that 'our *Plays*' are apt to 'produce a *levity* of Mind, and a *rambling* of Thought' and 'lead to *looseness* of Manners, and corrupt the *Principles* of Life, and bring Men by degrees either to a careless Neglect, or which is yet worse, a daring Contempt of *Religion* and *another World*' (Willis 1697a: 7). He regards such plays as directly opposite to 'the Genius of the *Gospel*' and 'the whole Design of *Christianity*', and argues that '*Jesus Christ*, whose Name we bear, and whose Religion we profess, came into the World to make us a People *zealous of good works*, to reclaim us from Folly and Vanity, and to engage us in the great Work of improving our Minds, and saving our Souls' (Willis 1697a: 6).[45]

After criticizing 'our Plays', he attacks *A Letter to the Deists*, published in 1696. The author was Humphrey Prideaux (1648–1724), who became dean of Norwich in 1702.[46] Willis's criticism has four points:

I. That he [Prideaux] has too great a fondness for the Title of a *Deist*.
II. That he would establish Morality upon the Principles of meer *Deism*.
III. That he asserts That *to believe Jesus Christ to be the Messiah, is all that is required to denote a Man a Christian*.

IV. That he expresses an unfit Prejudice against the *Ministers* of Religion, and their *Office*. (Willis 1697a: 10)

The third and fourth points are related to *The Reasonableness of Christianity* because Prideaux referred to the book in bringing up the third point,[47] and because Willis criticizes the fourth point by connecting Prideaux's argument with Locke's. I examine these two points here.

Willis quotes from the *Reasonableness* the following sentences: '*All that was to be believed . . . for justification, was no more but this single Proposition, That Jesus of Nazareth was the Christ, or the Messiah*' and '*that above sixty Years after our Saviour's Passion, St.* John *knew nothing else required to be believed for the attaining of Life, but that Jesus is the Messiah, the Son of God*' (Willis 1697a: 19; *Reasonableness*: 33, 108). Then he points out that these are identical with the words from Hobbes's *Leviathan*, part 3, chapter 43.[48] Willis claims that 'though they [men] must indeed assent to the rest of the Christian Doctrine . . . it is no great matter whether they know it or not as long as they believe this one singe Proposition, That *Jesus is the Messiah*'. He fears that it brings about a 'very dangerous consequence' because they have 'an intire liberty to believe or disbelieve any of the *rest* of the Articles of Christianity' (Willis 1697a: 21–2). Willis says that some doctrines other than this one article should also be regarded as fundamental 'because their necessity is apparent and visible to the support of the whole'. One of those fundamental doctrines concerns 'the Ministers of the Gospel', that is, priests and their office, which he calls the '*Superstructure* . . . added to make a full and *compleat* System of Christianity' (Willis 1697a: 23). This criticism contained in Willis's argument is related to the fourth point.

Willis quotes some of Locke's remarks on priests from the *Reasonableness*. '*The Priests [are] every where, to secure their Empire excluded Reason from having to do in Religion*'; '*The Priests*' are the '*wary Guardians of their own Creeds, and profitable Inventions*'; and they are '[*t*]*he designing Leaders as well as the following Herd*' (Willis 1697a: 30; *Reasonableness*: 143, 144, 149). Willis understands that these words are against 'the *Heathen* Priest' and claims that 'our Author [Prideaux] . . . extends the same Aversion to the Ministers of the *Gospel*'. Willis objects that it is 'politick enough for those who are Enemies to Religion to wound it through the Sides of its Ministers; and in order to bring what is holy under Contempt, to vilifie those who are employed about it' (Willis 1697a: 30). As the example of Prideaux shows, these words against the heathen priests are used to condemn the priests and their office. That is why Willis criticized Locke, though he may not have actually intended to do so.

Locke argues against Willis's criticism in *A Second Vindication of the Reasonableness of Christianity* as follows: 'I borrowed it only from the Writers of the Four *Gospels*, and the *Acts*; and did not know that those words he quoted out of the *Leviathan*, were there, or any thing like them' (Locke 2012: 229). Locke also claims that 'affirming, as he does positively, this, which he could not know to be true, and is in it self perfectly false', was 'meant to encrease or lessen the Credit of the Author of the *Reasonableness of Christianity*' (Locke 2012: 229). As for the fourth point noted earlier, Locke says that 'I have spoke of none but the Priests before Christianity, both *Jewish* and *Heathen*', and that he hopes 'to find them such as becomes that Temper, and Love of Truth, which he professes' (Locke 2012: 232). Willis also replied to Locke's argument in *The Occasional Paper*, Number IV,[49] but their dispute did not continue further because Willis finally thought that they could reach an agreement if Locke would help and join him 'in convincing the world' that '*a true Christian*' needs to believe such other things as 'are necessary to give a tolerable Scheme of the Christian Religion' and to 'promote that purity of Heart, and true Faith in Christ Jesus' (Willis 1697b: 42).[50]

6 Conclusion

In this chapter I have, first, analysed Locke's theory of salvation to show that the unity of inward belief and outward behaviour has a significant place in it. In so doing, I have also examined the relationship between 'the Law of Works' and 'the Law of Faith', and then between faith and repentance, and finally clarified Jesus's way of conducting his mission. Those who seek salvation can hold the conviction that Jesus is the Messiah through his outward behaviour, which is described as miracles and good works again and again in the New Testament. This is the reason why Locke's description of how Christ conducted his mission is a very important part of the *Reasonableness*. Then they must perform their duties, that is to say, repent of their deeds and try to obey faithfully his commands based on the authority of God. Thus, it has become clear that Locke held the view that a mutual reconciliation of one's inward belief and one's outward behaviour (good deeds) was essential for salvation. According to Locke, even ordinary people can understand this through the example of Jesus by reading the Bible, because 'it suits the lowest Capacities of Reasonable Creatures'.

A few years later, Locke gave an example of 'A ploughman that cannot read' and explained 'a principle of Christianity' (Locke 1997b: 347). This explanation is similar to the argument in the *Reasonableness*. A ploughman 'knows in those few cases which concern his own actions, what is right and what is wrong'. If 'he is in doubt in any matter that concerns himself', 'he cannot fail to enquire of those better skilled in Christ's law, to tell him what his Lord and master has commanded in the case', and he can 'have his law read to him concerning that duty ... for the regulation of his own actions'. His 'business is to live well himself, and do what is his particular duty', and this is 'knowledge and orthodoxy enough for him'. Locke concludes that 'the right and only way to saving [this] orthodoxy, is the sincere and steady purpose of a good life'. This is 'a principle of Christianity' (Locke 1997b: 347). We can find here that Locke regards the unity of inward belief and outward behaviour based on faith as important for the salvation of the ploughman, just as it is for that of other human beings.

Second, in examining a contemporary criticism of *The Reasonableness of Christianity* I have shown that Richard Willis criticized it from an Anglican perspective. However, his criticism was based on his misunderstanding of the book, and as a result, the dispute between Willis and Locke ceased to be productive. As I explained in the introduction, *The Reasonableness of Christianity* has often been interpreted as taking a position very close to the Socinian (or Unitarian) one. As Marshall has also pointed out in his examination of the book, it is more likely that Locke's position is similar to the Anglican (latitudinarian) one.

Locke himself explains in his *A Second Vindication* that 'my Book was chiefly designed for *Deists*' (Locke 2012: 191). Furthermore, William Popple (1638–1708), a friend of Locke who produced an English translation of *Epistola de Tolerantia*, says in a letter to Locke, that 'The Reasonableness of Christianity (however Reasonable a Book it be) has I doubt had little Effect upon those that call themselves Deists in this Age' (Popple to Locke, 16 January 1696, Locke 1979: 519). Popple continues, saying that 'The men I mean are such as deny all Immaterial Beings', and that they 'laugh not onely at Revealed but even Natural Religion' (Locke 1979: 519). Judging from Locke's explanation and Popple's statements, it is plausible to think that Locke wrote his book in order to convince deists of true Christianity and prevent them from going to extremes. To do so, Locke had to show that people as rational creatures could understand true Christianity by reading the Bible for themselves, while he also added later that if they could not read the Bible, they could still understand true Christianity by having it read to them.

Notes

1 The first version of this chapter was presented at Gakushuin University in December 2016. I am deeply grateful to Kiyoshi Shimokawa and Peter Anstey for their useful comments and suggestions. I would also like to thank MARUZEN-YUSHODO Co., Ltd. (https://kw.maruzen.co.jp/kousei-honyaku/) for the English-language editing. In addition, this study was supported by JSPS KAKENHI Grant Numbers JP15K17034 and JP19K13664.
2 Locke, for example, argued that 'the freedom of Christ's subjects' was 'not of this world or of the outward but inward man', and that 'an outward set form of worship' imposed by the magistrate could not 'necessarily take away the spirituality of religion' (Locke 1997a: 18, 43).
3 He says as follows: 'If Jesus could demonstrate such forbearance toward manifestly evil men, how could Christian leaders approve the use of force against fellow believers?' (Loconte 2014: 179).
4 Here he cites the following passage from 'Error' (1698) written by Locke: 'and, therefore, I lay it down as a principle of Christianity, that the right and only way to saving orthodoxy, is the sincere and steady purpose of a good life' (Loconte 2014: 189; Locke 1997b: 347). Sherlock also pays attention to the role of Jesus Christ as a 'moral teacher'. He argues that the life of Jesus shows a moral character (Sherlock 1997: 19–49). Rabieh takes the same stance and says that 'he [Locke] vindicates the practice of morality . . . by presenting Jesus as practicing a mercenary morality' (Rabieh 1991: 933)
5 For Locke's minimal definition, see Shimokawa's discussion in Chapter 7 of this volume.
6 Foster also claims that 'Locke's retelling of the life of Jesus . . . shows that the story of Jesus in the Bible is the story of God's messenger bringing to humanity rational reasons to believe in his revelation' (Foster 2005: 137).
7 See Wallace (1984), Marshall (1994: 389–413) and Foster (2005: 131–4). Peter Anstey, however, argues that there is a third controversy contributing to the writing of *The Reasonableness of Christianity*. According to him, this is the dispute over *The Naked Gospel*, which Arthur Bury, the Rector of Exeter College Oxford, published in 1690. His book was burnt in Oxford because of its anti-Trinitarian claims. Newton and Locke, however, succeeded the spirit of Bury, who sought 'the naked truth of Christianity'. As a result, Locke wrote *The Reasonableness of Christianity* to 'recover the naked gospel and the fundamentals of the Christian religion' (Anstey 2017: 7–9). In contrast, John Edwards, who is a Calvinist Anglican, criticized not only *The Naked Gospel* but also *The Reasonableness of Christianity* as anti-Trinitarian (Edwards 1695: 104–5, 112).
8 Iliffe (2004: 121–2). For Nye's arguments, see also Lim (2012: 306–9).

9 For details about Sherlock's arguments, see Thiel (2000: 220–43).
10 Foster (2005: 132).
11 Baxter published 'A Breviate of the Doctrine of Justification' and 'A Defence of Christ, And Free Grace', which were both included in his *The Scripture Gospel Defended, and Christ, Grace and Free Justification Vindicated against the Libertines* (1690). The next year, he published *An End of Doctrinal Controversies*. For details, see Cooper (2001: 170–83).
12 See Marshall (1994: 391).
13 Marshall also quotes this letter; see Marshall (1994: 411).
14 See Parker (2004: 20–5).
15 See Nuovo (2016: 501). For example, see Bodleian Library MS Locke f. 30 from the early 1690s. This manuscript, especially, ff. 1–121, consists of some annotations of the New Testament by Locke and extracts from commentaries written by Jean Le Clerc, Joseph Mede, Simon Patrick and others.
16 As for Locke's intention to write, Marshall points out that 'Locke very probably wished to argue in the *Reasonableness* against deism, increasingly prominent in English and Irish thought at that moment' (Marshall 2000: 164). Herold takes the same view, and moreover claims that 'Locke is charting a middle course between traditionalists and Deists' (Herold 2014: 204, 206). As I will discuss later, Locke agrees with Richard Willis, later bishop of Winchester, on this point. Although Willis connected *The Reasonableness of Christianity* with deism and criticized this book, Locke cleared up his misunderstanding and brought the debate to an end.
17 Previous studies on *The Reasonableness of Christianity* in Japan can also be classified in the same way. Fewer studies, however, have examined Locke's religious thought in contrast to his political thought in Japan. A new Japanese edition was published by Takashi Kato in 2019, which it is expected will promote research on the *Reasonableness* in Japan.
18 While Locke argued that 'Revelation cannot be admitted against the clear evidence of Reason', he also argued that '*Revelation*, where God has been pleased to give it, *must carry it, against the probable Conjectures of Reason*' (*Essay* IV. xviii. 5, 7). It seems that these two propositions are contradictory. According to the Japanese scholar Takashi Kato, the dispute about the relationship between reason and revelation is about how these propositions cited earlier can be consistently understood (Kato 1987: 107). See also Grant (1987: 24–6) and Rabieh (1991: 933–9).
19 See also Stanton (2013: 32). Kato holds a similar view; see Kato (1987: 105). Tully understands Locke's position as 'a compromise between the voluntarist (Ockhamist) and rationalist theories' and explains it as follows: 'According to the former view, natural laws are imperatives, accepted on faith, and are binding solely because they are an expression of God's will. The rationalist holds that natural laws

are normative propositions, discoverable by reason, and are binding solely because they are rational' (Tully 1980: 41). In contrast, Rabieh emphasizes the compatibility between faith and reason by reinterpreting the meaning of Christianity in *The Reasonableness of Christianity*. He claims, 'by reducing Christianity to a simple faith in Jesus . . ., Locke has taken God off our minds. And by reinterpreting God as supporting his rational law of nature, Locke has left him in our conscience, but it is a conscience which sees little tension between self-interest and morality' (Rabieh 1991: 955). Herold revisits Rabieh's argument and reinterprets the meaning of Christianity in a different way from Rabieh. According to Herold, 'Locke implicitly suggests that traditional Christianity is unreasonable, and has been a political failure, because of its hostility to an ethic of enlightened selfishness' (Herold 2014: 199).

20 See Polinska (1999).
21 Marshall (1994: 413).
22 See also Marshall (2000: 116–17, 162–4). Wallace also holds a similar view and says that '*The Reasonableness of Christianity*, insofar as it was a treatise on justification, repeated . . . an understanding of justification which had been a commonplace of Anglican Latitudinarians and Baxterian Presbyterians' (Wallace 1984: 62). See also Wootton (1989: 48–9). The Japanese scholar Goko Seno also shows Locke's doctrinal position and the character of his thought by examining not only the *Reasonableness* but also other books by contemporaries in light of the historical context. He says that 'Locke's way of thinking about salvation is similar to Arminianism and, at the same time, overlaps widely with the Socinian position' (Seno 2005: 202–6, 644).
23 See also Rabieh (1991: 953–6) and Foster (2005: 128–40).
24 Rom. 2.6: 'Who [God] will render to every man according to his deeds', in the King James Bible Online: http://www.kingjamesbibleonline.org/ (the same is referred to hereafter).
25 1 Cor. 15.21-2: 'For since by man came death, by man came also the resurrection of the dead. For as in Adam all die, even so in Christ shall all be made alive.'
26 Mt. 25.46: 'And these shall go away into everlasting punishment: but the righteous into life eternal.'
27 Rom. 3.9: 'What then? are we better than they? No, in no wise: for we have before proved both Jews and Gentiles, that they are all under sin'; 20: 'Therefore by the deeds of the law there shall no flesh be justified in his sight: for by the law is the knowledge of sin'; 23: 'For all have sinned, and come short of the glory of God.'
28 Gal. 3.22: 'But the scripture hath concluded all under sin, that the promise by faith of Jesus Christ might be given to them that believe.'
29 Lev. 18.5: 'Ye shall therefore keep my statutes, and my judgments: which if a man do, he shall live in them: I am the LORD'; Ezek. 20.11: 'And I gave them my statutes,

and shewed them my judgments, which if a man do, he shall even live in them';
Rom. 10.5: 'For Moses describeth the righteousness which is of the law, That the man which doeth those things shall live by them'; Gal. 3.12: 'And the law is not of faith: but, The man that doeth them shall live in them.'

30 *Reasonableness* 18–19.
31 Rom. 3.31: 'Do we then make void the law through faith? God forbid: yea, we establish the law.'
32 This is based on Rom. 4.3, 5, 6, 8.
33 He repeats that 'it was not all that was required to be done for Justification' (*Reasonableness* 33).
34 See Leiter (2018: 370–1).
35 Mk 1.14-15: 'Now after that John was put in prison, Jesus came into Galilee, preaching the gospel of the kingdom of God, and saying, 'The time is fulfilled, and the kingdom of God is at hand: repent ye, and believe the gospel'; 6.12: 'And they went out, and preached that men should repent.'
36 Lk. 13.3, 5: 'I tell you, Nay: but, except ye repent, ye shall all likewise perish', 'I tell you, Nay: but, except ye repent, ye shall all likewise perish'; 16.30-1: 'And he said, Nay, father Abraham: but if one went unto them from the dead, they will repent. And he said unto him, If they hear not Moses and the prophets, neither will they be persuaded, though one rose from the dead'; 24.27: 'And beginning at Moses and all the prophets, he expounded unto them in all the scriptures the things concerning himself.'
37 Loconte also pays attention to the role of repentance in Locke's argument; see Loconte (2014: 176–7).
38 Foster also claims that 'the *Reasonableness* shows that Christianity teaches the need for rational faith not only by recounting Jesus' statements about miracles, but in the larger account of Jesus' life' (Foster 2005: 138).
39 Locke refers to Jn 6.15: 'When Jesus therefore perceived that they would come and take him by force, to make him a king, he departed again into a mountain himself alone.'
40 Locke repeats that 'it was not fit' to reveal himself to be the Messiah 'too plainly or forwardly, to the heady Jews' and '[t]hat was to be left to the Observation of those who would attend to the Purity of his Life, and the Testimony of his Miracles, and the Conformity of all with the Predictions concerning him' (*Reasonableness* 88).
41 Foster also claims that 'Locke stresses the complexity of Jesus' achievement in laying a rational groundwork for faith' (Foster 2005: 138).
42 Jn 14.11: 'Believe me that I am in the Father, and the Father in me: or else believe me for the very works' sake'; 20: 'At that day ye shall know that I am in my Father, and ye in me, and I in you.'
43 Locke also says a similar thing as follows: 'Hearing plain Commands, is the sure and only course to bring them [all the Day-Labourers and Tradesmen, the Spinsters and Dairy Maids] to Obedience and Practice' (*Reasonableness* 157).

44 See Numao (2010).
45 Although Willis criticizes *The Reasonableness of Christianity*, his view of Christianity, his emphasis on good works, for example, is in common with Locke.
46 See Quehen (2004).
47 Willis (1697a: 19).
48 Willis (1697a: 19).
49 Willis (1697b: 37–42).
50 Furthermore, Willis cites the following passage from Locke's *A Second Vindication of the Reasonableness of Christianity*: '1. That there is a Faith that makes Men Christians. 2. That the Believing Jesus to be the Messiah, includes in it a receiving Him for our Lord and King, promised and sent from God: And so lays upon all his Subjects an absolute and indispensable necessity of assenting to all that they can attain the Knowledge that he taught; and of a sincere Obedience to all that he commanded' (Willis 1697b: 42; Locke 2012: 230).

References

Anstey, P. R. (2017), 'Newton and Locke', in E. Schliesser and C. Smeenk (eds), *The Oxford Handbook of Newton*, Oxford Handbooks Online: http://dx.doi.org/10.1093/oxfordhb/9780199930418.013.8.

Baxter, R. (1690), *The Scripture Gospel Defended, and Christ, Grace and Free Justification Vindicated Against the Libertines*, London.

Baxter, R. (1691), *An End of Doctrinal Controversies*, London.

Bury, A. (1690), *The Naked Gospel*, Oxford.

Cooper, T. (2001), *Fear and Polemic in Seventeenth-Century England: Richard Baxter and Antinomianism*, Aldershot: Ashgate.

Crisp, T. (1690), *Christ Alone Exalted Being the Compleat Works of Tobias Crisp*, London.

Dunn, J. (1969), *The Political Thought of John Locke*, Cambridge: Cambridge University Press.

Edwards, J. (1695), *Some Thoughts Concerning the Several Causes and Occasions of Atheism, Especially in the Present Age*, London.

Foster, G. (2005), *John Locke's Politics of Moral Consensus*, Cambridge: Cambridge University Press.

Grant, R. W. (1987), *John Locke's Liberalism*, Chicago: University of Chicago Press.

Herold, A. L. (2014), '"The Chief Characteristical Mark of the True Church": John Locke's Theology of Toleration and His Case for Civil Religion', *The Review of Politics*, 76 (2): 195–221.

Iliffe, R. (2004), 'Prosecuting Athanasius: Protestant Forensics and the Mirrors of Persecution', in J. E. Force and S. Hutton (eds), *Newton and Newtonianism: New Studies*, 93–154, Dordrecht: Kluwer.

Kato, T. (1987), *Jon Rokku no Shisō Sekai: Kami to Ningen to no aida* (The World of John Locke's Thought: Between God and Human Beings), Tokyo: Tokyo University Press.

King James Bible Online: http://www.kingjamesbibleonline.org/ (accessed 11 December 2020).

Leiter, Y. (2018), *John Locke's Political Philosophy and the Hebrew Bible*, Cambridge: Cambridge University Press.

Lim, P. C. H. (2012), *Mystery Unveiled*, Oxford: Oxford University Press.

Locke, J. (1689), *A Letter Concerning Toleration*, trans. W. Popple, London.

Locke, J. (1975), *An Essay concerning Human Understanding*, ed. P. H. Nidditch, Oxford: Clarendon Press; abbreviated as *Essay*.

Locke, J. (1979), *The Correspondence of John Locke*, vol. 5, ed. E. S. de Beer, Oxford: Clarendon Press.

Locke, J. (1997a), 'First Tract on Government', in M. Goldie (ed.), *Locke: Political Essays*, 3–53, Cambridge: Cambridge University Press.

Locke, J. (1997b), 'Error', in M. Goldie (ed.), *Locke: Political Essays*, 345–8, Cambridge: Cambridge University Press.

Locke, J. (1999), *The Reasonableness of Christianity*, ed. J. C. Higgins-Biddle, Oxford: Clarendon Press, 1st edn, 1695.

Locke, J. (2002), *John Locke: Selected Correspondence*, ed. M. Goldie, Oxford: Clarendon Press.

Locke, J. (2006), *An Essay Concerning Toleration and Other Writings on Law and Politics, 1667–1683*, eds J. R. Milton and P. Milton, Oxford: Clarendon Press.

Locke, J. (2012), *A Second Vindication of the Reasonableness of Christianity, &c.*, ed. V. Nuovo, Oxford: Clarendon Press.

Loconte, J. (2014), *God, Locke, and Liberty: The Struggle for Religious Freedom in the West*, Lanham, MD: Lexington Books.

Marshall, J. (1994), *John Locke: Resistance, Religion and Responsibility*, Cambridge: Cambridge University Press.

Marshall, J. (2000), 'Locke, Socinianism, "Socinianism", and Unitarianism', in M. A. Stewart (ed.), *English Philosophy in the Age of Locke*, 111–82, Oxford: Clarendon Press.

Numao, J. K. (2010), 'Willis, Richard (1664–1734)', in S.-J. Savonius-Wroth, P. Schuurman and J. C. Walmsley (eds), *The Bloomsbury Companion to Locke*, 117–18, London: Bloomsbury.

Nuovo, V. (2011), *Christianity, Antiquity, and Enlightenment: Interpretations of Locke*, Dordrecht: Springer.

Nuovo, V. (2016), '*The Reasonableness of Christianity* and *A Paraphrase and Notes on the Epistles of* St Paul', in M. Stuart (ed.), *A Companion to Locke*, 486–502, Chichester: Wiley-Blackwell.

Nye, S. (1687), *A Brief History of the Unitarians, Called also Socinians*, London.

Parker, K. I. (2004), *The Biblical Politics of John Locke*, Waterloo: Wilfrid Laurier University Press.

Polinska, W. (1999), 'John Locke, Christian Doctrine and Latitudinarianism', *Zeitschrift für Neuere Theologiegeschichte / Journal for the History of Modern Theology*, 6 (2): 173–94.

Prideaux, H. (1696), *A Letter to the Deists*, London.

Quehen, H. de (2004), 'Prideaux, Humphrey (1648–1724)', in *Oxford Dictionary of National Biography*, Oxford: Oxford University Press, https://doi.org/10.1093/ref:odnb/22784 (accessed 6 October 2020).

Rabieh, M. S. (1991), 'The Reasonableness of Locke, or the Questionableness of Christianity', *The Journal of Politics*, 53 (4): 933–57.

Seno, G. (2005), *Rokku Shūkyōshisō no Tenkai* (The Development of Locke's Religious Thought), Osaka: Kansai University Press.

Sherlock, R. (1997), 'The Theology of Toleration: A Reading of Locke's "*The Reasonableness of Christianity*"', *Jewish Political Review*, 9 (3/4): 19–49.

Sherlock, W. (1690), *A Vindication of the Doctrine of the Holy and Ever Blessed Trinity, and the Incarnation of the Son of God*, London.

Stanton, T. (2013), 'Locke and His Influence', in J. A. Harris (ed.), *The Oxford Handbook of British Philosophy in the Eighteenth Century*, 21–40, Oxford: Oxford University Press.

Thiel, U. (2000), 'The Trinity and Human Personal Identity', in M. A. Stewart (ed.), *English Philosophy in the Age of Locke*, 217–43, Oxford: Clarendon Press.

Tully, J. (1980), *A Discourse on Property: John Locke and His Adversaries*, Cambridge: Cambridge University Press.

Wallace, Jr., D. D. (1984), 'Socinianism, Justification by Faith, and the Sources of John Locke's *The Reasonableness of Christianity*', *Journal of the History of Ideas*, 45 (1): 49–66.

Willis, R. (1697a), *The Occasional Paper*, Number I, London.

Willis, R. (1697b), *The Occasional Paper*, Number V: With a Post-script Relating to the Author of The Reasonableness of Christianity, London.

Wootton, D. (1989), 'John Locke: Socinian or Natural Law Theorist?', in J. E. Crimmins (ed.), *Religion, Secularization and Political Thought: Thomas Hobbes to J. S. Mill*, 39–67, London: Routledge.

9

Locke on sex, marriage and the state[1]

J. K. Numao

1 Introduction

Two 'Johns' – John Locke and John Finnis – both take the idea of natural law seriously, but they do not agree about sex and marriage. This opening line is somewhat misleading because this chapter is not intended to be a comparison between the two philosophers, nor is it intended to be an evaluation whether favourable or unfavourable of the latter. I introduce Finnis here simply to illustrate a more general point. Let me explain precisely what I mean. Finnis advances what we may call the slippery-slope argument against same-sex marriage: if you allow same-sex marriage, you will 'have no principled moral case to offer against (prudent or moderate) promiscuity, indeed the getting of orgasmic sexual pleasure in whatever friendly touch or welcoming orifice (human or otherwise) one may opportunely find it in' (Finnis 1997: 133). Or in the more concrete language of the late Justice Antonin Scalia in his dissenting opinion in *Lawrence v. Texas*, if you disallow discriminatory laws against gay men and lesbians, you will open the door to 'bigamy, same-sex marriages, adult incest, prostitution, masturbation, adultery, fornication, bestiality, and obscenity' (*Lawrence v. Texas* 2003: 590). The point, in short, is that if you allow any kind of sexual activity or relationship other than one that is coital, marital and monogamous, you will be unable coherently to oppose the whole range of what moral conservatives see as morally suspect sexual activities and relationships.[2] 'Yes' to one means 'yes' to all. Locke, I argue, disagrees with this formula.

While Locke is regularly noted for having unconventional views about marriage and divorce, he is also often portrayed as having a more conservative, a more traditionally Christian side when it comes to so-called 'sexual immoralities'[3] – for example, adultery, fornication, incest, sodomy – calling for a rather indiscriminate suppression of them all.[4] Polygamy is an interesting case in this context, where again Locke is frequently noted for making unorthodox and condoning remarks about the practice.[5] However, commentators focusing on Locke's later[6] writings on toleration argue that at the end of the day, he calls for its suppression alongside the other immoralities listed earlier.[7]

Challenging the portrayal of Locke as a Christian moral conservative and a blanket opposer of sexual immoralities,[8] I try to show in the first part of this chapter (Section 2) that Locke made careful distinctions between the different sexual activities and relationships, defining and measuring them against relevant standards of different types of societies – namely, political and religious – by which he determined their permissibility within them. To this end, I will be looking closely at the distinction made between adultery, fornication and polygamy in Locke's thought.[9] I hope to show that while natural law plays the central role in Locke's political thinking, 'yes' to one does not mean 'yes' to all, and also why that is the case. Through this investigation, I wish to show that Locke's political thinking is informed by natural law rather than Christian scriptural teachings, which, in turn, enables us to see and make sense of the distinctions he makes.[10] Given the growing interest in polygamy in modern debates, but by contrast, lack of coverage in Locke scholarship, I will be using more space to consider the peculiar place of polygamy in Locke's thought. Finally, in the second part of this chapter (Section 3), I ponder over how his insights on sex and marriage might be relevant for us when we think about how the modern state should (if it is to) involve itself in the marriage business today.

2 Locke on adultery, fornication and polygamy

For moral conservatives, there does not seem to be much of a difference between adultery, fornication and polygamy: they are all forms of sexual promiscuity, and, hence, they are all equally reprehensible. It is, however, not just the conservatives who see them as comparable sexual practices. Some liberals have also tried to emphasize the conceptual overlap between them, except they do this to defend the legality of these practices. So for example, Peter de Merneffe offers the following 'simple' argument for the decriminalization of polygamous cohabitation: 'The government can criminalize polygamous cohabitation only by criminalizing certain instances of adultery and fornication. Criminal penalties for adultery and fornication violate our rights to sexual freedom. Therefore criminal penalties for polygamous cohabitation violate our rights to sexual freedom and should be repealed' (de Merneffe 2016: 126).

What I want to show in this part of the chapter is that Locke treats these three practices as distinct, and also that as a consequence, he thinks the state should deal with them in different ways. In the process, I will be charting out how Locke views adultery, fornication and polygamy from the perspectives of Christianity, natural law and the state. I will show how the relation with natural law is key to understanding Locke's political and legal response to these practices. Let me start with adultery.

2.1 Adultery

Locke takes a firm stand against adultery. In the *Letter Concerning Toleration* (1689), he argues that 'Adulterers' alongside those who are 'Seditious, Murderers, Thieves, Robbers . . . Slanderers' ought to be 'punished and suppressed' (*Letter* 58). This staunchness is maintained in his *Paraphrase and Notes on the Epistles of St Paul* (1705–7): in this work, he notes that adultery was a crime in ancient Greece, adding, 'nor could it be tolerated in any civil Societie' (Locke 1987: 188). In the 'First Treatise' of the *Two Treatises of Government* (1690),[11] Locke refers to adultery, sodomy and incest as 'Sins' (TT I. 59). Given the context of the argument, he seems to have meant this both as a Christian sin and as a natural law violation (I will say more on this latter point later). More specifically for adultery as a sin under the Gospel, he cites the Apostle Paul's letter to the Galatians in the *Letter*, arguing that those who were serious about inheriting the kingdom of God would work hard to root out from their lives the '*Works of the Flesh*' or 'Immoralities', among which adultery is included (*Letter* 10). The content of the 'works of the flesh' is not contested in the *Paraphrase* either (Locke 1987: 154).

Thus, for Locke, adultery is both a Christian sin and a natural law violation, and it is not to be permitted by the church, or tolerated by the state. Wherein did its wrongfulness consist vis-à-vis the state? To answer this, let us look at how it contradicts the law of nature on which civil laws are based (TT II. 12). Fortunately, Locke actually says quite a lot about adultery in his various writings. Let me start by looking at his definition, which, I believe, will help to illuminate his reasons for objecting to it. In his discussion of the names of mixed modes in the *Essay concerning Human Understanding* (1690), adultery (*à la* Adam) is defined as 'the Act of Committing Disloyalty' (*Essay* III. vi. 44; see also §45). According to the *OED*, one sense of being 'disloyal' is to be 'Unfaithful to the obligations of friendship, or honour, to the marriage tie, etc.'. In the *Paraphrase*, another sort of talk is present. Perhaps to the dismay of feminists, it is the talk of property and dominion.[12]

Let us first take a look at the disloyalty part. In his paraphrase of Romans 7 where Paul is preaching to the converted Jews of their freedom from the Mosaic Law through Christ, Locke observes that a woman would not be a disloyal adulteress should she marry after her husband dies: Jews can follow Christ 'with as much freedom from blame or the imputation of disloyalty as a woman whose husband is dead may without the imputation of adultery marry an other man' (Locke 1987: 540–1).[13] The talk of property, in turn, comes up in his analysis of the 'fornication as is not so much as named amongst the Gentiles' in the Corinthian Church (1 Cor. 5.1). Here, distinguishing between fornication and adultery, Locke writes that if a man takes his father's wife while she is still legally his father's wife, this would not be fornication but adultery, or, in other words, 'that one man should have the use of a woman whilst she was an other mans wife, i e an other mans right and possession' (Locke 1987: 188; also, 540). The language Locke uses seems to be relative to one's position. The wife who commits adultery is being disloyal to her husband, and the man who takes another man's wife is wrongfully taking that man's property.[14]

This talk of the wife as the husband's property spiced with Locke's jokes about 'wife selling' in his correspondence (while a common practice in his time, this was probably just that, a joke)[15] would probably be enough to get the modern reader worried (Locke 1976–1989, 2: 32). However, the wife being the husband's property, in the first instance, does not mean he can do whatever he wants with her: a justly conquered man would be at the conqueror's mercy, but as for his 'Wives and Childrens', Locke maintains, 'I [i.e. the husband] could not forfeit their Lives, they were not mine to forfeit' (TT II. 183). This is consistent with Locke's remarks about how property in something does not entail arbitrary or absolute power over it, such as in his rejection of the right of committing suicide or consenting to enslave oneself (TT II. 6, 23; Shimokawa 2006: 192). Marriage being a 'voluntary Compact between Man and Woman', the terms of 'use', so to speak, are set by the end of the compact. And with Locke, the terms are much more equal than might appear at first sight. Locke says that in conjugal society both the man and woman have a 'Right in one anothers Bodies', that is, a property in each other's body (TT II. 78). Moreover, the husband does not have complete control over the wife's life plan as the wife maintains 'in many cases, a Liberty to *separate* from him' (TT II. 82, 83). This equality is also expressed in his paraphrase and commentary on 1 Cor. 7.1-5. Verse 4 is rendered as follows:

> For the wife has not power or dominion over her own body to refuse the husband when he desires, but this power and right to her body is in the husband. And on

the other side the husband has not the power and dominion over his own body to refuse the wife when she shews an inclination, but this power and right to his body when she has occasion is in the wife. (Locke 1987: 199)

Locke then elucidates this verse:

> The woman (who in all other rights is inferior) has here the same power given her over the mans body, that the man has over hers. The reason whereof is plain. Because if she had not her man, when she had need of him; as well as the man his woman when he had need of her, marriage would be noe remedy against fornication. (Locke 1987: 199–200)

While Locke's thought as a whole might not fully be egalitarian in a modern-day sense, the talk of the wife being the husband's property does not have to be disturbingly inegalitarian in its implication and his discussion of adultery might be seen as maintaining a kind of equality between the sexes given both man and woman have a property in each other's body.[16]

Now that we have a better understanding of what adultery is in Locke's mind, let us return to the question as to why it is not to be tolerated by the state. Locke's reason is connected to his idea about the purpose of marriage. Lockean marriage needs to be understood in relation to God's purpose for humankind. God through the law of nature wills 'the Peace and *Preservation of all Mankind*' (TT II. 7). In turn, the chief purpose of marriage, which, again, is 'a voluntary Compact between Man and Woman', is procreation and 'the continuation of the Species' (TT II. 78, 79). So for married couples,[17] in addition to a communion and right to one another's bodies, it comes with 'mutual Support, and Assistance, and a Communion of Interest too, as necessary not only to unite their Care, and Affection, but also necessary to their common Off-spring' (TT II. 78). Child rearing, together with the woman's biological capability of having more children before the older ones are out of a state of dependency, gives us an explanation as to why human marriages last longer than other creatures (that said, there is nothing 'in the nature of the thing' to make it always for life (TT II. 80–1)). Thus, thanks to the necessity of supporting their children, a couple's 'Industry might be encouraged, and their Interest better united'. By contrast 'uncertain mixture, or easie and frequent Solutions of Conjugal Society would mightily disturb' it (TT II. 80). The state does not have any business in taking away the couple's rights to procreate or offer mutual support, these being required by natural law and the state's purpose being to uphold it. The state's role in this affair is merely to decide 'any Controversie that may arise' between the couple concerning these rights (TT II. 83).

Adultery undermined marriage so understood. For Locke, the 'Principal Aggravation' of adultery (and likewise incest and sodomy) was that it went against 'the main intention of Nature', which was to increase and preserve the human species, and to that end, required 'the distinction of Families, with the Security of the Marriage Bed' (TT I. 59). Couples entered a voluntary compact to create a stable environment to bear and rear children. But adultery involves one party being disloyal, that is, being unfaithful to his or her obligation, and thereby destabilizing this environment of cooperation; and by this, it undermines the means to preserve the human species. Such is how adultery violates the law of nature. Added to this, recall also the talk of property. The law of nature teaches us that 'no one ought to harm another in his Life, Health, Liberty, or Possessions' (TT II. 6). As your spouse's body is your property, another person 'using' him or her can, as such, be seen as a natural law violation involving theft. For these reasons, adultery is not to be tolerated by the state.

2.2 Fornication

Let me turn to fornication next. The term has already appeared a few times in the discussion of adultery but was not defined there. So, I will start by looking at Locke's definition of it. Earlier, we saw that Locke distinguished fornication from adultery. This is important because, in the literature, fornication tends to get jumbled in the box of sexual immoralities alongside adultery without much discussion and then is described as an act that the magistrate should likewise punish. For example, John Marshall writes that Locke 'argued in the *Letter* itself that "adultery" and "fornication" were punishable as crimes and so not to be tolerated on civil grounds' (Marshall 2006: 715). Now in the *Paraphrase*, Locke notes that what the New Testament writers referred to as *porneia* in Greek was translated as 'fornication' in English, but that in the Bible, it had 'a larger sense' than in his day, encompassing uncleanness in general, and more specifically 'uncleaness of unlawfull copulation and Idolatry'. By contrast, the sense of fornication in his time was more simply 'the unlawful mixture of an unmaried couple' (Locke 1987: 192). So conceptually fornication is different from adultery. What then is Locke's take on it?

Fornication, as was the case with adultery, is a Christian sin. In the aforementioned part of the *Letter* concerning the works of the flesh, Locke marks out '*Adultery, Fornication, Uncleanness, Lasciviousness, Idolatry*' as immoralities that should be rooted out (*Letter* 10). Locke's paraphrase of 1 Cor. 6.9-10 in the *Paraphrase* also indicates that he believed that the scripture designated fornication as a sin: 'neither Fornicators, nor Idolators, nor adulterers, nor effeminate... shall inherit the Kingdom of god' (Locke 1987: 194). This is quite straightforward. The difficult question is whether fornication is a crime for Locke as some commentators have suggested. One thing we can say is that it is not a crime for the reason Marshall suggests. When Marshall notes that Locke argued in the *Letter* that both adultery and fornication were to be punished, it seems that he had the works of flesh list in mind, not least because there is no other explicit mention of fornication in the *Letter* itself.[18] However, if this is his basis, then it is unpersuasive. If we take a closer look at the list, leaving aside its peculiar selectiveness compared to the actual biblical text,[19] we can immediately observe that idolatry is also included. In the *Letter* itself, however, Locke painstakingly distinguished idolatry as a sin from a crime: 'But *Idolatry* (say some) *is a Sin*, and therefore not to be tolerated. If they said, it were therefore to be avoided, the Inference were good. But it does not follow, that because it is a Sin, it ought therefore to be punished by the Magistrate' (*Letter* 41). What Locke is trying to say here in the works of flesh passage is that if you truly wanted people to become Christians, if you were really serious about people becoming Christians, you would admonish them to correct their immoral lives. If you do not do this yet are ruthless towards people with different opinions about worship, then this shows that you are not sincerely keen on spreading Christianity but rather interested in something else, namely, building your own empire.[20]

In contrast to the evidence for punishing fornication, the other remarks about the subject Locke makes might be understood as lending support to the case against, or, at least, as rendering the case for punishing less conclusive. Again, in the *Paraphrase*, where Locke analyses Paul's response to the 'fornication as is not so much as named amongst the Gentiles', Locke takes note of the significantly *Christian* nature of the response:

> the arguments that St Paul uses... to prove Fornication unlawfull are all drawn Soley from the Christian institution. v.g That our bodys are made for the Lord ver. 13. That our bodys are members of Christ ver. 15. That our bodys are the temples of the holy ghost ver. 19 That we are not our own but bought with a price ver. 20. all which arguments concerne Christians onely; And there is not in all this discourse against Fornication one word to declare it to be unlawfull by the law of nature to man kind in general. (Locke 1987: 189)

Locke does add immediately after this passage that an argument to prove the unlawfulness of fornication was 'altogeather needless, and besides the Apostles purpose here, where he was teaching and exhorting Christians what they were to doe as Christians within their own Society by the law of Christ'. Thus, he leaves open the possibility that there could be an argument against fornication in natural law terms: it just was not pursued by the Apostle. At the same time though, Locke observes that fornication was lawful in some societies (he surmises that it was in Corinth), and that for some people, it was an 'indifferent' matter (Locke 1987: 187–8, 194n). In the *Essays on the Law of Nature* (1663–4), he also notes that in some societies 'it is lawful for unmarried girls to live dissolutely' (Locke 2007: 171). Then again, the particular context for this remark is how general consent of mankind is inadequate to derive the content of the natural law as the existence of diverse lifestyles demonstrates.

Turning back to the evidence for punishing fornication, if we take a look at what Locke says in his manuscript 'Atlantis', he writes 'marriage is to be encouraged' and 'fornication therefore to be hindered', so that children 'can be many' (Locke 1997: 255). The language here seems to be more about unsteadiness or ineffectiveness, that is, the ineffectiveness of unmarried, and, by implication, uncommitted, couples steadily to bring up children. In modern terms, Locke's worry may be akin to something like teenage pregnancy/poverty. If this is so, this would seem to be a weaker conflict with natural law than adultery.

In the end, what exactly is Locke's political and legal stance on fornication is rather hazy, but I think that we can appreciate the difference between adultery and fornication. Thus, we can accept the possibility that unlike adultery, while fornication remains a clear sin for Locke, it may not be a clear violation of the law of nature, or a criminal offence. Fornication may be officially discouraged, but that does not immediately amount to punishment (cf. *Second Letter* 66, where Locke talks about using both punishments and 'severities'[21] to impose a good life). 'No' to adultery does not automatically mean 'no' to fornication.

2.3 Polygamy

We now come to the *pièce de résistance* of this chapter: polygamy. Polygamy, Locke defines, is 'the having more Wives than one at once' (*Essay* II. xxviii. 4). Locke says 'wives' here, but he was aware of the opposite possibility as well, that is, polyandry: 'And what will become of this *Paternal Power* in that part of the World where one Woman hath more than one Husband at a time?' (TT II. 65) Is polygamy so defined a sin or a crime, or both? According to John Witte Jr, it was both a sin and a crime on Locke's account, although he admits that this is more implicit than explicit.[22] By contrast, Susanne Sreedhar and Julie Walsh (2016) argue that Locke's stance on polygamy is neutral and at times even positive. My own view is close to Sreedhar and Walsh – what Locke says about polygamy is incredibly open-ended.

Let me start with the evidence of Locke's neutral attitude towards polygamy. In the *Essays on the Law of Nature*, Locke avoids passing judgement on polygamy, saying, 'Let me pass over polygamy, which here is regarded as a right, there as a sin, which in one place is commanded by law, in another is punished by death' (Locke 2007: 171). Another instance is in his discussion of the names of mixed modes in the *Essay* (*Essay* III. vi. 44). In a hypothetical situation, Adam discusses with Eve about Lamech's melancholy, which he suspects is coming from the suspicion Lamech has of his wife Adah (it turned out that it was because he had killed a man). Lamech, Adah's husband, is the biblical figure in Genesis 4 who is said to have had two wives and also killed a man. In this example, Locke rather playfully uses Lamech, characterizing him only as a distraught killer who seems dearly to love his wife, and does not bring up or problematize his polygamous relationship (although it could be said that the latter characteristic was irrelevant to the point at hand).

Moving on to the more explicit and positive condoning of polygamy by Locke, in the manuscript 'Virtus', Locke suggests that polygamy is not necessarily contrary to reason or the law of nature, while it may be seen as a vice in some societies.

> & so many things naturally become vices amongst men in societys, which without that would be innocent actions thus for a man to cohabite & have children by one or more women, who are at their owne dispos<al> & when they think fit to part again I see not how it can be condemd as a vice, since no body is harmd supposeing it done amongst persons considerd as seperate from the rest of mankind but yet this hinders not but it is a vice of deep dye when the same thing done in a societie, wherein modestie the great vertue of the weaker sex, has often other rules & bounds set by custom & reputation, than what it has by direct instances of the Law of nature in a solitude or an estate seperate from the opinion of this or that societie. For if a woman by transgressing those bounds which the received opinion of her country or religion & not nature or reason have set to modesty, has drawn any blemish on her reputation she may run the risque of being exposd to infamy & other mischiefs amongst which the least is not the danger of looseing the comforts of a conjugall settlement & therewith the chief end of her being, the propagation of mankinde. (Locke 2006: 391)

If, as Locke says here, polygamy does not necessarily contradict natural law, how should the civil magistrate view it? In *An Essay Concerning Toleration* (1667),

Locke cites polygamy as an example of an 'indifferent' thing, things 'in their owne nature are neither good nor bad', nor do 'in them selves . . . inconvenience or advantage humane society'. For Locke, whether or not polygamy is lawful is something comparable to whether or not you choose to become a vegetarian (Locke 2006: 271, 289).[23] As such, therefore, polygamy deserves to be tolerated, but only to the extent that the magistrate judges that it does not 'tend to the disturbance of the state' or 'cause greater inconveniences, then advantages to the community' (Locke 2006: 276).

It is this conceptual space that allows Locke to flirt with the idea of polygamous morganatic relationships in 'Atlantis': 'He that is already married may marry another woman with his left hand. . . . The ties, duration, and conditions of the left hand marriage shall be no other than what are expressed in the contract of marriage between the parties' (Locke 1997: 256).

It is worth noting that the language of property in marital relationships fits neatly with Locke's openness towards polygamy.[24] Given that you work within the bounds of natural law, such as not being wasteful and leaving enough for others, you can acquire property for yourself. This might mean acquiring multiple wives (or husbands). Again, something becoming your property does not mean you can do anything with it.[25] And as we saw earlier, it also does not mean that the relationship will necessarily be unequal, the husband and the wife (or wives) having property in each other.

Now while there is certainly a lot going for the case to allow polygamy, how are we to view the case for Locke as an opponent of polygamy? I want to consider Witte's argument at this point. There are three points I will be examining and responding to. First, Witte argues that Locke did not think 'polygamy was a proper "moral relation" because it compromised a man's "readiness to acknowledge and return kindness received"' (Witte 2015: 366). But this must clearly be a misreading of the relevant passage. What Locke was doing in the said passage from the *Essay* (II. xxviii. 4) was simply talking about 'gratitude' and 'polygamy' separately as examples of mixed modes, making the point that in order to determine whether they are good or bad actions, you had to relate them to some kind of law.[26] Second, referring to Locke's comments in the *Essays on the Law of Nature*, Witte writes that Locke suggests that polygamy was a 'sin' (Witte 2015: 366). However, as we saw earlier, all that Locke does say is that in some societies it is considered a sin, not that Locke himself thought that it was.

Witte's third point is much more persuasive. Witte argues that Locke maintained that religious toleration 'did not prevent the state from punishing "the dishonesty and debauchery of men's lives" – which, for Locke, included "arbitrary divorce, polygamy concubinage, simple fornication", adultery, and incest'. He goes on and claims that Locke says that polygamy, like adultery and incest, is 'simply wrong' and 'must be prohibited without exception, religious liberty notwithstanding' (Witte 2015: 366–7). Witte is right to say that Locke distinguishes between speculative religious opinions and immoralities, and that what he says in the *Third Letter for Toleration* (1692), from which Witte quotes the philosopher, echoed the 'Essay', where he had said polygamy *qua* indifferent thing falls within the magistrate's power. However, what Locke says in the *Third Letter* and elsewhere is much less conclusive and hence much more open. First, to my knowledge, nowhere does he say in the *Third Letter* that polygamy, adultery and incest are 'simply wrong'. It is also noteworthy that the list of immoralities or 'vices' from arbitrary divorce to simple fornication was originally broached by Jonas Proast, Locke's adversary in the second to fourth letters on toleration. That said, it does seem that Locke does agree that the vices listed were immoralities societally understood when he makes the point through a rhetorical question that calling these vices and other things, including theft and murder, 'virtues' does not make them acceptable for that reason (*Third Letter* 241–2).

What are we to make of Locke's comment about the magistrate cracking down on vices? Locke does write, quoting the *Second Letter*, 'that if the magistrates would severely and impartially set themselves against vice in whomsoever it is found, and leave men to their own consciences in their articles of faith and ways of worship, true religion would spread wider, and be more fruitful in the lives of its professors', noting that vice here refers to 'immorality of manners' distinguished from religious opinions (*Third Letter* 241). I admit this sounds quite prescriptive. Moreover, the examples can be multiplied. Also in the *Third Letter*, of debaucheries, Locke writes: 'And for the toleration of corrupt manners, and the debaucheries of life, neither our author nor I do plead for it; but say it is properly the magistrate's business by punishments to restrain and suppress them' (*Third Letter* 416). Again: 'What you have said, plainly shows you that the assistance the magistrate's authority can give to the true religion, is in subduing of lusts; and its being directed against pride, injustice, rapine, luxury, and debauchery, and those other immoralities which come properly under his cognizance, and may be corrected by punishments' (*Third Letter* 468). Finally, even in the original *Letter*, he says, 'if some Congregations should have a mind to . . . (as the Primitive Christians were falsly accused) *lustfully pollute themselves in promiscuous Uncleanness*, or practise any other such heinous Enormities, *is the Magistrate obliged to tolerate them*, because they are committed in a Religious Assembly? I answer, No' (*Letter* 37).

There is a question as to what exactly is contained in the category 'debauchery' and 'promiscuous uncleanness' here. It might include adultery, fornication, polygamy and all other conducts typically dubbed sexually immoral. Or it might be used in a more limited sense, say, just to include adultery and perhaps fornication. Whichever it turns out to be, even in its most favourable reading for Witte's case (which would be the first), I do not think the previously cited passages can do the work he wants them to do. All that these passages show is that, for Locke, immoralities become the subject of punishment because of their presumed injury to the public good, and that the specific circumstances in *this or that* society demanded a response from the magistrate, or so Locke judged.[27] This seems to be the right place to say a word about the distinction Locke makes in the study of politics.

Locke identified two parts in the study of politics: one about seeking the origin and extent of political power, the other about the art of governing. Thus using this distinction, we may say that, for Locke, while all governments have a common source justifying their use of political power, that is to say natural law, they could diverge in how they ruled their society based on prudence acquired through experience and history (Locke 1997c: 351–2). Natural law, seen as a 'permissive' idea, rather than simply a prescriptive law, could allow for such space.[28] Recall too that in 'Virtus', Locke maintains that polygamy was not a vice 'by direct instances of the Law of nature in a solitude or an estate separate from the opinion of this or that societie'. Polygamy, for Locke, is not something that is always and everywhere the subject of punishment. It being censured was a contingent social fact.[29] We should therefore also recall that in his remarks about the suppression of debaucheries in the *Third Letter*, he and his interlocutor, Proast, reaffirm that they are speaking of 'England' (*Third Letter* 241). The upshot is this. Locke's opposition to polygamy that Witte identifies (granted that it was that) is not necessarily an objection against polygamy as such, but an objection in consideration of the social and moral climate of England in Locke's day. In other words, under different circumstances, it could be lawful. In fact, such a circumstance as an heirless Charles II may have just been it, and an option seriously considered by people around the king was divorce or polygamy.[30]

Whether societies tolerate polygamy or not, Locke maintains that polygamy per se is not a violation of the law of nature, that it does no injury to anyone. However, some modern commentators may argue that their objection to polygamy is not about cultural taste, but precisely about harm – harm to women and children. I will not be rehearsing all the objections in relation to this point; instead, I focus on one, the objection that polygamy tends to reduce the average parental investment per child, which, I think, puts Locke's argument to the test.[31] An example of this could be when male heads of household under polygamy compared with monogamy 'invest surplus resources in securing additional wives, leaving fewer resources for the education of rising generations' (Macedo 2015: 172). Let me, therefore, briefly turn to Locke's discussion of child provision and inheritance before bringing this section to a close.[32] While there indeed may be cases in which children of polygamous families are left with fewer resources than those of monogamous ones, what Locke says about parental and property rights seems to suggest that such cases will only count as harms under natural law if it does not meet a certain threshold, of which I will be presently elaborating. Thus, from this perspective too, I think Locke's thinking seems to have room to accommodate polygamy, albeit limited to certain kinds if it is to be practised in society.

Concerning parental duty, Locke argues that parents have a power over their children in their minority arising from a duty to bring up and educate them (TT II. 58–74). Children concomitantly have a right to be 'nourish'd and maintained by their Parents'; moreover, this right is not only a right to 'bare Subsistance but to the conveniences and comforts of Life, as far as the conditions of their Parents can afford it' (TT I. 89). So natural is this duty to care for and the right to be cared for that upon the parents' death, children have a 'natural Right of Inheritance to their Fathers Goods' exclusive of the rest of humankind. Locke reiterates this point later in the *Two Treatises*: everyone has a right 'before any other Man, to *inherit*, with his Brethren, his Fathers Goods' (TT II. 190). This is plain both from 'Laws of God' and the 'Law of the Land' (TT I. 88). Now Locke also holds that this right of inheritance is not limited to the first born, but equally to all the children under the guardianship of the parents: 'the First Born has not a sole or peculiar Right by any Law of God and Nature, the younger Children having an equal Title with him founded on that Right they all have to maintenance, support and comfort from their Parents' (TT I. 93). Locke does observe that as a matter of practice, fathers generally have the power to bestow their inheritance in different degrees to their children according to their behaviour (TT II. 72). Further, Locke maintains that a father could 'dispose his own Possessions as he pleases'. But there is a proviso immediately after, and this is 'when his Children are out of danger of perishing for want' (TT II. 65; cf. 'Atlantis' in Locke 1997: 259). So important is children's welfare that according to the 'Fundamental Law of Nature' even a just conqueror seeking reparation who has a just claim to their father's property must 'give way to the pressing and preferable Title of those, who are in danger to perish without it' (TT II. 183). Children by the law of nature have a 'Title' to 'share in', or a title 'to a part' of their parents' property (TT I. 88).

Let me return to polygamy. Whether a monogamous or polygamous family, while the parents may distribute their resources differently to their children, each child must equally receive not only the bare minimum for survival in that society[33] but also as far as possible what is necessary for a comfortable life. This applies not just to money but education as well. In other words, if your particular financial situation, say, does not allow for this, then you will not qualify for a polygamous marriage, or for that matter, not even a monogamous one. By contrast, if this level of resources is met, then in natural law terms, there is no harm done. True, had the man who meets this criterion not entered a polygamous union, in theory he could have given more to the child of the first and only wife. That, however, is not required by natural law, although it may require that all the children's needs be met at the level of what they would expect of a standard monogamous family.[34] In this sense, while this discussion on inheritance has space to accommodate polygamy, it seems that it will restrict it to a few cases: in short, polygamy will not be a general practice. Indeed, this seems consistent with what Locke pondered. Although he deleted the passage from 'Atlantis', Locke considered the option of married men entering another left-hand marriage, that is, someone of higher rank than the woman and presumably of wealth (say, someone like the king) entering into plural marriages.

This manuscript entry raises a final point I want to consider in this section, of what Locke calls 'bastards' or children born out of wedlock. In 'Atlantis' Locke writes: 'Bastards shall be incapable of inheritance or legacy by will' (Locke 1997: 256). Again, this is not his final word on the matter, as it was deleted. What he seems to have wanted to do was to distinguish between children born outside wedlock (i.e. as a result of adultery or fornication) and children born within albeit polygamous. Of the children of the left-hand marriage he writes: they 'shall be legitimate, but not capable to inherit but as younger to all those of the right hand marriage, though elder in years, i.e. shall have in succession the place of the next brother's children' (Locke 1997: 256). Thus, while polygamous children can inherit, bastard children cannot. This seems inconsistent with what he says in the *Two Treatises*. True, begetting in itself does not give you the power over your child, and you might un-father yourself, say, from your bastard son (TT II. 65: see also I. 100); but the parents have an 'Obligation bound to preserve what they have begotten', which in turn gives their offspring a right to inherit (TT I. 88). Maybe the assumption is that the bastard son would have received enough by the time of the father's death. In any case, in the *Two Treatises* Locke cites the 'bastard' Jephtha routinely as an example challenging Sir Robert Filmer's primogeniture narrative of the inheritance of Adamic political power (TT I. 163; II. 109), and also interrogates

Filmer about whether there is a natural law explanation ruling out inheritors of political power, including bastards, in the absence of the first born: 'Whether the Elder Son by a Concubine, before a Younger Son by a Wife? From whence also will arise many Questions of Legitimation, and what in Nature is the difference betwixt a Wife and a Concubine? . . . Whether a Sister by the half Blood, before a Brothers Daughter by the whole Blood?' (TT I. 123).[35] Given this, it seems unlikely Locke was saying that we could simply cut off bastards. If the deleted passage in 'Atlantis' is to have a part in Locke's thought, the point to be taken is that solemnized relationships were to be better rewarded materially than a monogamous plus an adulterous one. Polygamy, for Locke, was about commitment, not promiscuity.

So for Locke, polygamy in itself is not a natural law violation. Surprisingly, it is not a Christian sin, given that it is indifferent. If it were to be practised in society, it would be limited in scope. There is, of course, a question of whether society would ever find it acceptable, for the magistrate could only allow it if it did not cause social and civil instability. The legality of polygamy rested in effect on public opinion. In this respect, Locke was not J. S. Mill who would go on to challenge the effects of public opinion on one's liberty.

2.4 A summary of Section 2

Let me summarize the discussion so far. For Locke, adultery is a sin. It is also a natural law violation: you are unfaithful to your marital contract, you undermine your marital relationship and you take someone else's property. And for that, it is also a crime. Fornication is likewise a sin. It also seems to compromise the end of natural law – propagation of the human species – due to unsteadiness and insecurity, but the language against it seems weaker than adultery (i.e. suppress/punish vs hinder). It should be discouraged, but whether or not it is to be seen as a crime is not entirely clear. Finally, polygamy *qua* indifferent thing is not a sin. It is not a natural law violation as such. Given public opinion and in consideration of civil peace, magistrates can, if they so judge, regulate it (see Table 9.1).

Table 9.1 Locke's Responses to Adultery, Fornication and Polygamy

	Sin	Natural law violation	Crime
Adultery	Yes	Yes	Yes
Fornication	Yes	Not clear	Not clear, but may be officially discouraged
Polygamy	No	No	Depends on public opinion and judgement of magistrates

I think that I have said enough to show that Locke made distinctions between adultery, fornication and polygamy, and in relation to how the state should view and deal with these practices, measured them against natural law, rather than Christian scripture. Locke did not indiscriminately oppose sexual immorality, and neither did his pattern of thought take a slippery-slope logic, that 'yes' (or 'no') to one immorality means 'yes' (or 'no') to the others.

To conclude this first part, Locke's general stance towards sexual immoralities might be summarized as follows. For Locke, sexual vices that (1) completely breach natural law (e.g. adultery) could be punished and criminalized, while sexual vices that (2) potentially come into conflict with natural law (e.g. fornication) could be officially discouraged, say, by severities. This is akin to legalizing marijuana but to campaign against its use. Sexual vices that (3) do not usually come into conflict with natural law could be tolerated. However, under certain cultural circumstances, when the said vices undermined civil peace, they could become the subject of punishment.

3 Locke and marriage today

In this section, I want to turn from the question 'what we can learn about Locke's way of thinking through sex and marriage' to 'what we might learn from Locke's ideas about sex, marriage and the state'. I will use the debates over polygamy as my starting point. In his book *In Defense of Plural Marriage*, Ronald C. Den Otter has cast doubt on whether we can learn from past political theorists about polygamy, particularly from the case against it. As I understand him, he seems to think that past theorists tend to base their arguments on 'old religious texts', which tend to be 'outdated' and 'sectarian', and even for the more secular theorists, that their understanding and treatment of the subject tend to be limited and prejudiced, and so as a whole they are unlikely to be able to contribute to discussions in today's complex pluralistic society.[36] I agree with Den Otter that it is indeed difficult to translate and apply the insights of past thinkers to contemporary cases. But for one, Locke's arguments are not based on Christianity but on natural theology, and in the sense that the state does not exist to uphold religion, it is secular. Perhaps that does not make things more palatable for the modern reader, but the difference is important. The other point is that while Locke's conceptualization of marital relationship and consequently how the state should relate to marriage may be 'outmoded' to the modern liberal, I want to suggest that his conceptualization of how the state should relate to marriage is much more radical than one might suppose. By contrast, I point out that the newer liberal models are more connected to the 'outdated' model than they admit, and to that extent, we might say that Locke is still very much in the race. As a competitor, I think that Locke's model is quite flexible and broad even compared to some liberal societies today. Let us look at the broadness of Locke's model in more detail.

As Sreedhar and Walsh have highlighted, Locke holds that moral judgements – 'Good, Bad, *or* Indifferent' – about mixed modes are made in relation to a rule or law.[37] The law that has the most normative force for Locke is the law of nature promulgated by God through reason. What God makes manifest through natural law, especially in relation to sex and marriage, leaves us with considerable options. What Sreedhar and Walsh call the 'permissive' reading of Locke on marital forms is based on the law of nature being permissive.[38] Locke's idea of marriage is based on procreation, its chief goal, which in turn creates an obligation to sustain the vulnerable dependant, and, therefore, the necessity to continue in that relationship until the dependant becomes capable of becoming independent. Less emphasized but present as an aim is also to unite the care and love of the married. Thus marriage is about bearing, rearing *and* caring.

Marriage so conceived, polygamy, including both polygyny and polyandry, would be capable of satisfying this condition. One might venture to say incest would also pass the test, but Locke clearly objected to incest (TT I. 59). Yet if his definition of incest in the *Essay* is assumed to be final, which limited the circle to father, mother, son and daughter (*Essay* III. v. 6), it may be possible to talk about some sorts of incest in a less restrictive sense being justified.[39] While the emphasis on procreating might seem to bar elderly couples from marrying despite the encouragement of the 100-year-old Abraham and 90-year-old Sarah of the Old Testament, the aims of rearing and caring might do the work. I think that this is implicit in his discouragement of fornication and adolescent marriage and childbearing (Locke 1997: 255–9): if marriage was just about procreation, then there would be no reason to object to them. Also, given that you could become a parent fully as a foster parent, childrearing is possible without bearing yourself, and so there is a point in getting married without bearing yourself.[40] Of course, the elderly couple may not consider childrearing as an option. Locke did consider infertility after seven years a reason for divorce and remarrying, and so if the elderly couple are incapable of procreating – and moreover, we might add, not interested in childrearing – the ties may be looser, but this was only what one could do and not what one had to do (Locke 1997: 256). Marriage is chiefly about procreating and rearing, but it is also about caring. After all, if mutual support helps you and your spouse to live longer, it is consistent with the goal of natural law of preserving humankind. Thus, while old-age marriage might be more dissolvable given childlessness from the outset, it need not be excluded as an option. This gives Locke the conceptual resources to say that marriage is not just about reproductive sex (although it is chiefly about that).

If elderly couples can pass the test, can same-sex couples? Locke clearly opposes 'sodomy', but by this he could simply be talking about a specific sexual conduct, namely, anal sex or other non-coital, non-penile-vaginal sex. If that is the case, we could distinguish a particular sexual act from a relationship, again because not all marriages are just about sex.[41] Thus, as in the case of the elderly couple becoming foster parents, might not adoption and guardianship by same-sex couples but with no sex pass the test? And if we emphasize the caring part, would not there be space to include same-sex marriages (again without sex) even without an eye to adoption? However, the crucial difference between the elderly couple or the childless couple and the same-sex couple is that Locke explicitly states that a conjugal society is a compact between a man and a woman (so with polygamy, you will be making a number of contracts, depending on the number of spouses). If we are to follow Locke to the letter, this would exclude same-sex couples from getting married. The most that Locke's model could allow for in this respect, therefore, is cohabiting same-sex couples without sex, or such couples becoming foster parents, say, as partners or friends, rather than as a conjugal unit.

As we can see, in some areas (i.e. polygamy) Locke is much more open than liberal societies today, and in others (i.e. same-sex marriages), more conservative than liberal societies yet perhaps more liberal than conservative liberal societies.[42] The goal of natural law being the preservation of humankind through the preservation of society, Locke can say that there are many roads to Rome. While at present some may be temporarily closed, crucially they are not necessarily *fore*closed. What as a matter of fact is allowed under civil law might be less than what the full extent of natural law allows, because in consideration of civil peace, magistrates need to take into account the temperament of the people in their society: if magistrates judge that making something legal might lead to civil unrest, they might not give the green light to the said law. So for Locke, the social and moral culture of a society acts as a buffer, for better or worse, before something which in natural law terms can in principle become law actually becomes a positive law or not. Proponents of Burkean gradual change might applaud this, while Millian liberals might deplore the tyranny of public opinion. The significant point, in any case, is that Locke's model creates a landscape of possibilities and a space for dialogue.

While there is considerable latitude in Locke's model, there is undeniably an emphasis on procreation and preservation of the species, and because the state protects this relationship, it seems as if the state is privileging and promoting this particular type of relationship. In fact, in 'Atlantis', Locke precisely gives the law a role in incentivizing procreative marriages. For example, he writes: 'He that is married or has a child shall not be pressed to the wars' (Locke 1997: 255). Today, however, revisionists are calling into question the state's involvement in marriage. Does this render Locke obsolete in the eyes of liberals? I do not think so. As far as the *Two Treatises* goes, Locke's idea of how the state is to be involved in the marriage business is much closer to the revisionists than it first appears. For example, Den Otter defends what he calls 'Semiprivate Intimate Contracts (SPICs)'.[43] Eschewing complete privatization of marriages, SPICs are customized contracts, which the state is to recognize and require others to recognize. Now recall that for Locke the state simply reaffirms and protects a couple's natural right to procreate and offer mutual support, and only intervenes to adjudicate 'any Controversie that may arise' between the couple concerning these rights (TT II. 83). However, the specifics of the marriage (e.g. duration) is determinable and determined by what the couples themselves put in their original contract (TT II. 81–3).[44] So the state itself does not promote this or that arrangement but protects a lawful one in terms of natural law, and intervenes when a problem arises concerning the contract.[45] Moreover, its business is also to protect, in a manner consistent with civil stability, what is in natural law terms permitted, so if it does pass the test, same-sex couples as foster parents will be protected, although it will not go under the name of marriage. While this last point does have a 'separate but equal' tone to it, and so for some liberals will be inadequate, the general direction approaches revisionists' arguments for less state involvement in promoting certain kinds of marriages, and, in turn, opening up the range of recognized relationships seen as contracts.[46]

Superficially there might be a similarity between Locke and modern liberals, but the snag is that natural law is a way of understanding the good, and so while broad, Locke's model based on natural law would not be neutral in a modern liberal sense. But for many modern liberals, state neutrality matters. The state should remain neutral towards different conceptions of the good, hence different, forms of marriages. It should not privilege this or that kind of marriage, or for that matter, perhaps, marriage at all. By contrast, the state today is, as a matter of fact, deeply involved in promoting marriage, and for very Lockean-sounding reasons. For example, it is believed that marriage helps with population growth and creates a non-state rearing labour force. In other words, marriage is thought to provide a stable framework for procreation and childrearing. It is beneficial for the partners, for the children and as such for society as a whole. Other reasons as to why the state is in the marriage business might include an interest in reinforcing societal beliefs about appropriate sexual and marital relations, and, more technically and logistically, securing a way to mete out benefits through the creation of legal categories.[47] Both the 'traditional' state and Locke seem to fail the test of neutrality then. But how feasible is neutrality? And connectedly, how neutral are liberals themselves? It seems that liberals are faced with two, if not three, challenges.

The first challenge is that of libertarianism. Libertarians argue that if neutrality really matters, the solution would be for the state to pull out of the marriage business altogether. In other words, the question that needs to be answered is why you have to be in the marriage business at all? It seems, however, that liberals do not want to go as far as to withdraw completely because, today, many important material benefits are conferred through marriage (spousal visas, the right not to testify against your spouse, etc.), and also, more symbolically, because so many people have settled expectations about the recognition of their marriage by the state, the consequences of complete retreat of the state in reality seem enormous.[48] Moreover, for the state to leave at this precise moment will also leave intact the structural and symbolic biases in society that favour amatonormative relationships. Thus, liberals try to preserve some form of marriage, but try to make it more inclusive. Their aim is corrective: to rectify past injustices against hitherto marginalized relationships.[49]

However, liberals encounter a two-pronged challenge here, namely, the slippery-slope and strict anti-perfectionism. While liberals want to make marriage more inclusive, they want to draw a line somewhere and exclude some things from being called marriage, say, the unrequited feelings and the imaginary relationship that a stalker has with his or her object of affection.[50] So Elizabeth Brake, for example, defends what she calls 'minimal marriage', wherein the 'liberal state can set no principled restrictions on the sex or number of spouses and the nature and purpose of their relationships, *except* that they be caring relationships' (Brake 2012: 158, emphasis added). While caring relationships may indeed be broad, as for Brake it includes friendship, if you stop short of abolition, the anti-perfectionist challenge awaits you. That is, by supporting or incentivizing one sort of arrangement over others, even if it is not amatonormative, you are putting value on a particular conception of the good.

For example, Tamara Metz advocates a scheme of 'Intimate Caregiving Unions' (ICGU), which broadens the range of to-be-recognized relationships, but this in effect says being in a certain kind of relationship (i.e. intimate, caregiving) is better than not.[51] Do you, then, go down the slippery slope?

Den Otter's response to the slippery-slope and anti-perfectionism is to say that while complete neutrality might not be possible as long as the state is in the marriage business, you might try to minimize the effects by widening the net as much as possible; thus, SPICs. These customized contracts give greater flexibility to the types of recognizable marriages than Metz's or Brake's scheme as they do not have to be predicated on intimacy.

Comparing Locke's and Den Otter's model, then, we might say that while there is a structural similarity between the two in that marriages are contracts, and that the content of these is flexible, on the point of neutrality, Den Otter (and Brake) is better equipped to navigate around the anti-perfectionist challenge. By contrast, we might point out that all things considered, Locke is better prepared to answer the libertarian challenge paradoxically thanks to the non-neutral law of nature. Against Den Otter, libertarians might ask what motivation the state has simply for the sake of neutrality to be involved in a costly business of enforcing SPICs (or, in Brake's case, minimal marriages), when neutrality might be achieved by pulling out of the business altogether. As seen above, Den Otter (and Brake, likewise) would respond that it is to rectify past injustices of exclusion, and the state pulling out now would leave things as they are, that is, in an unequal state.[52] But what motivation would the state have to stay in the business after things are levelled out (or can be levelled out by other means than state intervention[53]), especially given that the anti-perfectionist challenge has not been completely met while minimized? Once again, the liberal model is a corrective, rather than a constructive, one. And so in this sense, it is parasitical on the fact that the state is in the marriage business already, that the state does give certain benefits through marriage, that people do attach a special meaning to marriage and from *that* starting point, it tries to make things more inclusive.[54] What they do not explain therefore with much force is why from a zero-base perspective the state should be in the marriage business at all.[55] While blatant, but not unreasonable, from a human rights perspective, Locke has an explanation, which is the preservation of humankind. This fact alone does not make Locke's scheme superior to the rest, but given too its flexibility, we might say at the very least that it does have a certain robustness that could give us reason to consider it to be on a par with other modern arguments for or against marriage as it stands today.

4 Conclusion

This chapter has attempted to clarify Locke's way of thinking about how the state should regulate matters concerning sex and marriage by fleshing out and comparing his responses to adultery, fornication and polygamy in particular. A close examination has shown that Locke responded differently to each of these practices according to how each related to natural law, and, therefore, that as a political theorist he did not approach the question from a religious perspective, nor did he take a blanket approach against these practices simply as comparable sexual immoralities. Noteworthy too was his peculiar openness towards polygamy.

In relation to modern discussions of democratizing marriage, we saw how Locke could vie with other modern liberal accounts. While Locke does not try to go 'beyond conjugality' (Law Commission of Canada 2001) and remains within it, he shows us that even within it, there is considerable flexibility, perhaps more than modern commentators have allowed, and, indeed, more than some actual liberal societies allow. Sex and marriage are central to Locke's vision, and while what he has to say about the subject may have a greater appeal to countries facing an ageing and shrinking population such as Japan and Italy, to the extent that states are still 'traditional' or have developed from or are parasitical on them, Locke's 'pastness' does not seem to be a good reason automatically to disqualify him or to presume him to be incapable of contributing to complicated modern debates about sex, marriage and the state.

Notes

1. I have benefitted from friendly exchanges in seminars and workshops at Keio University and Gakushuin University, especially comments by Peter Anstey. I am also obliged to Takuya Furuta, Giuliana di Biase and Kiyoshi Shimokawa for comments on earlier drafts of this chapter.
2. See March (2011: 247).
3. I say 'so-called' because their morality is precisely being explored here.
4. See Dunn (1991: 187), Israel (2006: 142), Marshall (2006: 715–19), Goldie (1993: 167–8), Goldie's note at *Letter* 37n, Watson (2011). For general studies on sex and marriage in early modern England, see Laslett (1977), Stone (1977), Dabhoiwala (2012).
5. For example, Pfeffer (2001), Yenor (2011), Dabhoiwala (2012), Schmidgen (2013), Achinstein (2016), Sreedhar and Walsh (2016).

6 See also Locke's remarks about 'tithingman' in his middle writings. See 'Atlantis' in Locke (1997).
7 See Witte (2015).
8 My focus is on *sexual* vices and not vices in general. Also, the view I challenge is not so much that Locke was sympathetic to the cause of the Societies for the Reformation of Manners (SRM) (Goldie 1993: 167n) as that he indiscriminately opposed all sexual immoralities, and thought that they were all equally punishable by the state because they were the same sort of conduct. In fact, I believe Locke could show sympathy towards the SRM while seeing different ways in which the state could face sexual immoralities. See also Shimokawa's note 24 in his chapter in this volume.
9 To a much lesser extent, I will say something about sodomy and incest too.
10 See also Stanton (2008); see also Israel (2006: 142), Forster (2011); cf. Waldron (2002). My argument in this chapter might be seen as reinforcing the reservations Takei expresses in his chapter to this volume about Loconte's (2014: 178) argument that 'Locke was thinking seriously about the Biblical basis for toleration while writing *The Reasonableness of Christianity*'.
11 Cited by treatise and paragraph number.
12 On feminist views on Locke and the family, see, for example, Hirchmann and McClure (2007), Ward (2010: ch. 4).
13 In 'Atlantis', Locke writes that if a woman converses in private 'i.e. out of sight of witnesses, with a man, whose company has been forbidden her by her husband solemnly before two witnesses', she shall be accountable for adultery (Locke 1997: 256).
14 For a comprehensive study on being a 'cuckold' (i.e. the husband of an adulterous wife) in early modern England, see Foyster (1999).
15 I thank Giuliana di Biase for her comment about the commonness of the practice in the seventeenth century.
16 See also Waldron (2002: 29, 122–5).
17 I say 'couple' for convenience's sake.
18 The term appears only once in the Popple translation, but in the modern translations from the Latin original (i.e. the Klibansky and Gough edition (Locke 1968: 61) and the Vernon edition (Locke 2010b: 4)) it also appears in a different place. However, it is basically used to make the same point.
19 See Wolfson (2010: 85–7).
20 See also *Second Letter* 65.
21 See *OED*, sense 1c in the plural: 'severe rebukes or criticisms'.
22 Witte (2015: 366).
23 I do not mean to trivialize the fact that for many vegetarians and vegans, the choice to become what they are is of paramount ethical significance.

24 I am grateful to Takuya Furuta for pointing this out to me.
25 See Simmons (1992: esp. ch. 5) and Shimokawa (2006).
26 See also Sreedhar and Walsh (2016).
27 See Harris (2013: 93) and Marshall (1994: 380–3).
28 See Tierney (2014); cf. Locke (1976–1989, 1: 559; 2007: 193–7).
29 See also Schmidgen (2013: 107–8).
30 See Wootton (2003: 72), Marshall (1994: 199–200), and Dabhoiwala (2012: 220).
31 *Reference re: Section 293 of the Criminal Code of Canada* (2011: para 499), Macedo (2015: 172). For a general case against polygamy, see Brooks (2009).
32 I am grateful to Peter Anstey for suggesting this line of inquiry.
33 We might infer this from Locke's views expressed on just pricing in 'Venditio', namely, at the market price where one sells one's products (Locke 1997: 340).
34 Ibid.
35 This last part about half-sisters does not necessarily imply the existence of a concubine or a polygamous wife (although some did see remarriage by a divorced person as a form of polygamy (Witte 2015)).
36 See Den Otter (2015: 39–41).
37 Sreedhar and Walsh (2016: 97); *Essay* II. xxviii. 15.
38 Sreedhar and Walsh (2016: 92) and Tierney (2014).
39 See also Sreedhar and Walsh (2016: 106).
40 See Sreedhar and Walsh (2016: 107).
41 And so we might say Thomas West is too quick to reject considerations of Locke and same-sex marriage just based on the *Two Treatises* where the latter says procreation is the chief end of marriage and sodomy is a sin (West 2012. 25; TT I. 59). For a coverage of the debate over Locke and same-sex marriage, see Henry (2016).
42 Japan, for example, did not allow foster parenting by same-sex couples until 2017.
43 Den Otter (2015: 274–5, 301ff).
44 See also Nolan (2016) for 'temporary' marriages.
45 See also Witte (2012).
46 Den Otter (2015) and Chartier (2016).
47 See Vanderheiden (1999: 179–85), Corvino and Gallagher (2012: 116–20) and Chartier (2016: 178–9).
48 See Volokh (2014) and Den Otter (2015: 264ff, 278ff).
49 Brake (2012: 188).
50 Brake (2012: 164).
51 See Metz (2010: 113ff) and Den Otter (2015: 318).
52 See Den Otter (2015: 264ff) and Brake (2012: 185ff).
53 Chartier (2016).
54 See also Warner (2010).
55 See also Chartier (2016).

References

Achinstein, S. (2016), 'Early Modern Marriage in a Secular Age: Beyond the Sexual Contract', in B. Hoxby and A. B. Coiro (eds), *Milton in the Long Restoration*, 363–78, Oxford: Oxford University Press.

Brake, E. (2012), *Minimizing Marriage*, Oxford: Oxford University Press.

Brooks, T. (2009), 'The Problem with Polygamy', *Philosophical Topics*, 37 (2): 109–22.

Chartier, G. (2016), *Public Practice, Private Law*, Cambridge: Cambridge University Press.

Corvino, J. and M. Gallagher (2012), *Debating Same-Sex Marriage*, Oxford: Oxford University Press.

Dabhoiwala, F. (2012), *The Origins of Sex*, London: Penguin Books.

de Marneffe, P. (2016), 'Liberty and Polygamy', in E. Brake (ed.), *After Marriage*, 125–9, Oxford: Oxford University Press.

Den Otter, R. C. (2015), *In Defense of Plural Marriage*, Cambridge: Cambridge University Press.

Dunn, J. (1991), 'The Claim to Freedom of Conscience: Freedom of Speech, Freedom of Thought, Freedom of Worship?', in O. P. Grell, J. Israel and N. Tyacke (eds), *From Persecution to Toleration*, 171–93, Oxford: Clarendon Press.

Finnis, J. (1997), 'The Good of Marriage and the Morality of Sexual Relations: Some Philosophical and Historical Observations', *The American Journal of Jurisprudence*, 42 (1): 97–134.

Forster, G. (2011), 'Locke, Christianity, Evangelicals, and Marriage'. Available online: https://www.firstthings.com/blogs/firstthoughts/2011/03/locke-christianity-evangelicals-and-marriage (accessed 7 October 2020).

Foyster, E. A. (1999), *Manhood in Early Modern England*, New York: Longman.

Goldie, M. (1993), 'John Locke, Jonas Proast and Religious Toleration 1688–1692', in J. Walsh, C. Haydon and S. Taylor (eds), *The Church of England, c.1689–c.1833*, 143–71, Cambridge: Cambridge University Press.

Harris, I. (2013), 'John Locke and Natural Law: Free Worship and Toleration', in J. Parkin and T. Stanton (eds), *Natural Law and Toleration in the Early Enlightenment*, 59–105, Oxford: Oxford University Press.

Henry, C. (2016), '*Obergefell*, Locke, and the Changing Definition of Marriage', *Catholic Social Science Review*, 21: 55–70.

Hirschmann, N. J. and K. M. McClure, eds (2007), *Feminist Interpretations of John Locke*, University Park: Pennsylvania State University Press.

Israel, J. (2006), *Enlightenment Contested*, Oxford: Oxford University Press.

Laslett, P. (1977), *Family Life and Illicit Love in Earlier Generations*, Cambridge: Cambridge University Press.

Law Commission of Canada (2001), *Beyond Conjugality*.

Lawrence v. Texas (2003), 539 U.S. 558.

Locke, J. (1823a), *A Second Letter Concerning Toleration*, in *The Works of John Locke*, vol. 6, 61–137, London: T. Tegg; abbreviated as *Second Letter*.

Locke, J. (1968), *Epistola de Tolerantia A Letter on Toleration*, ed. R. Klibansky, trans. J. W. Gough, Oxford: Clarendon Press.

Locke, J. (1975), *An Essay concerning Human Understanding*, ed. P. H. Nidditch, Oxford: Clarendon Press; abbreviated as *Essay*.

Locke, J. (1976-1989), *The Correspondence of John Locke*, 8 vols, ed. E. S. de Beer, Oxford: Clarendon Press.

Locke, J. (1987), *A Paraphrase and Notes on the Epistles of St Paul*, ed. A. W. Wainwright, 2 vols, Oxford: Clarendon Press.

Locke, J. (1988), *Two Treatises of Government*, ed. P. Laslett, Cambridge: Cambridge University Press; abbreviated as TT, and cited by treatise and section number.

Locke, J. (1997), *Political Essays*, ed. M. Goldie, Cambridge: Cambridge University Press.

Locke, J. (2006), *An Essay Concerning Toleration and Other Writings on Law and Politics, 1667-1683*, eds J. R. Milton and P. Milton, Oxford: Clarendon Press.

Locke, J. (2007), *Essays on the Law of Nature and Associated Writings*, ed. W. von Leyden, Oxford: Clarendon Press.

Locke, J. (2010a), *A Letter Concerning Toleration and Other Writings*, ed. M. Goldie, Indianapolis: Liberty Fund; abbreviated as *Letter*, and cited by page number.

Locke, J. (2010b), *Locke on Toleration*, ed. R. Vernon, Cambridge: Cambridge University Press.

Loconte, J. (2014), *God, Locke, and Liberty*, Lanham, MD: Lexington Books.

Macedo, S. (2015), *Just Married*, Princeton: Princeton University Press.

March, A. (2011), 'Is there a Right to Polygamy?: Marriage, Equality and Subsidizing Families in Liberal Public Justification', *Journal of Moral Philosophy*, 8 (2): 246-72.

Marshall, J. (1994), *John Locke: Resistance, Religion and Responsibility*, Cambridge: Cambridge University Press.

Marshall, J. (2006), *John Locke, Toleration and Early Enlightenment Context*, Cambridge: Cambridge University Press.

Metz, T. (2010), *Untying the Knot*, Princeton: Princeton University Press.

Nolan, D. (2016), 'Temporary Marriage', in E. Brake (ed.), *After Marriage*, 180-203, Oxford: Oxford University Press.

Pfeffer, J. (2001), 'The Family in John Locke's Political Thought', *Polity*, 33 (4): 593-618.

Reference re: Section 293 of the Criminal Code of Canada (2011) BCSC 1588.

Schmidgen, W. (2013), *Exquisite Mixture: The Virtues of Impurity in Early Modern England*, Philadelphia: University of Pennsylvania Press.

Shimokawa, K. (2006), 'Locke's Concept of Property', in P. R. Anstey (ed.), *John Locke: Critical Assessments*, Series II, vol. 1, 176-216, Abingdon: Routledge.

Simmons, A. J. (1992), *The Lockean Theory of Rights*, Princeton: Princeton University Press.

Sreedhar, S. and J. Walsh (2016), 'Locke, the Law of Nature, and Polygamy', *Journal of the American Philosophical Association*, 2 (1): 91-110.

Stanton, T. (2008), 'Locke the Thinker', *Locke Studies*, 8: 23–58.

Stone, L. (1977), *The Family, Sex and Marriage in England 1500–1800*, London: Harper & Row.

Tierney, B. (2014), *Liberty and Law*, Washington, DC: The Catholic University of America Press.

Vanderheiden, S. (1999), 'Why the State Should Stay Out of the Wedding Chapel', *Public Affairs Quarterly*, 13 (2): 175–90.

Volokh, E. (2014), 'Why Not Get the State Out of the Marriage Business'. Available online: https://www.washingtonpost.com/news/volokh-conspiracy/wp/2014/04/10/why-not-get-the-state-out-of-the-marriage-business/?utm_term=.a4946e189b27 (accessed 7 October 2020).

Waldron, J. (2002), *God, Locke, and Equality*, Cambridge: Cambridge University Press.

Ward, L. (2010), *John Locke and Modern Life*, Cambridge: Cambridge University Press.

Warner, M. (2010), 'Response to Martha Nussbaum', *California Law Review*, 98 (3): 721–29.

Watson, M. (2011), 'John Locke and the Evangelical Retreat from Marriage'. Available online: http://www.thepublicdiscourse.com/2011/03/2904/ (accessed 7 October 2020).

West, T. (2012), 'The Ground of Locke's Law of Nature', *Social Philosophy & Policy*, 29 (2): 1–50.

Witte, Jr., J. (2012), *From Sacrament to Contract*, 2nd edn, Louisville: Westminster John Knox Press.

Witte, Jr., J. (2015), *The Western Case for Monogamy over Polygamy*, Cambridge: Cambridge University Press.

Wolfson, A. (2010), *Persecution or Toleration*, Lanham, MD: Lexington Books.

Wootton, D. (2003), 'Introduction', in *John Locke: Political Writings*, 7–122, Indianapolis: Hackett.

Yenor, S. (2011), *Family Politics*, Waco: Baylor University Press.

Index

Aaron, R. 106
Abraham 196, 210 n.36
   and Sarah 230
Adam
   Adam's fall 191, 194–5,
      209 n.25
   Adam's political power 227
   adultery 216
   and Eve 222
affirmation and negation 38–40, 43
agreement 103, *see also* compact
agreement and disagreement of ideas 16, 29–47 *passim*
Aikyo, K. 12
anarchy 122, 128
Anderson, J. 46 n.13
Anstey, P. R. 1, 15–16, 18–19, 29, 68 nn.3, 9, 10, 69 nn.11, 12, 17, 78, 91 n.2, 93 nn.11, 14, 15, 164 n.6, 207 n.7
Antinomianism 192, 197, 202
Aoki, S. 16, 52, 91 n.2
Aquinas, *see* Thomas, (Saint)
Arbuthnot, J. 92 n.8
Aristotle 3, 52, 61, 68 n.2, 125–9, 140 nn.21, 22
Arnauld, A. 46 n.5
Arneil, B. 11
Ashcraft, R. 10, 179–80
Ashe, St George 75, 92 n.5
assenting 41–4
atheist 17, 170, 181–3, 186 n.37
Augustine of Hippo, (Saint) 153
Ayers, M. 47–8 n.29

Bacon, F. 127, 140 n.19, *see also* natural history
   Baconian natural philosophy 76, 78, 91 n.2
Bagshaw, E. 12, 185 n.27
Barrovian case 76, 92 n.9, 95 n.28
Bates's Case 132, 133
Baxter, R. 192, 208 n.11

Bayle, P. 183 n.3
Beran, H. 111
Berkeley, G. 2, 11, 16, 52, 67 n.1, 70 n.32
   analysis and synthesis 83, 85, 87, 94 n.22
   attraction 76, 79–81, 88
   consciousness 87
   distance perception 85–8, 95 n.28
   experimental philosophy 74–95 *passim*
   laws of nature 81, 93 n.19, 94 n.20
   metaphysical causes 76, 77, 82, 85, 90
   New Theory of Vision 16, 75–6, 81–94 *passim*
   Theory of Vision Vindicated 76, 82–3
   Philosophical Commentaries 75, 77, 78, 80
   principles 82–3, 87, 88, 90, 94 n.20
Bodin, J. 126, 128, 140 n.15
Boyle, R. 2, 16, 52–71 *passim*, 74, 76, 78, 79, 89, 93 n.15, 95 n.30
   corpuscularianism 16, 53–5, 58, 59–64, 67 n.1, 91 n.2
   critique of scholasticism 55, 58
   experimental philosophy 76, 78, 79
   Forms and Qualities 52–60, 69–70 n.19
   texture 56–8, 61, 67, 70 n.29
   theory of qualities 54–8
Brake, E. 233–4
Buckle, S. 11
Bury, A. 207 n.7

Calvert, B. 165 n.8
Calvinist 192, 197, 202
Caron, F. 2
charity 171, 178, 190, 198
Charles II, (King) 124, 225
Charleton, W. 68 n.3
Christ (Jesus, Messiah) 190–211 *passim*
   miracles 18, 190, 199–202, 205, 210 nn.38, 40
   self-disclosure 199–202

Cicero   127
civil interests (*bona civilia*)   174, *see also* property
civil society   117, *see also* political society
civil wars (England and Scotland)   132, 134, 138, 189
clear and present danger   183
colonialism   12, 15
community   102–4, 120, *see also* society
compact   103, *see also* consent, marriage
consciousness   14, 87, 154–5, 159
consent   12, 16, 101–18 *passim*, 122
   conditions for valid   112–14
   tacit   16, 104–7, 112–13, 115–16
Constitution
   American   119
   ancient   129, 132
   of the Empire of Japan (Meiji Constitution, 1889)   20 n.18, 21 n.27
   of Japan (New Constitution, 1946)   7, 9, 20 n.18, 147, 149, 161
constitutionalism   11, 17, 119–41 *passim*
Cooper, T.   192
Copernicus, N.   3
Corbett, R. J.   130, 135
corpuscular hypothesis   11, 16, 59, 60–5, 67, 70 nn.24, 26, 32, 71 nn.39, 45, 74, 79, 91 n.2, 95 n.30, *see also* Boyle
covenant   181
   new covenant (of grace)   192, 196–8, 201
Cranston, M.   179
Crisp, T.   192
   son Samuel   192

D'Ailly, P.   133
death   102, 112, 194–5, *see also* death penalty
   Epicurean view   164–5 n.7
death penalty   2, 17, 145–65 *passim*
   abolitionism   157–8, 161
   impossibilism   17, 157–62
   and Japan   146, 158, 161
   retentionism   157, 158, 161, 162
Declaration of Independence (1776)   147
Declaration of Rights of Man and of the Citizen (1789)   147

Deism   203, 206, 208 n.16
de Merneffe, P.   215
democracy   6, 8, 120, 146
   democratically elected legislature   16, 114, 116
   democratic values   7
Den Otter, R. C.   229, 232, 234
Descartes, R.   3, 58, 61, 68 n.3, 70 n.25, 74, 84, 90, 95 n.30
   and ideas   61
divine right of kings   126, 129–30
Dublin Philosophical Society   75, 76, 78, 80, 91 n.4, 92 nn.5, 6, 9, 10
Dunn, J.   10, 17, 124, 170, 179, 193

Edwards, J.   12, 207 n.7
empiricism   6, 89, 91 nn.1, 3
   British   8, 74
   idea-empiricism   64–5
Epicurus   58, *see also* death
   Epicureans   56
equity   125, 127, 128, 132
Euclid   47 n.17
Exclusion crisis   122, 124
experimental philosophy   16, 53, 74–6, 89–90, 91 n.1, 94 n.24
   experimental/speculative distinction   68 n.10, 77–81, 93 n.14

Fall (The), *see* Adam
Fatovic, C.   124–6, 135
Filmer, (Sir) R.   12, 13, 17, 21 n.26, 112, 123, 126, 138, 139 n.4, 141 n.34
   Patriarcha   122, 126–9, 136–7, 140 n.21, 227–8
Finnis, J.   214
Fleming, (Chief Baron) T.   132–3
force   16, 62, 66, 84, 93 n.17, 102, 103, 112–13, 131, 170–2, 174, 178–9, 184 n.6, 207 n.3
   civil   171
forfeiture   17, 156–9, 162, 164 n.5
freedom of expression   170, 182
Furuta, T.   12

Galilei, G. (Galileo)   3, 68 n.3
Gassendi, P.   58, 61
Gaukroger, S. W.   16, 74–5, 89–90, 91 nn.1, 2, 3, 95 n.30

God 80, 81, 90, 112, 122, 126, 129, 133, 135, 153, 158, 160, 161, 171–2, 176, 181–2, 190, 194–7, 201–3, 205, 209 n.19, 218, 230
  Deus 182
  kingdom of 195, 199, 210 n.35, 216, 220
  miracles 133
  numen 181
Gough, J. W. 179
gravity (attraction) 76, 79–81, 88, 93 n.18
Gray, J. 124
Grotius, H. 11, 147, 174

Hamabayashi, M. 9
harm 174, *see also* injury
  applications of the harm principle 175–82
  harm argument 169–70, 173–82
  harm principle 173–4
Hart, H. L. A. 150
Hartlib, S. 93 n.14
Hatta, S. 6
Hattori, T. 10
Hill, B. 40
Hill, J. 60, 62–3
Hirano, A. 9, 21 n.34
Hobbes, T. 6, 68 n.3, 137, 147, 202
  Hobbist 186 n.37
  Leviathan 204, 205
Hodgskin, T. 22 n.43
Holmes, (Justice) O. W. Jr 186 n.39
Hooke, R. 93 n.15
Hume, D. 11, 16, 74, 89–90, 101–2, 105–16
  criticisms of tacit consent 112–13
  critic of social contract theory 101–2, 105–16
  on de facto government 112, 115
  descriptive critique of Locke 105–6
  normative critique of Locke 106–7
  on the obligation to obey a particular government 111–12
  on the original contract 106–7, 109–10, 115, 117
  on property 150
Hume, D. (Works)
  'Of the Original Contract' 101, 102
  Treatise 89, 102, 105, 112

Humphrey, J. 2
Hunton, P. 141 n.31
Huygens, C. 53
hypotheses 78, 80, 87, 91 n.2, 93 n.15, 94 n.24, *see also* corpuscular hypothesis

Ichinose, M. 11, 14, 17, 145, 165 n.7
idolatry 174, 176, 219–20
Imamura, K. 12, 15
impulse 60, 62, 79, 90
inheritance 149, 226–7
injury (concept of) 174
Inoue, K. 9
intermediate ideas (proofs) 32, 33
Ito, H. 12

James VI and I, (King) 127, 129, 140 n.17
Japan, *see also* Constitution
  Catholic missionaries in 3
  and the Dutch 3–4
  isolationism 3–5
  persecution of Christians in 2
Jefferson, T. 182
Josephson, P. 114
judgement 15, 42, 127
  fallibility of 185 n.19
  liberty of 172
  moral 230
  political 131, 134, 138
  practical (*phronesis*) 128
justice
  conformity to 126
  corrective 233–4
  flexible exercise of 127
  and Locke 177, 185 n.26
  negative 171
  restorative 162
  retributive 156–7, 162, 163
justification (by faith) 192, 197, 198, 202, 204, 209 n.22
  sola fide 173, 184 n.16

Kanno, K. 21 n.42
Kato, T. 10
Kato, U. 6
King, W. 92 n.9
Kiyomiya, S. 7

knowledge   5, 11, 15–16
   by acquaintance   36–8, 44, 45, 47 n.24
   definition of   29
   demonstrative   31, 32, 37, 42, 47 n.16
   of individual ideas   36–7, 45
   intuitive   31, 32, 37, 42, 47 n.24
   propositional   16, 29, 31, 33–6, 38, 47 n.24, 154
   sensitive   30, 31, 44, 48 nn.35, 39, 49 n.54
Kobayashi, S.   6
Kojo, T.   1, 12, 16, 101

law of nature   16, 80, 102–3, 112–13, 115–16, 195, *see also* natural law
law of works/law of faith   195–8, 202
Lawrence v. Texas   214
Le Clerc, J.   192, 208 n.15
Leibniz, G. W.   3, 48 n.40, 95 n.30
Letwin, S. R.   137
liberalism   126, 137, 139
libertarianism and marriage   233–4
liberty   7, 102, 103, 109, 113, 123, 124, 149–50, 176, 219
   of conscience   172, 182, 189, 202
   of judgement   172
   of the press   203
   of religion   9, 21 n.27, 170, 176, 224
Lightfoot, J.   192
Limborch, P. van   192
Locke, J. (Works) 'Atlantis'   221, 223, 226–8, 232, 236 n.13
   Drafts of the *Essay*   47 n.29, 48 n.33, 60, 70 nn.26, 33
   Elements of Natural Philosophy   34, 35
   Essay concerning Human Understanding   6, 8, 10, 14, 29–71 *passim*, 74–5, 89, 90, 92 nn. 5, 6, 154–5, 164 n.4, 193, 208 n.18, 216, 222, 223
   Essay Concerning Toleration   2, 9, 12, 180, 189, 190, 222–3
   Essays on the Law of Nature   8, 10, 221, 222, 223
   'First Treatise'   216
   Letter Concerning Toleration   9, 13, 169, 190, 216, 219–20, 224
   Letter to Stillingfleet   42–3
   Of the Conduct of the Understanding   13, 184 n.18

Paraphrase and Notes   216–20
Reasonableness of Christianity   10, 13, 18, 184 n.16, 189–211 *passim*, 236 n.10
'Reasons for Tolerating Papists Equally with Others'   180
Second Letter   171, 179, 183 n.2, 184 n.6, 221
Second Reply to Stillingfleet   33, 34, 47 n.20, 48 n.35, 49 nn.52, 54
'Second Treatise'   7, 8, 17, 20 n.17, 102, 120, 148, 164 n.4, 232
Second Vindication   41–2, 192, 205, 206, 211 n.50
Some Thoughts Concerning Education   5, 71 n.39
'Some Thoughts Concerning Reading and Study for a Gentleman'   110
Third Letter   224–5
Two Tracts on Government   10, 184 n.5, 189, 190
Two Treatises   8, 10, 12, 101–5, 107–14, 122, 123, 126, 128, 174, 184 nn.5, 11, 226, 227, 232
'Virtus'   222, 225
Locke and Japan   1–15
Loconte, J.   190–1
logic, early modern   41
   syllogistic   45
love   171, 190–1
   of truth   205
Luther, M.   197

MacArthur, (General) D.   7
Machiavelli, N.   125, 126
Macpherson, C. B.   10, 22 n.43
majority   103–4, 113–14, 146
Malebranche, N.   75, 91 n.3, 95 n.30
Mansfield, H. C. Jr   124, 125
Manwaring, R.   129
marriage   214–37 *passim*
   adultery   216–19, 221, 228
   bastards   227–8
   contract (compact)   217, 218, 219, 223, 228, 231, 232, 234
   fornication   215–18, 219–21, 228
   incest   216, 224, 230
   parental duty   226
   polygamy   215, 221–8

polygamy contemporary
    perspectives   229–31
  same-sex marriage   18, 214, 230–2,
    237 n.41
Marshall, J.   183 n.3, 193–4, 206, 208
  n.16, 219, 220
Marušić, J. S.   46 n.5, 47 n.29
Matsushita, K.   8, 13
Matsuura, K.   8
Mattern, R.   29, 46 n.5
Mede, J.   192, 208 n.15
Meiji government   9
Metz, T.   234
Mill, J. S.   173, 174, 228
Miura, N.   11, 12, 15
Miyazawa, T.   21 n.42
moderation   6, 21 n.41
modernity   7, 137
  modern political principles   7–8
Molyneux, S.   75, 92 n.8
Molyneux, T.   75, 92 n.8
Molyneux, W.   75, 76, 92 nn.5, 9
Moon illusion   76, 89, 92 n.9
morality   10, 161, 164 n.6, 190, 193, 198,
    201–3, 207 n.4, 209 n.19
Morimura, S.   11
Moses   195–6, 210 n.36

Nakano, Y.   16, 74
native Americans   11, 12, 15, 17, 176,
    181, 183
  dispossession of   12, 15
natural equality   108, 109, 115
natural freedom   103, 109, 115, 122–3,
    128, 148
natural history
  Baconian   76, 78, 80, 81, 91 n.2, 92
    n.8, 93 n.11
natural law   8, 18, 121, 122, 126, 131,
    137, 139, 149, 155, 215, 216,
    218–19, 221–9, 231–2, see also
    the law of nature
Newman, L.   49 n.46
Newton, (Sir) I.   3, 16, 53, 68 n.10, 74,
    76, 77–81, 83–4, 88, 89, 93
    nn.11, 16, 17, 18, 94 n.25,
    207 n.7
  Principia   76, 78–81, 84, 88, 93 n.16,
    94 nn.20, 24
Nicole, P.   46 n.5

Nishi, A.   5, 6
Nishitani, K.   6
Nuchelmans, G.   41, 49 n.47
Numao, J. K.   18, 185 n.24, 214
Nuovo, V.   194, 200
Nye, S.   191, 207 n.8

oaths   104, 109, 181, 186 n.32
Ockham, W.   46 n.8, 133, 208 n.19
Oshima, M.   6, 20–1 n.24
Otsuki, H.   8, 20 n.12, 20–1 n.24
Ott, W.   48 n.34
Ottoman Empire   181, 185 n.27
Owen, D.   29, 40–1

Panaccio, C.   46 n.8
Pangle, T. L.   124
Parker, H.   132–4, 138, 141 n.31
Parker, K. I.   192
Parker, S.   12
Pasquino, P.   124
Patrick, S.   208 n.15
Paul, (Saint)   216, 217, 220
Pembroke, (8th Earl) Herbert, T.   92 n.6
Perry, (Commodore) M.   5
persecution   2, 171
persons   11, 14–15, 147–9, 151–5, 158,
    160, 164 n.4
Plato   3
  Crito   101
Pocock, J. G. A.   125
Pococke, E.   185 n.27
political society   7, 8, 110, 113–14, 122,
    131, 169, 183 n.5
Popple, W.   177, 184 n.12, 185 nn.20, 23,
    186 n.28, 206, 236 n.18
prerogative   17, 119–41 *passim*
Prideaux, H.   203–4
primary and secondary qualities   52–71
    passim
principles of reason   42, 43, 201
Proast, J.   12, 169, 170, 183 n.2, 224, 225
probability   145
promise   106, 107, 112, 178, 181–2,
    186 n.37, 196, see also covenant;
    oath
property   6, 8–12, 14–15, 155, 174, 217,
    223, see also native Americans
  concept of   11, 14, 150, 152, 163 n.3,
    174, 185 n.22

labour theory of 6, 12, 13, 15, 22 n.43, 149–53
  in a wife's (or husband's) body 217–19
propositions 29–30, 38
  mental propositions 31, 38–44, 48 n.33
  verbal propositions 16, 31, 32, 35, 39, 43–4, 48 nn.34, 40
Pufendorf, S. 11, 147, 174
punishment 5, 14, 17, 103, 145–8, 154–60, 161, 162, 164 nn.4, 5, 6, 165 nn.8, 9, 177, 178, 182, 221, *see also* death penalty; forfeiture
Pythagoras 3

Rawls, J. 101, 116 n.4, 139
reason of state 127, 132–5, 137
repentance 184 n.16, 191, 197–9, 201, 202, 205
Republicanism 123, 126, 140 n.5
resistance 6, 13, 21 n.42, 113, 122, 128, 130, 131, 147
revelation 10, 193, 194, 201, 208 n.18
Rickless, S. 30, 46 n.10
rights 13, 17, 102, 116, 136, 147–53, 155, 156, 161, 162, 174, *see also* divine right of kings; inheritance; property; resistance
  choice theory of 150–1
  civil 175, 176
  interest theory of 151
  natural 11, 102, 103, 131, 134, 136, 147
  perfect *vs.* imperfect 174
  to procreation 218
  to sexual freedom 215
Roman Catholics 2–3, 11, 17, 169, 170, 173, 175, 179–81, 183, *see also* toleration
Roman law 14, 126, 127
Royal Society 68 n.10, 74–6, 78, 80, 89, 92 n.8, 93 n.14
Russell, B. 16, 21 n.26, 36–7, 44, 47 n.24, 68 n.4
Rye House Plot 123
Ryle, G. 67

salus populi 126, 127, 132, 133, 135, 141 n.31

salvation 18, 172–3, 184 n.16, 189–211 *passim*
Sasaki, T. 12
Scalia, (Justice) A. 214
Schochet, G. 119, 120
Selden, J. 193
Seno, G. 12, 209 n.22
separation of church and state 9, 21 n.27, 178
separation of powers 120, 124, 128–9, 134
September 11 attacks 124
Sergeant, J. 45
Sermon on the Mount 198
sex, *see* marriage
Shaftesbury, (1st Earl) Cooper, A. A. 122
Sherlock, W. 191, 207 n.4, 208 n.9
Shimokawa, K. 1, 11, 14, 17, 116 n.12, 163 n.3, 169, 185 nn.19, 22, 26, 207 n.5, 217, 236 n.8
Ship Money Case 132
Sidney, A. 123–4
Simmons, A. J. 11, 116 n.3, 156, 165 n.8
Simon, R. 192
Skinner, Q. 123, 140 n.5
slavery 112, 129, 152, 153
Sloane, (Sir) H. 92 n.8
Smith, A. 6
social contract 16, 101–17 *passim*, 122
society, *see* will of the majority
Socinianism (and Arminianism) 191, 193, 194, 206, 209 n.22
Socrates 3
Soles, D. 46 n.7
solidity 65–7, 71 n.44
sovereignty 7, 20 n.18, 126–8, 132–4, 138, 140 n.15, 141 n.32
speculative philosophy, *see* experimental philosophy
Spencer, J. 193
Spinoza, B. 95 n.30, 173
Sreedhar, S. 221–2, 230
state of nature 16, 102–3, 105–9, 115, 130, 131, 148, 149, 155, 160
  and children 109
State Shintō 9, 21 nn.27, 29
Stillingfleet, E. 12, 33, 34, 42
Stubbe, H. 185 n.27
suicide 153, 160, 217

Sydenham, T.   53, 68 n.10
Symner, M.   93 n.14

Takano, C.   3–4, 19 n.7
   (Works) *Bojutsu Yumemonogatari*
      (The 1838 Tale of a Dream)   4
   'Seiyo Gakushi no Setsu' (Doctrines of
      Western Philosphers)   3
Takei, K.   12, 18, 189
Tanaka, S.   8, 22 n.43
texture   52, 56–61, 67, 70 n.29
Thales   3
Thomas, (Saint) Aquinas   128, 153
Toinard, N.   192
Tokugawa, I.   3
Tokugawa government   3–5, 19 n.6,
   20 n.10
toleration   8–9, 11, 12, 17, 169–86
      passim, 189–90, 215,
      218–25, 236 n.10, *see also*
      atheist
   dangerous practical opinions   178–82
   extensive scope of   169, 173, 182–3
   four considerations   170–3
   of Jews   169, 175–7, 183
   minimal definition of   170–1, 190
   of Muslims   169, 177, 181, 183,
      185 n.27
   of native Americans   176, 181, 183
   of pagans   169, 173, 175–7, 181
   and persuasion   172–3
   of Roman Catholics   11, 17, 169,
      170, 173, 175, 179–81, 183,
      186 nn.29, 30, 31, 32, 33, 34
   and salvation   172–3, 184 n.16,
      190–1
   and sincerity   172–3
   speculative opinions   175, 177, 180
   and truth   173, 175
   worship   172, 175–7, 179–80
Tomida, Y.   11
Toyotomi, H.   3

Trinitarian controversy   12, 191–3,
   207 n.7
trust   7, 8, 17, 104, 120, 132, 135–8,
   184 n.11
Tully, J.   10, 15, 208 n.19

Unitarianism   191, 193, 206
US Constitution   119

Vanzo, A.   93 n.14
Vernon, R.   179
Voluntarism (versus
   intellectualism)   133, 208 n.19

Waldmann, F.   180
Waldron, J.   186 nn.31, 33
Walmsley, J. C.   60, 180
Walsh, J.   221–2, 230
war   129, 131, 134, 137, 138,
   156, 176, 232
   just war   11, 156
Watanabe, K.   4
Watanabe, Y.   12
Wilkins, J.   46 n.15
will   19, 45, 108, 123, 137, 172,
   173, 175, 198, *see also*
   Voluntarism
   free will (versus determinism)   12
   of the majority   104, 113–14
   of the people   7, 20 n.18, 104,
      113–14
Willis, R.   202–5, 206, 208 n.16,
   211 n.45, 50
Witte, J. Jr   221, 223–5
Wolfson, A.   179
Wolin, S.   137
Wootton, D.   179
World War II   7, 9, 19 n.7, 101
Wynne, J.   63–4, 71 n.38

Yamada, S.   7, 12
Yamaoka, R.   17, 119

www.ingramcontent.com/pod-product-compliance
Lightning Source LLC
Chambersburg PA
CBHW062135300426
44115CB00012BA/1933